BLACK FLAG

BLACK FLAG

THE SURRENDER OF GERMANY'S U-BOAT FORCES 1945

Lawrence Paterson

Seaforth
PUBLISHING

First published in Great Britain in 2009 by
Seaforth Publishing,
Pen & Sword Books Ltd,
47 Church Street,
Barnsley S70 2AS

www.seaforthpublishing.com

British Library Cataloguing in Publication Data
A catalogue record for this book is available from the British Library

ISBN 978 1 84832 037 6

Typeset and designed by MATS Typesetters, Leigh-on-Sea, Essex
Manufactured in the United States of America by The Maple-Vail Manufacturing Group, York, PA.

Contents

Foreword

In May 1945 Nazi Germany surrendered to the Allied nations with whom it had waged war over the previous six years. During the course of this great conflict the lands conquered by the Third Reich stretched from the sands of North Africa to the frozen steppes of Russia, with the greater part of mainland Europe and Scandinavia falling under occupation. However, the high tide of German empire-building broke in 1942 and nearly three years of retreat followed. Germany had neither the men or resources required to maintain what it had taken in the face of the enormous reserves accumulated by the Allies, notably the United States and Soviet Union.

At sea, the Kriegsmarine had waged war in four oceans and five seas, this onslaught spearheaded by Grossadmiral Karl Dönitz's U-boat service. However, as on land, it was a battle of attrition that he could not win. Bested by Allied numbers, tenacity and technology, the German U-boat service's chance at victory ended in May 1943 and they, too, fought a defensive battle for the remainder of the war. Despite this fact, the boats – which were largely becoming obsolete by the end of 1944 – continued to sail and attack wherever they could. Brief successes against an all-powerful enemy, whether localised success in small group offensives, or single 'kills' made in lone-wolf patrols, were achieved right up to the final days of combat, whereupon the U-boats were ordered to cease fire and face the certainty of a humiliating surrender.

On land, the dispirited remnants of military formations, savaged in combat, were herded into confinement by the victorious armies. However, as well as the task of disarming thousands upon thousands of soldiers, there also existed large enclaves of Kriegsmarine personnel which still stretched from France to Norway in ports and bases from which the U-boats had operated. These men remained fully armed and almost unbroken in battle as Allied forces arrived to disarm them. In France, several of the harbour towns that had hosted the U-boat flotillas had been successfully defended against Allied siege troops, and were forced to surrender only because of the ending of the war. The complicated task of taking Germany's U-boat men into captivity often fell to small units of Allied troops, vastly outnumbered by crowds of unbowed German troops, many of them youngsters unwilling to consider their nation vanquished.

Coupled with the men ashore were those U-boats which still operated on a war footing around the United Kingdom, off the coasts of the United States, and as far away as Malaya. These had to be located before being shepherded into harbours where their surrender could be effected. For many Allied naval and air force personnel it was their first glimpse of the dreaded U-boat menace, and both sides were forced to exercise considerable restraint to avoid compromising the terms of Germany's surrender.

After this surrender, Dönitz's men were incarcerated with varying degrees of severity. Several were brutally interrogated by American intelligence officers in attempts to discover what potential weapons had been developed in conjunction with the Japanese, with whom the Allied powers were still at war. Elsewhere, German submariners found themselves held in prisoner-of-war camps that stretched from Canada and the United States to Britain. Many would not see their homeland until years after the end of the war. In the Far East, their erstwhile allies, the Japanese, incarcerated many U-boat men until Japan's eventual surrender some months later. The surrendered German forces were witness to much of the agony of Japan's troops and civilians in the dying months of the war which saw frequent bombing.

Meanwhile, Germany's underwater weaponry was eagerly seized and examined by the victors, particularly the Type XXI and XXIII electro-boats and Walter's hydrogen peroxide propulsion units installed aboard a handful of experimental boats. Interest was so high that even the American President Harry Truman boarded the Type XXI U-boat that had been commanded by the Ace Erich Topp; this resulted in an almost comical episode as the boat submerged and suffered a brief power failure, at which point the Secret Service men surrounded their Commander-in-Chief, amidst fears of a *coup d'état* aboard the dreaded German U-boat.

Eventually, the majority of Dönitz's surrendered U-boat fleet was to be disposed of by the Allies in various ways, some providing targets for a certain limited amount of firing practice by Allied aircraft and naval vessels, whilst others represented a small measure of symbolism about Allied triumph over the much-feared U-boat threat.

Germany's submariners were much maligned in Allied propaganda, this image of savage cunning being reinforced by their seeming unwillingness to refrain from offensive action right up to, and regretfully beyond, their orders to cease fire being transmitted from Germany. Allied reasoning that only the hardcore Nazi element would continue to fight such a clearly lost war was naïve and incorrect. This assumption was mostly made by people who were not only unaware of the grim realities accepted by most U-boat men about their slim chances of survival, but who had also forgotten that a similar kind of dogged determination had led to Britain remaining steadfast when faced with disaster in 1940, Soviet forces counter-attacking in the winter of 1941 even after being roundly beaten by the Wehrmacht, and American troops summoning the strength and determination to hold their position at Bastogne in the face of overwhelming German assault. Such courage in the face of almost certain annihilation did not require the political motivation often ascribed to Nazi forces, or indeed to the Soviet troops who suffered the most within the ranks of the Allies.

In May 1945 the task of disarming and accepting the surrender of the U-boats fell primarily to the invading Allies from the West. Those that were taken by the Soviets were largely swallowed up into the unforgiving Gulags and the quest for secrets that would become hidden behind the rapidly-descending Iron Curtain. This is the story of the surrender of Dönitz's Grey Wolves at sea, in trenches on the French Atlantic coast, and in the battered cities of northern Germany.

Acknowledgements

There are always many people involved in the writing of a book such as this. I would like to begin by thanking Aki, Megz and James of the Paterson clan (British Section), Nami, Ernie (American Section), Audrey 'Mumbles' Paterson and Don 'Mr Mumbles', and Ray and Philly Paterson of the New Zealand branch. Plus, special mention to Julia Hargreaves who has been a constant source of encouragement throughout this and other books.

Special thanks for help and inspiration go to a long list of people, particularly Jak Mallmann-Showell; Mike, Sheila, Mitch and Claire French; Cozy Powell (RIP); Dave Andrews; Cath Friend; Tina Hawkins; Paul 'The Rög' Rogne; 'Blaze' Bayley Cooke; Dave Leonardo Bermudez; Jeremy Walsh; Nicolas 'Petit Porc' Bermudez.

Many men from the ranks of the Kriegsmarine, Bundesmarine, and Royal Navy, and their families have offered unparalleled glimpses into their experiences and much hospitality during visits. My thanks to all of them, but if I could single out some particular people I would like to mention the late Ludwig Stoll and his wonderful wife Inge; Jürgen and Esther Oesten; Gerhard and Traudl Buske; Georg and Frau Högel; Georg and Frau Seitz; Gesa and Hannelore Suhren; Karl and Annie Waldeck; the late Volkmaar König and Jürgen and Gisela Weber. Also, special thanks to all at the München U-Bootskameradschaft for many memorable evenings in Munich.

For the many people who have not been mentioned here, I have not forgotten your help and support, and it is always appreciated.

Glossary

Abwehr	German Military Intelligence Service.
ASDIC	Royal Navy term for Sonar, used for submarine location.
B-Dienst	German radio listening service for gathering intelligence of enemy transmissions.
BdU (Befehlshaber der Unterseeboote)	U-Boat Commander-in-Chief.
Coastal Command	Royal Air Force arm of service dedicated to defending Britain from naval threats. Formed in 1936.
Enigma	Name for coding machine used by German Armed Forces.
Falke	T4 acoustic torpedo designed to home on low-pitched merchant propellers.
FAT (Felderapparattorpedo)	German T3 pattern-running torpedo.
FdU (Führer der Unterseeboote)	Regional U-boat command responsible primarily for the logistical coordination of that area's U-boat flotillas and bases.
FuMB (Funkmessbeobachtungs Gerät)	Radar detector.
G7a	Standard German air-driven torpedo.
G7e	Standard German electric torpedo.
Heer	German Army.
HMCS	His Majesty's Canadian Ship.
HMS	His Majesty's Ship.
HMSAS	His Majesty's South African Ship.
HMT	His Majesty's Trawler.
HNMS	His Norwegian Majesty's Ship.
Ing. (Ingenieur)	German Engineer designation inserted after rank, eg Leutnant (Ing.).
Kriegsmarine	German Navy.
KTB (Kriegstagebuch)	German unit War Diary kept as daily record of military activities.
LI (Leitender Ingenieur)	Chief Engineer.
Liberty ship	Mass-produced cargo ships manufactured in

	the United States, originally of British conception. Quick and easy to produce they became a backbone of Allied mercantile traffic.
Luftwaffe	German Air Force.
MV	Motor vessel.
OKM (Oberkommando der Marine)	German Naval Command.
OKW (Oberkommando der Wehrmacht)	German Military Forces High Command.
SKL (Seekriegsleitung)	German Naval War Staff.
SS	Steamship.
Stab	German staff.
Vorpostenboot	German patrol boat, typically a converted trawler.
VP	US Navy Patrol Squadron (aircraft).
VPB	US Navy Bomber Patrol Squadron.
Wehrmacht	German Armed Forces, excluding the Waffen SS.
Wintergarten	Nickname given to open-railed extension of the conning tower to accommodate flak weaponry.
WO	German Watch Officer. Thus, IWO is First Watch Officer, IIWO is Second Watch Officer and IIIWO, Third Watch Officer. There were three Watch Officers aboard a combat U-boat, the IIIWO a senior non-commissioned officer, the others commissioned.
Zaunkönig	T5 acoustic torpedo, designed to home on higher-pitched warship engines.

Comparative Rank Table

German (Abbreviation)	British/American
Grossadmiral	Admiral of the Fleet/Fleet Admiral
Admiral	Admiral
Vizeadmiral (VA)	Vice-Admiral
Konteradmiral (KA)	Rear-Admiral
Kapitän zur See (KptzS.)	Captain
Fregattenkapitän (FK)	Commander
Korvettenkapitän (KK)	Commander
Kapitänleutnant (Kptlt)	Lieutenant-Commander
Oberleutnant zur See (ObltzSzS)	Lieutenant
Leutnant zur See (LzS)	Sub Lieutenant/Lieutenant (jg)
Oberfähnrich	Senior Midshipman
Fähnrich	Midshipman
Stabsobersteuermann	Senior Quartermaster/Warrant Quartermaster
Obersteuermann	Quartermaster (also U-boat Navigation Officer)
Obermaschinist	Senior Machinist/Warrant Machinist
Bootsmann	Boatswain
Oberbootsmannmaat	Boatswain's Mate
Bootsmannmaat	Coxswain
-Maat (trade inserted as suffix)	Petty Officer
Maschinenobergefreiter	Leading Seaman Machinist
Matrosenobergefreiter	Leading Seaman
Mekanikergefreiter	Able Seaman Torpedo Mechanic
Maschinengefreiter	Able Seaman Mechanic
Matrosengefreiter	Able Seaman
Matrose	Ordinary Seaman

1

May 1945

On 1 May 1945, Grossadmiral Karl Dönitz had sixty-two U-boats at sea. Although he was now the head of Germany's entire navy, Dönitz, the architect of Germany's seemingly inexorable U-boat campaign which had begun at the outbreak of war in 1939, maintained a close connection with the submarine service. In truth, U-boats also remained the primary offensive power within the Kriegsmarine, Germany's capital ships being either disabled, sunk, or penned ineffectually to German coastal ports, while the smaller vessels of the S-boat, minesweeping, patrol and security flotillas were constrained to coastal actions which, though often fast-moving, violent clashes with the enemy, yielded little by way of influencing the war at sea. By the end of April 1945, U-boats, too, were a blunt weapon, their last major offensive in inshore waters around the United Kingdom and North America finally brought to heel by momentarily embarrassed Allied defences. Nonetheless, the U-boats continued to sail, and their very positions on the first day of May demonstrated their still far-flung operational zones.

The beginning of May had also been especially significant to Dönitz himself. During the previous day he had been in Lübeck, meeting with Reichsführer SS Heinrich Himmler, following a radio signal from Martin Bormann in Berlin accusing Himmler, rightly, of negotiating via Sweden to surrender Germany. Bormann had urged Dönitz to take 'instant and ruthless' action against the traitorous head of the SS, but Dönitz justifiably balked at the idea, opting instead for a meeting during which Himmler assured him the accusation was false.

> By about six o'clock on the evening of April 30 I was back in Plön. Waiting for me there I found Admiral Kummetz, the naval Commander-in-Chief, Baltic, who wished to report on the situation in the Baltic and on the progress of our rescue activities. Speer, the Minister of Munitions, who had been in north Germany for a long time, was also there. In the presence of these two, my aide-de-camp, Commander Luedde-Neurath, handed me a radio signal in the secure naval cipher [*sic*], which had just arrived from Berlin:
>
> 'Grossadmiral Dönitz.
>
> The Führer has appointed you, Herr Admiral, as his successor in place of Reichsmarschall Göring. Confirmation in writing follows. You are hereby authorised to take any measures which the situation demands. Bormann.'[1]

Indeed, although Dönitz was unaware of the fact, Hitler was already dead, having shot himself that afternoon. It was not until the following morning, at about 0740hrs, that he

The crew of *U47* departing the Reich Chancellery after being decorated by Adolf Hitler. The so-called 'Happy Times' of the U-boats made national heroes of many of the early commanders and crew. By 1945, most of them had either perished or moved ashore to staff positions.

received a further signal from Bormann in Berlin informing him that the dictator's will was 'now in force', but with no indication of how Hitler may have perished. Dönitz relocated his hastily-formed government from Plön to the Kriegsmarine School at Flensburg, occupying the Sports Hall, and accommodation aboard the liner *Patria*, which was docked in Flensburg harbour. From there, Dönitz transmitted the following broadcast over national radio to the shattered remains of the German nation to inform them of what he thought had happened.

German men and women, soldiers of the armed forces: our Führer, Adolf Hitler, has fallen. In the deepest sorrow and respect the German people bow.

At an early date he had recognized the frightful danger of Bolshevism and dedicated his existence to this struggle. At the end of his struggle, of his unswerving straight road of life, stands his hero's death in the capital of the German Reich. His life has been one single service for Germany. His activity in the fight against the Bolshevik storm flood concerned not only Europe but the entire civilized world.

The war at sea had been lost to Germany since 1943, although the Kriegsmarine's U-boats refused to admit defeat and sailed until the final days of the war.

The Führer has appointed me to be his successor. Fully conscious of the responsibility, I take over the leadership of the German people at this fateful hour.

It is my first task to save Germany from destruction by the advancing Bolshevist enemy. For this aim alone the military struggle continues. As far and for so long as achievement of this aim is impeded by the British and the Americans, we shall be forced to carry on our defensive fight against them as well. Under such conditions, however, the Anglo-Americans will continue the war not for their own peoples but solely for the spreading of Bolshevism in Europe.

What the German people have achieved in battle and borne in the homeland during the struggle of this war is unique in history. In the coming time of need and crisis of our people I shall endeavour to establish tolerable conditions of living for our women, men and children so far as this lies in my power.

For all this I need your help. Give me your confidence because your road is mine as well. Maintain order and discipline in town and country. Let everybody do his duty at his own post. Only thus shall we mitigate the sufferings that the coming time will bring to each of us; only thus shall we be able to prevent a collapse. If we do all that is in our power, God will not forsake us after so much suffering and sacrifice.[2]

And so, particularly mindful of the peril faced by German civilians in the east in the face of the advancing Russian juggernaut, Dönitz elected to continue the fight and buy crucial more time in which to evacuate all he could from the eastern provinces. Thus the U-boats continued their fight alongside the rest of the beleaguered Wehrmacht.

On the day that Dönitz took control of the German state, five U-boats were

The glory days of the German U-boat service in France had faded into distant memory by 1945.

operational in North American waters: *U190* was south of Halifax, Nova Scotia; *U853* in the Gulf of Maine; *U530* off New York; *U805* and *U858* part of the Seewolf group south of Halifax. *U802, U881, U889, U1231* and *U1228* were all en route to the United States. *U873*, on the other hand, was outbound to the Caribbean, whilst *U234* was also off the coast of the United States, but en route to the Indian Ocean, on what was primarily a transport mission rather than American combat patrol. Returning from the Far East at that time was *U532* carrying a cargo of tin, rubber, quinine, opium and tungsten, having sailed from Jakarta on 13 January. *U539* was returning to Norway defective after failing to reach the North Atlantic on the first leg of its long-distance voyage. *U485* and *U541* were both bound for operations off Gibraltar, whilst *U516* was engaged on transport duty to the besieged city of Saint-Nazaire.

Sailing for the North Atlantic were the Type VIICs *U320* and *U907*, while closer inshore to the United Kingdom *U245* and *U2324* were returning from operations in the Thames; *U764, U901, U979, U1009* and *U2336* were also either returning from, engaged on, or sailing to the waters off the British east coast. Off the British west coast were *U287, U739, U1058, U1305, U956, U1165, U293, U1105, U1272* and *U218*. In the Irish Sea, *U1023* was soon to be joined by *U825*. Finally, *U249, U776, U1010, U1109, U963, U244, U1277, U826, U991* and *U1058* were all designated for operations in the English Channel and Western Approaches, *U534* sailing the treacherous path between Kiel and Norway, following overhaul in Germany and due for fresh operational deployment. Further north, another fourteen U-boats had sailed from Narvik or Harstad for Arctic war patrols: *U278, U295, U312, U313, U318, U363, U427, U481, U711, U968, U992, U1061, U1163* and *U1165*.

Though only days were left in the now unevenly-matched U-boat battle against the Allies, their combat ardour still appears to have remained relatively intact, loyalty to Dönitz possibly more profound even than their patriotic duty. The dangers of war at sea remained, and within days seven of the above boats would be lost in action. On 2 May, BdU (Befehlshaber der Unterseeboote), the U-Boat Commander-in-Chief, ordered all operational U-boats in Germany to head for Norway – the exodus providing one last chance for Allied aircraft to batter their fleeing targets.

On 4 May Dönitz ordered all combat U-boats to cease offensive operations and return to their bases. His message was brief and succinct: 'All U-boats cease fire at once. Stop all hostile action against allied shipping. Dönitz.' However, off Point Judith, Rhode Island, *U853* was submerged and prepared for action as the message was transmitted. Shortly thereafter, at 1745hrs local time, the solo-sailing American 5,353-ton steamship SS *Black Point* was hit in the stern by a single torpedo fired by Oberleutnant zur See Helmut Frömsdorf's submerged Type IXC-40 boat. The American steamer was hauling coal from Newport to Boston in such thick fog that Captain Prior had been forced to drop anchor twice during the passage through Long Island Sound. Prior was not sailing in convoy, as the US Coast Guard considered the coastal waters now safe from U-boat attack. Frömsdorf had departed Norway on 23 February for American waters, and had already attacked and sunk the American patrol vessel USS *Eagle 56* off Portland, Maine, on 23 April. The German torpedo ripped off the aftermost forty feet of *Black Point*, which began to sink rapidly, four miles from land. Of the eight officers, thirty-three crewmen, and five armed guards, eleven crewmen and one guard died. The remainder managed to make it to the rail and leap overboard, before the steamer rolled to port and sank with a large exhalation of air. The *Black Point* was the last American-registered ship to be sunk by U-boat attack. Yugoslav freighter SS *Kamen*, one of the ships which arrived to begin rescue of the crew, radioed a report of the torpedo attack and the US Navy immediately despatched a hastily assembled 'hunter-killer' group which comprised the destroyer USS *Ericsson*, escort destroyers USS *Atherton* and *Amick*, and frigate USS *Moberley*.

Within two hours USS *Moberley* arrived, shortly followed by two others from the group. They formed a loose scouting line and it was USS *Atherton* which discovered *U853*, lying

The crew of a Type IXC-40 docked in Norway after the successful patrol completion. Of particular note are the two hand grenades carried by the man at right of the photograph in the U-boat leathers. As the end of the war drew nearer, security whilst in port became of greater concern: local resistance movements were beginning to become emboldened by the German's imminent defeat.

U2524 photographed while in training, shown by the pale band (yellow) on the conning tower. This boat was severely damaged by Beaufighters whilst attempting the run to Norway, and was scuttled on 3 May with two crewmen killed.

bottomed in thirty-three metres of water. The escort destroyer obtained a firm sonar trace and carried out a depth-charge attack on the Type IXC-40 U-boat. Thirteen magnetically-fused depth charges were dropped, but contact was lost in the swirling eddies of water following this initial barrage. Meanwhile, three more destroyers had arrived to join the hunt, alongside two former Royal Navy corvettes and an auxiliary destroyer. With this fearsome array of weaponry present, USS *Amick* was able to depart and continue with the previous high-priority mission in which it had been involved before the diversion to hunt *U853*.

While USS *Atherton* continued to stalk *U853* throughout the night, with periodic combined depth-charge and hedgehog attacks, USS *Moberley* held the sonar trace on the target, in what was a textbook example of a hunter-killer unit in action. The remaining ships blocked the German's escape routes towards possible sanctuary in deeper water. However, the same shallow water that imperilled *U853* also caused damage to its attacker, USS *Atherton* suffering damage to its electronics array, due to shock waves from its own depth charges reflecting off the bottom and bouncing back at the destroyer. USS *Moberley* then made its own depth-charge attack on the target, rather than allow any diminishing of the pressure on *U853*. Unfortunately for the American, the shock waves disabled the frigate's steering, momentarily creating a lull while emergency repairs were speedily completed. With steerage once more, the frigate made a second attack, this time discharging hedgehogs on the creeping target, this barrage being the one that probably destroyed *U853*. Amidst the turbid water were various bits of debris that had floated to the surface, including a pillow, escape gear, a lifejacket, and a U-boat officer's peaked cap.

As dawn broke, two US Navy K-Class blimps from Lakehurst, New Jersey (*K16* and *K58*), joined the attack. They located a large oil slick and marked the U-boat's suspected location with smoke and dye markers. *K16* obtained a firm MAD (Magnetic Anomaly Detector) contact on what was, in all likelihood, the hull of a destroyed U-boat. USS *Atherton*, *Ericsson* and *Moberley* mounted further hedgehog and depth-charge attacks which brought further wreckage to the surface: the boat's chart table, oilskins, cork and a life raft. The final nail in *U853*'s battered coffin was delivered by the blimps, which also attacked with 7.2in rockets. Finally, *U853* was declared as confirmed sunk, with USS *Atherton* and *Moberly* receiving joint credit for the destruction, and both returning to port with brooms attached to their mastheads, an international naval symbol for a 'clean sweep'.

The U-boat wreckage had been marked by a buoy and later that day US Navy salvage vessel *Penguin* arrived on the scene, and a diver was despatched to enter the sunken boat and locate the captain's safe. However, the hard-hat diver was tethered by his air line to its surface supply, and had great difficulty in attempting to enter *U853*, reporting massive damage to the U-boat's hull, and the presence of unexploded depth charges. The following day, the smallest diver aboard the vessel, Ed Bockelman, volunteered to attempt to enter *U853*. Accompanied by Commander George Albin, Bockelman was able to recover the body of Matrosenobergefreiter Herbert Hoffmann, one of the shattered bodies, clad in their Dräger escape gear, which were blocking the conning tower hatch. Bockelman was able to help identify the boat by observing the insignia which had been painted on to a shield that had been attached to the conning tower: beneath the hooves of a trotting horse, the artist had, somewhat unusually, painted the U-boat's number. The primary colours of the insignia were distorted by the effects of light absorption at depth, but comprised yellow and red – the two colours identified by survivors of *Black Point* as they glimpsed their attacker briefly surfacing. *U853* was the penultimate U-boat to be sunk in action by the US Navy.

That same day, southeast of Cape Race, Kapitänleutnant Dr Karl-Heinz Frische's *U881* was detected by USS *Farquhar* of the hunter-killer group centred on the carrier USS *Mission Bay*, while returning to New York. They had been on an extended hunt for the inbound German U-boat group, Seewolf, when firm sonar contact was made. *U881* had sailed independently, rather than as a member of the group, after snorkel problems had forced Frische to abort for repairs to Bergen, forcing a delay on the boat's departure. Sailing for the American coastline, Frische was detected by an Avenger aircraft from USS *Bogue* on 23 April, narrowly avoiding damage from two depth charges which straddled the diving boat. This time the successful hunt was short and dramatic, the American escort destroyer firing thirteen depth charges in a single attack, which destroyed *U881* with all hands. It was the last U-boat kill for the US Navy on a boat that in all probability had not received Dönitz's ceasefire order of 4 May, nor the instructions that followed on 5 May to prepare to surrender according to instructions to be transmitted thereafter.

The American forces hunting Seewolf were not the only Allied units to destroy U-boats in the days after Dönitz's ceasefire order had been transmitted. On 4 May, the

Type XXI *U2521* was sunk by Typhoons of 184 Squadron, 2nd Tactical Air Force. The boat was hit as it departed from Geltinger Bay on its way to Norway, and sank in seconds, with Oberleutnant zur See Joachim Methner and forty of his crew being killed in the attack.

That same day *U236*, *U2503* and *U2338* were all in the Little Belt, sailing from Kiel to Kristiansand Süd when they were attacked by twelve rocket-firing Coastal Command Beaufighters of 236 and ten of 254 Squadrons, under escort from Mustang fighters. The three U-boats were spotted while travelling surfaced in shallow waters close inshore, under escort from two Vorpostenboote, which acted as flak cover, augmenting those guns that the U-boats possessed themselves. Squadron Leader S R Hyland, of 236 Squadron, sighted the small German convoy, which promptly came under attack by all twenty-two aircraft. The leading boat immediately crash-dived, as the first arcs of cannon fire thundered against its superstructure. The two remaining U-boats and their escorts came under sustained cannon and rocket attack, with the third U-boat appearing to explode and one of the Vorpostenboote sinking. The Beaufighters suffered minor damage from gunfire, but all returned safely from what was the final operation mounted by the North Coates Strike Wing of Coastal Command. *U236* surfaced after the aircraft had departed, but was so badly damaged that she was later scuttled off Bogense, Denmark, after the crew had abandoned her.

The Type XXIII *U2338*, which carried no defensive flak armament, was sunk during the attack, and the commander, Oberleutnant zur See Hans-Dietrich Kaiser and eleven of his men were killed, with only two surviving. The remaining boat, Type XXI *U2503*, was severely damaged during the attack. It was this boat which had appeared to explode, a rocket projectile entering the control room through the conning tower before exploding inside. The men in the control room were killed instantly, one of them being Kapitänleutnant Karl-Jürg Wächter, who died alongside thirteen of his men. Limping ashore under the command of IIWO Leutnant zur See Oskar Curio, the boat was beached on the Danish island of Omø in the Great Belt where the survivors scuttled what was left of their boat.

It was not just in German and Danish waters that the threat remained for U-boats. In the fjords near Narvik, Allied aircraft were also active. On 4 May, the Fleet Air Arm launched Operation Judgement against the U-boat bases at Harstadt, its aim being to neutralise U-boat depot and store ships which supplied the boats operating against Russian Arctic convoys. The carriers HMS *Trumpeter*, *Searcher* and *Queen* were all allocated to the mission, mustering between them twenty-eight Wildcat VI and sixteen Avenger aircraft from 846 (*Trumpeter*), 853 (*Queen*) and 882 (*Searcher*) Squadrons. With take-off from the carriers completed at 1623hrs, the aircraft were above their target at 1701hrs, the depot ship SS *Black Watch*, found in Kilbotn Bay. Alongside the ship's port side was the Type VIIC *U711* having returned from patrol two days previously.[3] The anti-flak escorts made their initial attack, swiftly followed by the dive-bombers. The Norwegian ship MV *Senja*, under German control, was also hit and sunk during the attack; the old Norwegian coastal defence ship *Harald Hårfrage*, which had been commissioned in 1897 and transformed by the Kriegsmarine into a floating flak battery, was ignored by the British aircraft, not being considered a target worthy of the ammunition.

The four Wildcat and eight Avenger aircraft from Strike Leader HMS *Trumpeter* then began their main attack on the *Black Watch*. After the fighters strafed the stationary ship, the Avengers proceeded to launch their own glide bomb attacks, each dropping four 500lb bombs, scoring seven direct hits between them and four near misses. Temporarily obscured by plumes of water, *Black Watch* began to burn as *U711* struggled to escape. Aboard Kapitänleutnant Hans-Günther Lange's *U711* there was a skeleton crew of only twelve men, who cut her free of the depot ship and made for deeper water. The remaining forty crewmen were aboard the depot ship as the aircraft attacked. *U711* managed to get underway only a short distance when she began to sink rapidly, having been severely damaged by the compression waves of the near misses. As fire gripped the depot ship, she exploded shortly after the final Avenger attack, breaking in two and sinking, all forty men aboard from *U711* being lost with the depot ship. Those who had remained aboard *U711* had managed to escape.[4]

On 5 May, six more U-boats were destroyed at sea. The Type VIIC *U393* was sunk following an attack by aircraft. Caught once more on the surface, the U-boat was hit by rocket and cannon fire from Typhoons of the 2nd Tactical Air Force. Veteran U-boat commander Oberleutnant zur See Friedrich-Georg Herrle and Maat Erich Schneider were killed in the attack, and the boat scuttled in Geltinger Bay the following day.

The Type IXC-40 *U534* was also sunk while headed north in the Kattegat. A Royal Air Force Liberator VIII of 86 Squadron had been on its patrol station over the Kattegat for only twenty minutes when it detected the radar signatures of three surfaced U-boats dead ahead (*U534*, *U3017* and *U3503*). Another nearby aircraft, a 547 Squadron Liberator, had also detected the trio which was travelling in staggered line astern. This latter aircraft made two separate attacks, missing on both, before being hit by the fierce barrage of

U2506, U2511 and *U3514* photographed in Norway. Schnee opted to paint his boat's superstructure white after observing it from the air.

U-boat commanders in Norway just before the end of the war. Among this highly
decorated group are Rolf Thomsen (second from left), Jürgen Oesten (fifth from left),
Adi Schnee (sixth from left), Heinrich Lehmann-Willenbrock (commander of
11th U-Flotilla, second from right) and Gerd Suhren (right).

flak and crashing in flames into the sea. A single survivor was picked up by a rescue ship
from the nearby Anholt lighthouse on the small Danish island. Warrant Officer J D Nicol
immediately took his 86 Squadron aircraft into the attack. One of the German trio had
dived already and the other Liberator's main target was in the process of diving, so Nicol
concentrated on the third boat, still charging at speed on the surface and putting a strong
curtain of flak into the air. The first attack delivered six depth charges that missed, the
bomber's machine guns strafing the German flak weapons below and clearing the way for
a second attack with four depth charges, one of them this time hitting the stern deck,
rolling into the water alongside and exploding, rupturing the pressure hull at the stern
and sending the boat stern first to the bottom. The bombardier aboard the attacking
Liberator was Neville Baker, who recalls:

> As we lowered to get down to bombing height, I saw another B-24 ahead of us. It was
> lower and heading approximately northwest on a bombing run. As I saw no disturbances
> in the water, I presumed it was its first run. No sooner had I this thought, than I realized
> all three U-boats were firing at it.
> The B-24 was hit. All signs indicated that it was struck in the port engines. The
> port wing dipped, the B-24 slewed to port – right in front of us – the port wing tip
> touched the water and the entire port wing tore from the fuselage and the plane struck,
> head first, into the sea. As we passed over the spot, I saw only a tyre and a yellow
> dinghy floating in the debris.

Our front gunner, Jack Lanning, was now firing at the rear U-boat and, to my surprise (after all, they had shot down one B-24), saw that the two front U-boats were submerging and would be completely gone before we reached their position.

We zeroed in on the remaining U-boat. The bomb bay doors were open. While peering through the bombsight, I released the six selected depth charges at what I was sure was the correct moment. I remember thinking at the time that the U-boat was a sitting target and a dead duck. To my dismay, the rear gunner, John Hurrell, announced that all six depth charges had badly overshot.

I remember the skipper coming on the intercom and saying, 'Nev, if you can't handle it, I'll send Lionel down to do it.' Still not knowing what had gone wrong, I selected four more depth charges – leaving two for Lionel in case I missed again. I called Lloyd, our Second Pilot, and asked him what speed we had at the time of attack. He replied 'Just over 190,' and THAT cleared up my mystery. We were supposed to attack at 150 and the bombsight was set for that speed. As Nic brought the B-24 around for another run in the same direction as the first, I reset the bombsight. At the same time, I noticed the U-boat was no longer firing at us. Guns were either jammed or our front gunner was responsible. I believe the latter, as his firing was very accurate on the first run.

As we went into the second run, we again went over the spot where the first B-24 crashed. We noticed that there was a survivor hanging onto the dinghy. As I watched, on his fourth attempt, he hooked his right foot inside the dinghy, pulled himself in, and then waved to us as we passed overhead.

One other observation ... On the first run, I saw a sailor in a white sweater in front of the conning tower, in a running position. On our second run, he was more than halfway to the bow of the U-boat. I nicknamed him 'Hans' and hoped he was one of the survivors.

Then I thought we were going in at a little less height than the first run. My estimate then was 200ft. A minute adjustment on the bombsight, and I again released the fused depth charges. I held my breath until the rear gunner yelled that the first depth charge had actually landed on the U-boat and then rolled off into the water before exploding.

We returned and circled the sinking U-boat, counting at least thirty survivors, and also checked on our survivor in the dinghy. Close to the scene was a lightship, approximately one mile northwest, which launched lifeboats for the survivors. On picking up the survivors of the U-boat, they headed back to the lightship, but we laid smoke floats and flares in a line to our survivor and then machine gunned ahead of the lifeboat until they got our message and went back and picked up our survivor. I saw him get into the lifeboat, stand and wave to us. As they headed back to the lightship, we saw another B-24 arrive and circle the area. We headed home.

Crossing Denmark in a feeling of elation, we flew at about 100 feet, rising for towns and waving to the citizens in the streets. They waved back to us in jubilation as though they knew what we had done; however, it was probably because they knew the war was almost over.[5]

Unfortunately, Baker was wrong, as the man who had waved to the circling Liberator was not the survivor from the other aircraft. When the lifeboat arrived to pull him from his raft, he had died. Rumours circulating after VE-Day that the U-boat survivors had shot him and pushed him overboard were totally groundless.

The remaining German U-boats had successfully evaded attack and as the Liberator circled above, Kapitänleutnant Herbert Nollau and forty-seven of his men were rescued by the Anholt lifeboat. Three of the German crew died, though not from wounds, but rather from exposure as they floated in the frigid Danish waters. The three dead were Maschinenobergefreiter Georg Büssgen, Oberleutnant zur See Hans Endemann, the boat's IWO, and Funkgefreiter Josef Neudorfer. Neudorfer was German, but had been born in Argentina, leading to much ridiculous post-war speculation about the U-boat's mission and its possible passengers. There is no evidence to support theories that the boat was sailing on anything other than a transfer to Norway.[6]

Nearby, Liberator 'S' of 224 Squadron was also engaged on the anti-U-boat sweep. Squadron Leader J C T Downey flew over the area in which *U534* had been sunk, noting German survivors in six dinghies, the sole survivor from the 547 Squadron Liberator which had been downed, and indeed the wheels of the Liberator itself, protruding from the sea where it lay upside down. As two bombers continued to circle the area, Downey moved on and overflew a fully surfaced Type XXIII, but he spotted the German too late to attack:

> The attack was a complete balls up ... When we first sighted the U-boat it was travelling so fast we thought it was a speed boat and therefore turned too late to get lined up, toppling the gyros in the Mk14 bombsight in the process of a very steep turn. The depth charges missed by miles and only our gunfire could have done any damage. The boat crash dived but almost immediately reappeared and, since there was much discoloration of the sea surface, we thought that it must have ricocheted off the bottom in shallow water. However, we had another go, quite well lined up this time, but the bomb aimer had mis-selected his switches and nothing came off the racks. The sub then resubmerged and stayed down.[7]

Despite the seemingly botched attack, enough damage had been inflicted on *U2365* that Oberleutnant zur See Uwe Cristiansand was forced to scuttle his boat in the Kattegat.[8]

The training boat *U579* had also departed Kiel on orders to reach Norway when it was attacked by a 547 Squadron Liberator. Flying Officer A A Bruneau was the pilot aboard Liberator 'K'.

> I only qualified as a 1st pilot in late March or early April 1945. Then an epidemic of 'pink eye' (conjunctivitis) developed and our crew, which seemed particularly affected, was unable to do sufficient training to undertake operations until 5 May. Even then we had several non-regular crew members. Thus a rather patched up crew, with a 1st Pilot on his first operational trip as skipper, had the good fortune to sink a U-boat ...
>
> On the 5th, a number of aircraft were detailed to seek out the U-boats attempting to sail from the Baltic to the Norwegian fjords. We were to fly at low level over Denmark where, although the Germans had surrendered, they were still shooting at aircraft. The flight over Denmark was exciting; many Danish flags had just been raised for the first time in years and people on the roads were waving to us.
>
> Not long after reaching the Kattegat we picked up two submarines on radar at about 14 miles and soon saw them visually. Having seen sunken shipping sitting on the sea

Brigadeführer Walter Schellenberg, pictured here with Otto Skorzeny. It was Schellenberg who attempted to broker a surrender deal for Norwegian-based German forces to be interned in neutral Sweden. Dönitz ultimately refused.

bed with masts and funnels out of the water, we realised that U-boats would not submerge. As we approached, both subs opened fire, which seemed heavy to me, and which we of course returned. We took pretty severe undulating evasive action and the German gunners must have been terrified and not too accurate; in any case we were not hit. We attacked the leading U-boat at low level and as we passed over, the rear gunner reported that it had broken in half. We made a wide turn to try to get to the second sub but it had changed its course to a direction which would not have allowed us to get at it quite directly, only my rear gunner did not report this and by the time we got on the line of attack, another aircraft was already attacking. Soon after we had to start for home because of petrol levels and, as final excitement, we made a rough landing at Leuchars in foul weather.[9]

Oberleutnant zur See Hans-Dietrich Schwarzenberg was among the 24 men lost with *U579*.

The same aircraft that had destroyed *U534* scored its second victory the following day, albeit with a different crew aboard. The Type XXI *U3523* was making the dash for Norway, running submerged, when the boat's periscope and snorkel were both detected by radar

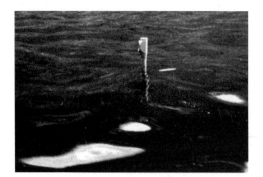

German U-boats would spend far more time submerged in 1945 than they had previously. This was partially facilitated by use of the snorkel, but made necessary by the fearsome power of Allied air superiority and naval forces.

Lookout aboard one of the Norwegian-based U-boats. Service in the Arctic was arduous in the extreme, and never seriously hampered Arctic convoy traffic, except for the notable success against PQ17 in conjunction with the Luftwaffe, aided by bad Allied intelligence work.

aboard the Liberator at a range of two and a half miles. An immediate attack was made and six depth charges released, which exploded around the U-boat and forced it partially to the surface. The conning tower emerged from the disturbed sea and the British crew observed black objects and debris blown into the air. Slowly the boat submerged for a final time, leaving oil and large air bubbles behind. Oberleutnant zur See Willi Müller and his fifty-six men went to the bottom with their boat. Oberleutnant zur See Hans Gessner's *U1008* was scuttled on 6 May after damage suffered the previous day in a bombing attack by a Liberator of 224 Squadron, as the boat made its run for Norway.

The instructions issued by the Allied Naval Command were very specific: all U-boats should proceed surfaced and flying a black flag of surrender, or be considered hostile. In the early hours of 7 May, a Catalina IV of 201 Squadron sighted a snorkel and periscope northwest of Bergen, the white smoke of diesel exhaust clearly visible. Within one minute the submerged U-boat, Oberleutnant zur See Heinz Emmrich's *U320*, was attacked, as it still appeared to be operating on a war footing. Four depth charges exploded astride the diving boat and a large patch of oil soon appeared on the surface. Hours later a sonobuoy contact was made with *U320*, an audible sound of hammering being picked up, indicating that repairs were underway on the bottomed boat. The hammering sounds continued for two hours as oil continued to rise to the surface. After eleven hours, the Catalina was forced to leave the scene and *U320* completed some measure of emergency repair, as the following day the boat surfaced and headed for Sotre Island, west of Bergen. There the crew scuttled their boat, Emmrich later lying to British authorities and claiming that they were sunk at the spot that the Catalina had attacked them. She was the last U-boat sunk as a direct result of enemy action.

The declared end of hostilities that Dönitz's ceasefire order should have ushered into being was not as complete as he had hoped. On 1 May, *U2336* had sailed from Norway, bound for Scottish waters as part of Dönitz's last-gasp offensive in British coastal waters. When the U-boat service had been bested in blue-water battles within the Atlantic, and virtually cleared from Biscay by relentless Allied air patrols, Dönitz had decided on a fresh strategy with which to take the fight to the British once more. Capitalising on the jumbled underwater topography that surrounds the British Isles – augmented with centuries of shipwrecks, many dating from this war and the previous one, and thus made of the same type of traceable iron as a U-boat hull – Dönitz ordered his boats inshore into the British shallows. This sudden and unexpected change in tactics came as a major shock to the primarily British and Canadian naval forces within the area. The U-boats now relied on their snorkels to keep them submerged where the advantage of radar was nullified. Their prolonged ability to stay beneath the surface meant less radio traffic, which counteracted in one stroke both Enigma decryption and radio direction-finding. The tangled mass of wreckage, from myriad shipwrecks littering the seafloor, played havoc with Magnetic Anomaly Detectors and ASDIC both. In one fell swoop, the U-boats had become invisible again. Established Allied hunter-killer tactics which had seen ocean success were found sorely wanting as the Kriegsmarine appeared to have turned the tables once more. There was great consternation in Whitehall as the U-boats preyed on inshore shipping with what appeared comparative ease, and the threat of new, deadlier, and more powerful U-boat types entering service, at long last, painted a bleak picture for the Allies.

Dönitz's success was, of course, transient. Eventually the Allies managed to adapt, and they bested their opponents once more. Technologies were refined, tactics were shaped, and the temporary sanctuary that U-boat commanders had discovered was removed once again. However, that is not to say that the U-boats did not continue to take their toll, even if on a vastly reduced scale compared to their glory days, when the tenure of the 'Ace' commanders had been in full swing.

Kapitänleutnant Emil Klusmeier was new to *U2336*, the previous captain Oberleutnant zur See Jürgen Vockel, who had taken the boat from its Hamburg shipyard in September 1944, having been killed by splinters from Royal Air Force bombing of the Deutsche Werft on 30 March. During the same raid, *U2340*, Klusmeier's boat, had been destroyed as it lay within the yards. The expedient of taking Klusmeier, his IWO, senior non-commissioned officers, and a single rating from the latter boat, and placing them aboard the undamaged *U2336* brought the small Type XXIII quickly to operational readiness once more, and no doubt spared Klusmeier and his men from action in the trenches around Hamburg. The boat sailed for Norway on 18 April in preparation for its maiden war patrol at the beginning of May.

At 2000hrs on 1 May, *U2336* sailed within a small convoy of escort vessels for the North Sea, diving and proceeding on snorkel once free of the coastal waters and its Vorpostenboote escorts. The boat was lashed with squalls of rain and drizzle as it headed for Scottish waters in the Firth of Forth, oblivious to developments in the war as radio reception suffered with the poor atmospherics. On 7 May, at around midday, the first hydrophone traces of convoy traffic were detected aboard *U2336* and Klusmeier turned his boat to investigate. By nightfall, the young captain recorded within his KTB (Kriegstagebuch), or war diary, the presence of three freighters escorted by a trio of destroyers in view, and he prepared to attack. In fact, it was five freighters escorted by armed trawlers HMS *Angle*, *Wolves* and *Leicester City*, forming the small coastal convoy EN91, sailing outbound from Methil bound ultimately for Belfast. The crews within the convoy were relaxed for the first time in years as news of Dönitz's order to cease fire at sea became common knowledge within Britain.

That same evening, far to the southwest, *U1023* also was preparing for its last torpedo attack. Kapitänleutnant Heinrich Schroeteler had been at sea since early March aboard the Type VIIC/41 *U1023*, his first claimed kill of the patrol dating from April. On 9 April, *U1023* had fired a spread of three LUT torpedoes, at what it took to be an 8,000-ton freighter that was part of convoy SC171 in the North Channel. Two clearly-heard detonations led to a claim of a damaged ship, though he had in fact missed his target. The explosions had buffeted nearby escorting frigate HMCS *Capilano*, but Schroeteler escaped unscathed. Schroeteler's claimed success was not merely the act of a deluded wishful thinker. As the war progressed, German captains had been provided with improved weaponry in their hunt for Allied merchant tonnage. Often these weapons were not so much developments spurred by the desire for greater offensive capabilities, but rather to provide the U-boats with improved *defensive* capabilities. With radar and direction-finding becoming increasingly effective aboard Allied escorts, and the hunter-killer technique of one ship fixing the position of a submerged U-boat, while the other attacked with any applicable weaponry, submerged conventional U-boats were at an incredible disadvantage. They were slow underwater and of limited battery capacity, which, once exhausted, forced the boat to surface beneath the waiting guns of any Allied warship determined enough to destroy it.

The introduction of LUT pattern-running torpedoes and Zaunkönig acoustically-guided weapons were two such developments which allowed the U-boat commander greater flexibility of operation. The T5 Zaunkönig was designed to home in on the high-pitched propeller noise generated by enemy warships. Once fired, the U-boat was forced to dive below torpedo-shooting depth, lest the weapon circle and home in on its own propellers. Therefore, the only hint of success was acoustic, picked up either on hydrophone or to the naked ear. An explosion was often erroneously taken to signify success, the U-boat captain unable, or unwilling, to rise to periscope depth and attempt to verify the kill. Instead, he could use the time until estimated torpedo impact to leave the area at depth, hopefully managing enough distance to thwart an effective hunt. The LUT offered a similar choice. When fired, the torpedo would follow a normal trajectory for a predetermined distance before running in programmed patterns, tracing a search pattern until it hit something. When fired into convoy traffic the rationale was that if the torpedo missed, it could still succeed in hitting an enemy ship in the course of its pattern-running. Once more it allowed the U-boat captain an opportunity to use the torpedo as a more effective 'fire and forget' weapon while the U-boat put some distance between itself and reprisal from escort ships. Also, if the torpedo did impact a ship during its change of direction, it would provide no clues at all to the escorts from which direction the attacker fired. However, once again, with German tactics reduced to this technique, the audible sounds picked up aboard the submerged and retreating boat – including premature detonation and the end-of-run detonation caused by the torpedo sinking into the depths until pressure caused an explosion – were all that could be used to verify success. Frequently, wish was the father to thought, and the claims of U-boat skippers differed wildly from the truth.

U1023 next passed into the Irish Sea where it made another attempt on convoy traffic on 19 April, firing a further three LUTs, this time recording a detonation that was observed through the periscope and another audible from the convoy body. Schroeteler claimed an 8,000-ton freighter as sunk and moved on to continue his aggressive patrol.

Four days later *U1023* attacked convoy TBC135 with a pair of LUT torpedoes, hitting and damaging 7,345-ton British steamer SS *Riverton* travelling in ballast. Wishfully claiming the steamer as a confirmed sunk 10,000-tonner, Schroeteler moved on and would make one final attack on 7 May at 2145hrs. Schroeteler had impressed Dönitz with his zeal in attack even before his final strike. He had previously served as captain of *U667* within the Atlantic for four patrols before being posted ashore to the BdU staff to replace 'Adi' Schnee who had returned to front-line duty as captain of *U2511*. But the fiery Schroeteler had pleaded with fellow Staff Officer and veteran captain, Günter Hessler – Dönitz's son-in-law – to be returned to active duty. Thus he had been assigned to *U1023* for the boat's maiden patrol. His reported successes of three large freighters totalling 26,000 tons sunk by 2 April prompted the award of the Knight's Cross from Dönitz, granted by radio that day. It was the last Knight's Cross to be awarded within the U-boat service.

On the evening of 7 May the target was military, and a single Zaunkönig hit 335-ton Norwegian minesweeper HNMS *NYMS 382* off Lyme Bay, Schroeteler claiming the victim as a corvette. The small ship sank within two minutes: her captain and twenty-one crew members lost, whilst other Norwegians of 3rd Minesweeping Unit picked up ten injured survivors stationed in Cherbourg. Less than an hour later, to the northeast, *U2336* fired its two torpedoes at the small convoy being stalked by Klusmeier. Both were direct hits: 2,878-ton Canadian freighter SS *Avondale Park*, followed by 1,791-ton

Test diving in Norwegian waters. The fjords offered excellent testing grounds for the U-boats as they became increasingly dependent on local facilities, after withdrawing first from France, and then from Germany itself in the last days of the Reich. However, Norwegian yards were never able to keep pace with demand.

The *Black Watch* and *U711* are obscured by plumes of water as they are sunk by attacking aircraft of the Fleet Air Arm at Harstad, 4 May 1945.

Norwegian steamer SS *Sneland I* hit squarely amidships. SS *Avondale Park* slewed to a stop as the ship began to sink rapidly, with the Chief Engineer George Anderson and donkeyman William Harvey being lost in the attack. The Norwegian was in the convoy's starboard column when SS *Avondale Park* was hit. *Sneland I* was forced to alter course to port in order to avoid the torpedoed Canadian, but suddenly was also struck on the starboard side. Within two minutes the ship had sunk. The First and Third Mates attempted to launch the ship's port lifeboat, but the rapidity of the ship's sinking prevented them from doing so. SS *Sneland I* capsized and the survivors were pitched into the sea. There they clung to debris before being picked up by HMT *Valse* and *Leicester City*. Seven men, including the captain, were killed. HMT *Leicester City* blindly dropped several depth charges before proceeding to pick up survivors from the torpedoed ships, and nearby Norwegian destroyer HNMS *Stord* arrived and also began a hunt for *U2336*. Klusmeier evaded the ensuing depth charges and escaped unscathed, beginning his return to base. Two days later *U2336* received news of Germany's capitulation.

Tragically, all three sinkings directly contravened Dönitz's ceasefire order transmitted on 4 May to all U-boats at sea. Whether these final U-boat attacks were deliberate, or not, will remain a speculative matter, the answer unlikely ever to be known for certain. The destruction of the two freighters by Klusmeier was the last attack carried out by a U-boat during the Second World War.

One final postscript to this part of Germany's war at sea was the mock attack mounted by one of only two Type XXI U-boats to sail on a combat patrol footing. After months of training and preparation, at the war's end the following Type XXIs were almost ready for operations:

U2503 (Oberleutnant zur See Raimund Tiesler) in transit to the 11th Flotilla, Bergen;

U2506 (Kapitänleutnant Horst von Schroeter) in Bergen, 11th U-Flotilla;

U3514 (Oberleutnant zur See Guenther Fritze) in Bergen, 11th U-Flotilla;

U2511 (Korvettenkapitän Adalbert Schnee) in Bergen, 11th U-Flotilla;

U3035 (Oberleutnant zur See Ernst-August Gerke) in Stavanger, though still nominally part of Stettin's 4th U-Flotilla;

U2529 (Kapitänleutnant Fritz Kalipke), in Kristiansand Süd 31st U-Flotilla;

U2502 (Kapitänleutnant Heinz Franke) in Horten, 11th U-Flotilla;

U2513 (Korvettenkapitän Erich Topp), in Horten 11th U-Flotilla;

U2518 (Kapitänleutnant Friedrich Weidner) in Horten, 11th U-Flotilla;

U3017 (Oberleutnant zur See Rudolf Lindschau) in Horton, 4th U-Training Flotilla;

U3041 (Kapitänleutnant Hans Hornkohl) in Horton, 4th U-Training Flotilla;

U3515 (Oberleutnant zur See Fedor Kuscher) in Horton, 5th U-Training Flotilla;

U3008 (Kapitänleutnant Helmut Manseck) in Wilhelmshaven, 11th U-Flotilla.

U2503 was badly damaged by aircraft on 3 May 1945 and later scuttled. Also on 3 May, *U2511* departed Bergen for its maiden war patrol, and *U3008* departed the northern German port of Wilhelmshaven that same day. Kapitänleutnant Helmut Manseck, a veteran, though largely unsuccessful, U-boat commander, took *U3008* out into the Jade estuary destined for the Atlantic, although the boat was soon returned after Dönitz's order to cease fire and abort any patrols. Korvettenkapitän Adalbert 'Adi' Schnee's *U2511* was the sole Type XXI to brush with enemy naval forces. Schnee was a highly decorated veteran of operations since the early stages of the war, taken ashore to a staff position once he had been awarded his Oak Leaves to the Knight's Cross in October 1942. He had managed to gather an equally experienced crew to the new boat, including his LI Korvettenkapitän (Ing.) Gerd Suhren. *U2511* was easily distinguishable from its sister boats, as Schnee had had the boat's superstructure painted white after noticing, during the course of a flight above the U-boat base in a Fieseler Storch, how visible the U-boats tied at the piers had been in Norway.

Schnee received the ceasefire order from Dönitz just hours before sighting a British task force bound for Norway which centred on the cruiser HMS *Norfolk*. The cruiser had provided cover for the carriers that had been engaged in Operation Judgement alongside the cruiser HMS *Diadem*. With the mission completed, *Norfolk* was returning to Scapa Flow when detected by Schnee. Deciding to test his boat under combat conditions, Schnee plotted an attack and carried it out, refraining only from firing his torpedoes. Once satisfied that he could have devastated the cruiser with a full salvo of torpedoes, he dived deeper and retreated at speed, completely undetected by the Royal Navy ships.

2

Surrender at Sea

We have seen how Grossadmiral Dönitz had issued the order for all U-boats to cease fire on 4 May, with his commanders still yet at sea being ordered to avoid further attacks against the enemy, and await further instructions while returning to port. Shortly thereafter, the predictable surrender was also received, broadcast repeatedly in order for all boats to receive it. At the time of Germany's surrender Dönitz had 398 U-boats in commission, although only twenty-six were on station within their patrol areas. The remainder were either in harbour or still engaged in their 'working-up periods'. Ironically, many Type XXIs were included in the figure of commissioned U-boats, though only two were ever put on a war footing. The opportunity with which Dönitz had tantalised his men, to take to the sea in a radical new U-boat design that could render Allied defences ineffective, was over. There would be no final reckoning with the Allies at sea, no last minute reversals for their enemy's convoy traffic which still shuttled men and material to the United Kingdom and to mainland Europe. The war had been comprehensively lost. Despite Dönitz's U-boats having fought a valiant losing battle since 1943, always in the hope of some kind of reward for their steadfastness with the introduction of the electro-boat, the end was simply the inglorious surrender of a fleet to the Allied powers for the second time in thirty years. Germany's humiliation was complete.

Indeed, Dönitz had been compelled to cancel his issued order to scuttle the U-boats and thus preserve the honour of the Kriegsmarine. Admiral Sir Max Horton, Commander-in-Chief Western Approaches, had strongly urged the caveats within the Allied conditions for the surrender of northern Germany which stipulated that the U-boats and all other intact vessels remain so. Horton wished for a formal surrender of the U-boat fleet. This was more for the impact of the gesture itself than for any practical purpose. Following the end of the First World War, Germany had clung to the mythology that its military had been stabbed in the back, the navy betrayed by Communists, and never defeated in battle. Horton would not allow a repeat of this, and the surrender would illustrate that the Kriegsmarine had been beaten by the Allies.

So the surrender instructions had been radioed to all U-boats at sea; these, as well as the specific orders to surface and fly a black flag of surrender by day, stipulated that navigation lights were required to be burning by night. To reiterate Dönitz's instructions, on 8 May 1945, Admiral H M Burroughs, RN, transmitted over the U-boat radio network, on the behest of Supreme Headquarters Allied Expeditionary Force (SHAEF), orders for all U-boats to surface immediately and fly a black flag or pennant. Next, they were

U532 surrenders in Liverpool, on 10 May 1945 on its return voyage from Jakarta. Amongst the valuable cargo which was destined to reach Germany was a large quantity of rubber.

told to report to the nearest Allied radio station for directions as to which Allied port to proceed. Torpedoes and mines were to be made safe, ammunition jettisoned, and all gun breech blocks were to be removed. Also, the crews were strictly forbidden to damage their U-boats in any way. There then followed a specific set of navigational instructions for the surrendering boats to follow to enable them to reach Allied harbours safely. All incoming and outgoing messages were also to be transmitted in plain language, deviation from any of these rules being deemed as hostile.

Interestingly, Dönitz also directed his U-boat commanders to release their men from military duty and to regard them as civilians thereafter. According to German crewmen, the British also relayed this procedure and thus, at their time of capture and internment, the crew were in fact no longer military personnel and were 'volunteering' their service to bring the U-boats to port. Therefore, the crews expected to be released within four weeks of landing on enemy territory as civilian non-combatants rather than military prisoners. Events would soon prove otherwise.

Two U-boats surrendered to Canadian forces days after the surrender on 8 May. *U889* was the first, Friedrich Bräucker having been destined for combat patrol off New York, after spending the latter half of April as weather boat for BdU. The surfaced boat was spotted by an RCAF Liberator 250 miles southeast of Flemish Cap on 10 May. The boat flew a black flag as the bomber approached, the German crew being observed to be waving their arms wildly as if to emphasise their message. Canadian escort group W6 comprising HMCS *Oshawa*, *Rockcliffe*, *Dunvegan* and *Saskatoon* intercepted the boat later that day, heavy weather preventing the Canadians from placing a Prize Crew aboard. Instead, Bräucker was told by loudhailer to head for Bay Bulls, Newfoundland, with which he complied. *U889* was handed over to other ships the following day, and on 13 May, the boat's official surrender took place off the Shelburne Whistle Buoy just before the port.

Hans-Edwin Reith's *U190* was also taken by the Royal Canadian Navy. After Reith had transmitted his position, incorrectly, three Canadian corvettes homed in on the boat's radio transmissions until its running lights were spotted. A boarding party from HMCS *Thorlock* went aboard, following standard Allied procedure to loop a chain around the periscope base and throw it down through the open hatch into the control room to prevent any sudden diving. But there was nothing but full co-operation from the German crew, who officially surrendered on 12 May. Reith had followed Dönitz's instructions and jettisoned all secret material and ammunition, including the boat's Zaunkönig acoustic torpedoes, while Bräucker had not.

Twenty three U-boats surrendered themselves in British ports, and four in the United States, whilst seven returned to Germany or Norway. *U541* and *U483* both surrendered themselves to the Royal Navy at Gibraltar, as they were caught within the region specified as 'Area E' when the instructions for surrender were received.[10] However, two others, *U1277* and *U963*, opted to scuttle themselves off the Portuguese coast.

Oberleutnant zur See Johannes Meermeier's *U979* had been on operations in the Denmark Strait at the end of April 1945. On 2 May she hit and sank the British minesweeping trawler HMT *Ebor Wyke* with one of two torpedoes fired west of Reykjavik. The minesweeper's crew had apparently been quite disgruntled to have to put to sea once more, expecting to head from their base in Iceland back to the United Kingdom with Germany's imminent surrender. Their orders were issued from HMS *Boulder*, the shore base on Iceland, and two minesweepers, the *Ebor Wyke* and HMT *Clavella*,

Adalbert 'Adi' Schnee in happier times mid-war, aboard *U201*. Schnee would captain the only Type XXI to encounter the enemy at sea while on a war footing when he took *U2511* into action.

left first thing that morning, expecting to return the same night. The trawlers were to clear a path for a small convoy. A little before 1300hrs the compulsory daily rum ration was being issued, and the majority of the crew of the *Ebor Wyke* was in the mess, with only the skipper and a pair of crewmen on the bridge, an engineer and one more man elsewhere. Coxswain John Milne was standing next to the ladders when all the men in the mess heard the distinct whirring of torpedo propellers. Milne raced up the ladder, remembering another man immediately behind him in a yellow oilskin. When he had reached the hatch he was shocked to find his head in the water with only the stern end and the 'whale back' at the bow pointing upwards. Milne scrambled for safety toward the bow as the small trawler sank in seconds. He was dragged underwater by the suction created by the sinking ship, able to feel the metal under his fingers and feet, until a rush of escaping air broke the suction and pushed him to the surface, where the shocked survivor clung to debris. HMT *Clavella* closed in to rescue survivors and sighted only Milne.

Three days later *U979* struck again, firing a three-torpedo spread in the early hours of the morning at convoy RU161 and hitting the 6,386-ton British tanker MT *Empire Unity* on the starboard side with two of them. With six tanks flooded, the crew initially abandoned ship, but thirty-four of them reboarded the damaged vessel after she was brought to Hvalfjordur by the frigate HMS *Northern Spray*. The remaining twelve survivors were picked up by HMS *Northern Sky* and taken to Belfast. Allied counter-attack was prompt, and altogether fifty-five depth charges were dropped on and around *U979*, which only inflicted superficial damage to the U-boat, but did manage to bend the starboard propeller shaft slightly, resulting in noise when used and forcing that motor to be stopped. *U979* remained at periscope depth throughout the counter-attack and was rammed in the early morning darkness from astern, though again escaping crippling damage. According to later recollections from the IWO, the hunt was shaken off after about four hours, whereupon Meermeier decided to return to Bergen for repair to the starboard shaft. It was also apparent to him that a single depth charge had lodged on the bow deck casing, heard rolling about inside the U-boat. The following day it was heard to roll off the hull, an explosion following shortly thereafter.

Already overdue, and the tanker *Empire Unity* attacked after Dönitz's ceasefire order, the radio operator aboard *U979* finally picked up the transmission after the boat had dived to repair existing damage to the antennae. Rather than hand himself over to Icelandic authorities in Reykjavik, Meermeier instead opted to return with his crew to Germany. It was not until 23 May that the boat's surreptitious voyage ended, when *U979* reached the North Frisian Islands. The boat's E-Obermaschinist, Heinrich Jansen, remembered their final voyage:

Reykjavik would not have been far, but our commandant told us that we were going home. Using the northern route we steered for Norway, reaching Bergen, the last port that we had departed from, using it to confirm our navigation. We continued the voyage until we reached the North Frisian islands on 23 May. There, our Commandant wanted to sink the boat near the Föhr Island as we rounded the southern point of Amrum. There we unexpectedly ran aground and got stuck fast – all manoeuvring of the engines failing to move us. Thus we sat and waited for the tide to come in. All through the day people ashore could see us clearly and soon a single boat came out to us. We learnt that the island was only inhabited by interned German crews and that there were no English men there at all. So we set the boat on the bottom, allowed the electric motors to flood and ran the diesel so hard and long that sand was eventually crunching in the transmission. And so we abandoned our wreck and reported to the Island commander who accommodated us in a home in Wittdün.[11]

Meermeier was later arrested by Allied authorities for breaching the German ceasefire order with his attack on the MT *Empire Unity*. The Royal Navy Flag Officer in Western Germany communicated portions of the boat's translated KTB to the Admiralty during June 1945 before the trial began. Included was a brief interrogation report from the boat's IWO Oberleutnant zur See Opitz: 'Since the Commanding Officer of *U979* is awaiting trial for non-compliance with the Surrender Terms, it has not been considered practicable to glean any useful information from him pending his trial. The First Lieutenant of the U-boat, however, has been questioned and has provided useful information in amplification of the recorded entries in the Deck Log.'[12] Eventually, Meermeier and his senior radio operator were able to prove that at the time of the transmission of Dönitz's ceasefire order, his radio had been inoperative. A second U-boat that had attempted to return to Germany was sunk in the mouth of the Elbe River. Oberleutnant zur See Heinrich Meyer's *U287* had been operating in coastal British waters when the ceasefire order was received. Like Meermeier, Meyer was attempting to return to Germany when his boat sank near Altenbruch at the mouth of the Elbe. Information regarding the sinking has since become sparse: at one time attributed to a mine, it is also possible that the boat was scuttled as it approached the entrance to the Kaiser Wilhelm Canal, the crew reaching shore in lifeboats. Regardless of the reason, *U287*'s war ended on 16 May in the turbid waters where the Elbe met the North Sea.

Other German U-boat men had chosen internment in what they hoped would be friendlier neutral countries, rather than a return to base or sailing to an enemy port. The Type XXI *U3503* captained by Oberleutnant zur See Hugo Deiring had been alongside *U534*, headed to Horten, when the latter was sunk by a Liberator bomber. Deiring had dived despite the danger posed by ground mines and shallow waters. The boat had received light damage and under the continuous threat of air attack, *U3503* snorkelled toward Swedish waters. On 6 May, at 0500hrs, the boat entered Swedish waters and surfaced west of Göteborg. Deiring was approached by the Swedish destroyer *Göteborg* and reported a defective exhaust valve and rudder. The boat had developed an oil leak and the commander informed the Swedish captain that he required medical treatment for some crewmen who had carbon monoxide poisoning on account of fumes released by the faulty exhaust valve. Deiring also requested contact with the German Consulate in Göteborg and the Marine Attaché in Stockholm. Meanwhile, British aircraft had discovered the boat, but were unable to approach as she lay in Swedish territory. The destroyer *Stockholm* remained on station watching *U3503*. On 7 May, the Swedish authorities ordered Deiring to transfer the U-boat to shallower water north of the inlet to Gothenburg harbour, whereupon the crew could be interned. Deiring jettisoned his secret material and fired all torpedoes seaward. The following day at 1700hrs Deiring reported that his boat was sinking: flooding valves had been opened and the boat began to gently sink stern first as the crew assembled on deck with lifeboats. The Swedish ship *H57* arrived to take *U3503* in tow, but failed, some accounts claiming the line broke repeatedly, others that German crewmen threw the tow cable overboard. Flooding valves

U249 boarded by Royal Navy personnel after the boat's arrival in Portland.

were opened in the diesel room and the Germans abandoned ship, rescued by destroyer *Norrköping*. By 1955hrs, *U3503* had sunk at a depth of 20 metres, the crew destined for internment in Sweden.

On 20 May, *U963*, skippered by Oberleutnant zur See Rolf Werner Wentz, arrived off the coast of neutral Portugal. The Type VIIC had been ordered to sail from Trondheim to the seas off Hartlepool, England, after its departure on 23 April. Wentz, aboard *U963*, received the orders to cease fire and then surrender, but opted to stay at sea while he and his crew discussed their options. The voyage had been uneventful thus far: the sole cause for concern had been the malfunctioning of the dipole antennae of the radar detector atop the schnorkel, three days from port. Water had entered the cable from the aerial to the wireless compartment, with the result that the cable had to be severed and sealed off. The danger in which this placed the boat was finally demonstrated on 6 May, in the early hours of the morning, when *U963* was rocked by a single aircraft-launched depth charge while west of the Hebrides. Though *U963* evaded further attack, considerable damage

U249 escorted into harbour, the first U-boat to surrender.

had been caused already: the pressure hull was cracked abreast the conning tower to starboard, the port diesel engine was damaged and inoperative, starboard vents could be opened but not shut, and the boat's main aerial was destroyed, rendering *U963* 'deaf'. Wentz headed southwest, his determination being to land in neutral Spain or Portugal, rather than return to a defeated Germany. A continuous inflow of water from the cracked hull threatened to swamp the U-boat as they slowly trudged into the Bay of Biscay. *U963* developed a pronounced list to starboard, and frequent short circuits caused by regular failures of the overworked bilge pumps. Finally, on the evening of 19 May, near the Portuguese west coast, the main pumps failed altogether and were judged irreparable. The boat began to settle, and Wentz gave the order to abandon ship at 0300hrs the next morning near Nazaré, the crew paddling ashore in small rubber dinghies on 20 May. There Wentz and his crew surrendered to local authorities, who, to the chagrin of the Germans, directed them to the British Consulate where they were handed over to the British authorities.

Wentz's was not the only boat which had sailed in April and then chose to remain at sea following the German surrender. 11th U-Flotilla mate, Kapitänleutnant Ehrenreich Stever's Type VIIC-41 *U1277*, had been ordered to patrol the Western Approaches after sailing from Bergen two days before Wentz. *U1277* remained at sea far longer, while the crew deliberated the best course of action for them to follow. Plans to sail to South

America were thwarted by a lack of fuel, and like *U963*, the boat sailed east towards the Iberian Peninsula. Stever was an experienced seaman, having served in minesweepers, but this was his first operational command. He had clearly received Dönitz's surrender instructions but, instead, he and his crew chose internment rather than handing their boat over and cruised first toward Spain, where they were rebuffed by local authorities and then toward neutral Portugal. At dawn on 3 June, *U1277* surfaced off Cabo do Mundo, near Oporto, and was scuttled, the crew paddling for shore in rubber dinghies, and landing at the beach of Angeiras north of Oporto. There they were captured and interned by Portuguese authorities in the Castelo de Sao Jose da Foz in Oporto. A few days later they were handed over to a British warship in Lisbon, beginning their journey to a prisoner-of-war camp, where they were held for three years before they could return to Germany. Ehrenreich also faced punishment by British court martial for contravening the German surrender terms, and was tried in Hamburg by the British Judge Advocate as Case No 115 during 1946: he was not released from prison until 1948.

Elsewhere, only one other boat of the Type VIIs directed against England made a genuine bid for freedom. On 17 August 1945, the dishevelled appearance of *U977* in Mara del Plata, Argentina, marked the final act of Dönitz's last campaign. Oberleutnant zur See Heinz Schäffer had received the surrender order, but instead chose to put the matter to his men, barely able to believe that, after the fierce, defiant rhetoric broadcast in the last hysterical days of the Third Reich, a total collapse had taken place. Aware of the Allied demand for unconditional surrender and also the cruel intentions of the Morgenthau Plan publicised in the German press, Schäffer put three options to his crew. The first option was to surrender as apparently ordered, the second to scuttle the boat, the third was to escape and put into harbour in a country that had remained friendly to Germany throughout the war years. Eventually a majority, thirty of the forty-eight men aboard, opted for the third, two desired to be landed in Spain, and sixteen others with families still in Germany wanted to return to their homes. The men who wished to return were subsequently delivered under cover of darkness to a remote area of the Norwegian coast near Bergen, paddling ashore in rubber dinghies after *U977* inadvertently ran aground. Schäffer and his remaining crew extricated the boat from their perilous position as dawn approached and headed to sea.

> First slowly, and then with gradually increasing speed, we moved away as with every moment the coastline emerged more clearly from the darkness. We could dimly make out our shipmates signalling with lights. They had reached the shore and were flashing out a farewell message: 'Bon voyage. If they catch us we'll say the boat struck a mine and we were the only survivors.' Then, to our surprise, followed a short burst of gunfire as coastal batteries engaged. We sank thankfully to the bottom.
>
> Morale was high. There was complete unity amongst us and our decision was duly entered in the log book. Any suggestion of running our ship on democratic lines was ruled out ...We certainly worked efficiently, even with so few hands aboard. The youngsters in the engine room knew their jobs and carried on without the Petty Officers, and, incidentally, moved into their mess so that now we had room to stretch our legs.[13]

So began a marathon trek around the British Isles and into the Atlantic, sailing continuously for sixty-six days underwater on snorkel and electric motors. Constant radar detection from the antennae mounted atop the snorkel head showed that the Allies had still not given up the hunt for outstanding U-boats. Many of those that had been lost in the final months of the war were still believed by BdU to be operational, and with no proof otherwise, Allied naval forces continued their search.

> After eighteen days without a break the crew began to get on edge, with black rings under their eyes, and faces pale and even greenish-looking from lack of daylight and fresh air. The bulkheads too were turning green with damp. Since we were permanently dived now we couldn't get rid of the refuse from the galley and this piled up into a revolting mess, apart from the smell breeding flies, maggots and other vermin … With our bodies and minds both imprisoned, there was nothing to occupy or stimulate us, and nothing at all to enjoy, cut off as we were from nature and civilisation. However much we longed to let off steam somehow, to scream, pick a quarrel or hit someone, we dared not break down for fear of what that might lead to – self-control is the first essential for the caged.[14]

Conditions in the boat deteriorated as the voyage dragged on. The crew had not seen daylight for over two months, and their condition and that of the vessel became extremely difficult. The diesel engines were also beginning to show the strain of the unnaturally prolonged voyage. As *U977* cruised in equatorial waters, the internal temperature rose, compounding the men's misery. Finally, after sixty-six days Schäffer allowed the U-boat to surface in an area he at last considered safe and the marathon submerged journey was ended beneath a clear, starry night sky. *U977* continued south, alternating between surface and submerged runs as the crew began to recover slightly from their ordeal. Conditions aboard were still delicate, and it remains a testament to Schäffer's leadership that the crew remained relatively united and functional throughout the trek. On 10 July, a radio broadcast announcing the arrival at Mara del Plata of the other escaping U-boat, Type IXC-40 *U530*, which had been in operations off the American coast at the time of the surrender, raised morale within the crew aboard *U977*, although only temporarily, as it was also learned that the crew had been handed over to the United States for imprisonment.

Twenty-four year old Oberleutnant zur See Otto Wermuth had been patrolling off New York in the Type IXC-40 *U530* when the ceasefire instructions were received. He had experienced no success, having fired nine of his fourteen torpedoes at a scattered group of ships that loomed in and out of fog, but achieved not a single hit. His crew of young men were despondent when orders to surrender to the nearest Allied port were received. Neither their commander nor the majority of the crew desired to spend time in an American prisoner-of-war camp, and instead they elected to head south to Argentina which, although now an enemy country, was well known for sympathetic treatment of Germans. The men jettisoned their remaining ammunition and all secret materials before heading south.

On 10 July, *U530* surrendered at Mara del Plata where the crew were thoroughly interrogated amidst lurid speculation that Hitler, or Bormann, had arrived by U-boat and been smuggled ashore before *U530* surrendered. Wermuth was far more circumspect than other surrendered U-boat commanders. He did not explain why it had taken him more than two months to reach Argentina, and he also refused to explain why the boat had jettisoned its flak guns, he had ordered the boat's KTB destroyed, and the crew carried no identification. Immediately, the rumours began. Brazilian Admiral Jorge Dodsworth Martins blamed the destruction of the cruiser *Bahia* on *U530*, while Admiral Dudal Teixeira believed that the boat had sailed from Japan, and thus could have been carrying gold or secret weapons. An Argentine reporter claimed that he had seen a Buenos Aires provincial police report, to the effect that a strange submarine had surfaced off the lower Argentine coast, and had landed a high-ranking officer and a civilian, who might have been Adolf Hitler and Eva Braun in disguise. Theories also circulated that the captain who surrendered the boat was not actually Wermuth, but had replaced him by, variously, either coming aboard from a secret Argentine base, or taking command following a mutiny by the crew. Eventually, the Argentine Naval Ministry issued an official communiqué in which they stated that *U530* was not responsible for the sinking of the *Bahia*; no Nazi leader or military officers were aboard; and *U530* had landed no one on the coast of Argentina before surrendering.

Unaware of most of this pandemonium, Mara del Plata remained Schäffer's destination, and *U977* surfaced on 17 August outside the three-mile territorial limit, flashing the message 'German submarine' in English. After curious fishing boats had already inspected the stained and rusted U-boat, the Argentine minesweeper *PY10* arrived with two submarines to inform Schäffer that a second, more senior, party would be aboard shortly. Once the Argentine officers had arrived and boarded *U977*, Schäffer was allowed to bring his boat into harbour. There he was politely but firmly interrogated about his voyage. A primary cause for concern was indicated by the questions that enquired whether Schäffer had travelled with anyone of 'political prominence' aboard. The arrival of *U977* fuelled endless absurd speculation about U-boats smuggling high-ranking Nazis from Germany as the nation lay in its death throes. Whilst it is true that Argentina did indeed harbour many such men, the idea that they had been smuggled

U805 after being boarded by American sailors. The boat put into Portsmouth, USA, and later made a tour of the American East Coast on so-called 'Victory Visits' before being scuttled in February 1946.

U977 and *U530* in Mara del Plata, Argentina.

there via U-boat remains completely unsubstantiated. Even more fanciful were reports that Schäffer had taken Hitler and Eva Braun on his epic voyage, or, the height of absurdity, that Schäffer and *U530* had acted as escort for a small convoy transporting Hitler and his entourage to their new redoubt in the frozen wastes of Antarctica. The truth remains more prosaic. *U977* was the final fragment of Dönitz's doomed U-boat war, manned by young men whose displeasure at handing themselves and their boat over to their enemy outweighed the risks inherent in such a long and difficult voyage.

Aside from the unlikely charge of smuggling prominent Nazis to 'freedom', another charge that has been commonly levelled at Schäffer (as well as Wermuth), and one that he was immediately questioned about by the Argentinians, was that he torpedoed and sank the Brazilian cruiser *Bahia* on 4 July 1945. Upon the cessation of hostilities in Europe, the Brazilian Navy had allocated support ships to take up predetermined stations within the Atlantic in order to track the large number of American aircraft transferring from their Brazilian and American airfields to Europe. During September 1945 this allocation proved its worth when the fourteen crewmen of a crashed B17 bomber were rescued by Brazilian destroyer *Greenhalgh*.

The *Bahia* had departed the naval base at Recife bound for Station 13, five hundred miles offshore. There, the cruiser relieved Escort Destroyer *Bauru* on 2 July and commenced sailing its allotted station. The next day, the anti-aircraft weapons began a routine exercise that involved seven Oerlikon 20mm cannon using a towed kit for target practice. At approximately 0900hrs, the engines were secured for launching of the target, and firing commenced soon afterward. Unexpectedly, after only a few shots, the stern of the *Bahia* was ripped apart by a huge explosion. The rapid firing weapon had not been fitted with stops to prevent its trajectory being lowered so as to endanger other gun positions. As the weapon fired at the target, the kite descended, bringing the gunfire down until it impacted depth charges stored on the fantail. The destruction was immense and within three minutes *Bahia* was rapidly sinking stern first. Only seventeen life rafts had survived the blast, with 271 men cramming into them once their ship was gone. Many were severely injured, and for the next four days they faced shark attack, dehydration, the cold of night and intense heat of day, until the pitiful number of survivors were found by British merchant ship SS *Balfe*. Immediately, the Brazilian Navy despatched a group of ships to search for survivors. In total, from a complement of 372, a total of 336 men died, including four American servicemen who were in charge of the communication system used in connection with the American aircraft.

Immediately, suspicion fell on Schäffer after he had arrived off the Argentine mainland. However, his direct answers to the questions put to him, and the fact that he still carried his full complement of torpedoes, appeared to convince his Argentine captors that he was telling the truth, and had in no way been responsible for the *Bahia* tragedy. His Argentine questioner then enquired as to why Schäffer had opted to surrender to Argentina.

> That question wasn't hard to answer. The rules of war provide that all war material belonging to a defeated power shall become the property of the victors, and so the Soviet Union must now be in possession of all our improvements in technique. I had therefore to take care to carry out Admiral Dönitz's order to surrender – as soon as I had verified it – in such a way as to ensure that it should be advantageous to a nation which had already displayed such chivalry towards the German Navy in the matter of the pocket battleship *Graf Spee*. I had also to consider the welfare of my crew. There was no other enemy country from which they could expect such good treatment. There had never been any hatred between Germany and Argentina, only a condition of honourable belligerency, and that for a relatively short time only.[15]

In short order, Schäffer's hopes of imprisonment in Argentina were dashed. Already newspapers were recounting a tale of the dramatic escape of Hitler aboard his boat, with the German leader then supposedly continuing towards the newly-established Nazi base in Antarctica, and once an Anglo-American commission had begun to interrogate Schäffer in Argentina, with no progress towards the confession they desired, he was transferred to Washington, DC, where the questioning continued. Schäffer and Oberleutnant zur See Otto Wermuth from *U530* were even brought face-to-face to each other in a confined cell, where American listeners hoped their reunion would provoke careless discussions about their secret mission. Unfortunately, the two officers had never met previously, and their conversations yielded nothing of interest for Allied Naval Intelligence.

The claims that U-boats gathered off Argentina at the end of the war continue to be put forward as reality by many, including some reputable historians who have claimed to have been given access to recently-declassified documents, detailing the landing of Nazi officials by U-boat, and clandestine missions of re-supply carried out to establish bases in Argentina and Antarctica. Although it is indisputable that several wanted Nazis, such as Adolf Eichmann and Josef Mengele, made their way successfully to South America following the German surrender, there has never been a scrap of corroborated evidence that proves the complicity of Kriegsmarine U-boats in this. Discounting immediately the absurdity of a German National Socialist redoubt in the barren wilderness of Antarctica, the assorted eyewitness accounts of furtive U-boat landings on the Argentine coast have yielded nothing. Various underwater anomalies that have appeared to resemble the conning towers of sunken U-boats have been dived and yielded large flat rocks. From personal experience of searching for the wrecks of

U190 photographed following its surrender in Canada, 1945.

Vorpostenboote and minesweepers in the waters of Brittany, I can confirm that what often appears to be an unmistakable silhouette of a sunken military vessel can in fact be little more than nature's practical joke on the unwary underwater explorer.

Stories of U-boat landings have long fired the imagination. So much so that U-boats have been ascribed as putting men and equipment ashore in Ireland, New Zealand, Argentina, the Canary Islands, and various parts of the United Kingdom. Yes, they were used for the delivery of raiding parties, saboteurs and spies: this is all a matter of documented fact. But the theories that include a fleet of U-boats smuggling gold, treasure, Nazi politicians, religious artefacts and even the Führer himself (a notorious sufferer of seasickness) have never been supported by a single shred of evidence. The sinking of the *Bahia* has even been attributed to *U977* without the latter having fired a shot! The same reputable author who made this claim in public also theorised that Schäffer's boat had been loaded with so much in the way of food supplies for the support of the Patagonian U-boat fleet that it resembled a floating delicatessen. How this boat then managed to destroy a fully-armed Brazilian cruiser, without the use of a torpedo, remains an interesting question, and one that I am sure Dönitz himself would have been interested to have had answered. Finally, this matter does beg the question as to why such crucial and sacred missions as the transport of the beating heart of National Socialist Germany to a new future would be entrusted to junior commanders, in obsolete boats, when there were more politically-motivated and experienced seamen available aboard newer, revolutionary U-boats which could almost guarantee to escape detection. The matter is patently implausible: the stuff of fantasy novels and adventure films.

In the real world, while the dramatic bids for freedom made by *U977* and *U530* were just beginning, the first U-boat to respond to the surrender order was *U249*, spotted flying a black flag off the Scilly Islands on 8 May by a US Navy Liberator bomber. Two Royal Navy sloops were despatched to rendezvous with the surrendering boat. Oberleutnant zur See Uwe Kock was obeying Dönitz's instructions to the letter, and continued to transmit his position in plain language as the British warships approached. HMS *Amethyst* and *Magpie* eventually reached the stationary U-boat and led Kock into Portland Bight.

That same day, *U1009*, which had been on weather reporting duties in the North Atlantic, surrendered to HMS *Beaumaris Castle*, Telegraphist George A Smith later remembered the event:

> Tuesday, the eighth of May, 1945, turned out to be a memorable day for me, a 21-year-old Royal Naval telegraphist aboard a minesweeper at the top of the Minches in the Atlantic, near the Butt of Lewis in the Outer Hebrides. Our flotilla was on its second day out from Stornoway, with the ships stretched out on a routine sweep in full lookout for mines, but the ship's crew and officers were trying to come to terms with the fact that the war in Europe had ended, when in the late afternoon 'Action stations' were sounded aboard our ship. To our shock and surprise a German U-boat rose menacingly to the surface, and slowly at the masthead she hoisted a black flag. The German High Command had ordered all U-boats to surrender unconditionally to the nearest Allied naval ships, and the hoisting of the black flag was the surrender signal.
>
> After the panic had subsided messages were rapidly exchanged with our flotilla leader and the naval base at Loch Ewe, and finally we were instructed to order the German U-boat to follow in our wake into Loch Ewe. Hours later we steamed into this great loch where in the past few years convoys to Russia and the United States had gathered and left with naval escorts.

U805 surrendering in the mid-Atlantic.

Formal surrender was undertaken by senior British naval officers who boarded the U-boat and interrogated her captain and officers. Apparently other U-boats were also expected there. Our crew was ultimately allowed to board this U-boat and inspect what had been the hated scourge of all Allied shipping. Ironically, we had formally to salute the U-boat's officers before boarding their boat, but grudgingly we all knew this was the crème de la crème of the German navy.[16]

The U-boat was escorted toward Loch Eriboll where the minesweeper handed its charge over to crews of other Royal Navy vessels who would board and take the boat's final surrender.

I was serving in HMS *Byron*, an anti-submarine frigate built in the USA. On VE Day, we, together with the rest of the 21st Escort Group, were ordered from Belfast to Loch Eriboll, a sea loch near Cape Wrath on the NW corner of Scotland, remote, rugged, grand; a sheet of water about ten miles long with the hills of Sutherland in the background, to accept the surrender of the U-boat fleet operating in the North Atlantic and Arctic.

The Group arrived at Loch Eriboll during the early morning of 9th May. We waited. The boarding parties drew weapons and rations, a Motor Launch patrolled the entrance and then on 10th May at 8.15am DBST (Double British Summer Time), the first U-boat, *U1009*, arrived on the surface flying a tattered black flag from its periscope as a sign that it was ready to surrender. Everyone went to action stations.

Byron was guard ship and the motor boat was launched with the boarding party aboard. The U-boat was boarded, guns and torpedo firing pistols were thrown overboard and log books and other documents were removed in preparation for the escorted passage to Loch Alsh where the crew were to be taken into captivity. Next morning we arrived at Loch Alsh and took the boat alongside a submarine depot ship. The U-boat Captain read a message to his ship's company telling them that they were leaving their boat and I think there were a few tears.

The 21st Escort Group/Loch Eriboll surrender operation lasted from 10th to 21st May and during that time thirty-three U-boats gave themselves up. On 22nd May, the

Scuttled Type XXI U-boats. The codeword Regenbogen was officially countermanded by Dönitz to be in line with Allied surrender terms, although privately he applauded the actions of those commanders who chose to destroy their boats rather than hand them over to the Allies.

Group escorted four boats across the Irish Sea to Moville on the shores of Loch Foyle ready for the formal surrender to Admiral Sir Max Horton, C-in-C Western Approaches in Londonderry.

The Kriegsmarine? We found them to be sailors much like ourselves, well-disciplined, responsive to the orders of their officers, still motivated to work their ships and with their morale intact even at the moment of surrender, despite the U-boat service having sustained casualties unsurpassed by any other enemy or allied fighting service. When shown photographs in 'Picture Post' of Auschwitz and Belsen, they were unable to believe that their country could do such things and called it Allied propaganda.

Such was the drama of those days in May 1945, played out on the quiet waters of a Scottish loch when peace returned to the Atlantic, when history was made. My remaining memories are of the White Ensign flying proudly over the swastika ensign of Hitler's navy on the first U-boat to enter an Allied harbour and of the short service which was conducted by our Captain at 'divisions' on the first Sunday morning of peace. ... We were glad that the war in Europe was over, we 'spliced the mainbrace' and were thankful.

We now had to prepare ourselves for transfer to the Pacific war against Japan, which still raged. We heard that HMS *Byron* had been allocated to the British Pacific Fleet.[17]

On 10 May, HMS *Mermaid* gingerly approached *U825* which was running surfaced south-west of Ireland in the Western Approaches. The U-boat's commander, Oberleutnant der Reserve Gerhard Stoelker, had hoisted a black flag as ordered. Lieutenant-Commander John Mosse remembered the meeting: 'It was an eerie feeling approaching this black monster, which had so recently been our mortal enemy. He was probably as apprehensive as we were. We kept our guns trained on him, but he gave no trouble. Until this moment it had been hard to believe that the war against Germany was over.'[18]

The majority of U-boats surrendering to British forces were ordered to proceed to the sea area off Northern Ireland or Loch Ryan in Scotland. In Loch Eriboll, naval correspondent Eric Williams awaited the arrival of the U-boats to surrender.

Through the haze on the horizon, a black object shimmered inexorably towards the loch. A tattered green flag, not the swastika, flapped on its mast. The guns of the fleet remained trained on the dark shape, *U1109*, as it slithered towards the frigates and corvettes massed to take the surrender of their foe. A British boarding party clambered on to the U-boat, where its commander, a dour, archetypal German officer, one Friedrich von Riesen, limply gave the Nazi salute. Within minutes, *U1109* – which on two patrols had failed to sink a single Allied vessel – had raised the White Ensign and was escorted toward Culmore Point.

I built up a fascinating impression of these brave, clever and determined men. Discipline was the backbone of their character – implicit and unquestioning obedience. They preferred to be known as soldiers, not sailors, and they obeyed automatically. When I asked one officer whether he would obey an order he knew to be wrong, he smiled and said: 'But that would not happen. We do not get wrong orders.'[19]

On 6 May, the 21st Escort Group, under the command of Lieutenant-Commander

Raymond Hart, DSC and Bar, were in Milford Haven for refuelling after escorting a convoy into the Bristol Channel. The following day all shore leave was curtailed and the group was ordered to sea by Admiral Max Horton. Their instructions were to head to proceed to the desolate anchorage at Loch Erinboll off the northwest coast of Scotland, where they were to prepare for the surrender of the U-boats. The group arrived during early afternoon on 8 May, by which time the British crews knew that the war against Germany had ended. The five ships were HMS *Conn, Byron, Rupert, Deane, Fitzroy* and the Commander-in-Chief's yacht, *Philante*, which joined the group on 9 May as a replacement for HMS *Redmill*, which had been torpedoed in Donegal Bay on the morning of 27 April 1945. The crippled destroyer was laying up in Lisahally with a hefty portion of stern missing and thirty-two crewmen killed in the blast.

The first guard ship assigned the task of shepherding the surrendering U-boats into the Loch was HMS *Conn*. A motor boat was loaded with an armed boarding party as they awaited the Germans. However, it was something of an anticlimax as it was not until the following day, 10 May, at 0940hrs, that the sleek grey shape of *U1009* hove into view. By this time the guard ship had been replaced by HMS *Byron*, whose boarding party scrambled aboard the U-boat to take its surrender. Oberleutnant der Reserve Klaus Hilgendorf and his boat were escorted into the Loch and anchored near HMS *Byron*. Two further boats surrendered to the 21st Escort Group on 10 May, and from that point onwards they arrived almost at regular intervals: each time a boarding party put aboard to escort them to Loch Alsh for complete disarmament, the crews were removed, and the officers shepherded away for interrogation and internment in prisoner-of-war camps. Once the boats had been disarmed and tidied internally, a skeleton crew under armed guard sailed them to Lisahally, where they would be held until they were handed over for trials and testing, or disposed of in what became Operation Deadlight.

By 18 May, eighteen U-boats had surrendered in Loch Erinboll to the 21st Escort

U3503 scuttling, photographed from the deck of Swedish destroyer *Norrköping*.

Group. On 16 May, Norwegian destroyer HMNS *Stord*, with Rear Admiral E C Danielsen on board on passage to northern Norway, had intercepted a German convoy consisting of fifteen U-boats, two depot ships, one accommodation ship which had formerly been the King of Norway's private yacht, and one tanker from the 14th U-Flotilla en route from Narvik to Trondheim. The U-boats were diverted to Loch Eriboll under escort by HMCS *Matane* and the 9th Escort Group, which was detached from Russian convoy escort duty to escort the boats to Scotland and into the hands of the 21st Escort Group.

At 1800hrs on 22 May, the last of the U-boats were escorted to their dispersal point, arriving in the Foyle at 1630hrs on 23 May. Whilst en route to Lisahally on 21 May, the following signal was received from Admiral Max Horton: 'Goodbye. My most sincere thanks for the wholehearted and efficient co-operation you have given. When I knew I was coming to this job I asked for the best group they could find. I got it. Your final escort of ten U-boats to Lisahally is a fitting tribute to your career in the Western Approaches.' The 21st Escort Group then replied: 'Your extremely generous and kind signal is much appreciated. We are proud to have been selected for this job and fortunate to work under your orders. We will do our best to deliver them safely. Hart, Conn, SO 21st E/G, 21/5/45.'[20]

Thirty-three U-boats had surrendered in Loch Erinboll, by far the largest number of seagoing U-boats to surrender in any one port in the United Kingdom. Once its task had been successfully completed, the 21st Escort Group returned to Belfast for the last time. After the disbandment of the 21st Escort Group in early June, HMS *Conn*, *Byron* and *Fitzroy* were ordered to Norway to help in the relief of Bergen and joined the Victory Parade.

Whilst many U-boats within the Atlantic and Arctic Oceans were obeying Dönitz's orders, and the corresponding instructions issued from Allied naval commands, in the Baltic the last moments of a desperate struggle for survival were being played out, against a backdrop of the full brutality of the land war as Soviet troops arrived to repay tenfold the suffering inflicted by the Wehrmacht on their country. The Baltic Sea had long been the training ground of the Kriegsmarine. Alongside their surface vessels, the U-boats used the area for training throughout the war, until these very last days when it was denied them by increasing Russian pressure and eventual evacuation. Stretching along the southern Baltic shore, the following ports had U-boat training flotillas established there:

Pillau (now Baltiysk, Russia)	19th U-Flotilla (general boat handling, commander training)
	20th U-Flotilla (basic tactical theory)
	21st U-Flotilla
	26th U-Flotilla (shooting instruction)
Danzig (now Gdansk, Poland)	6th U-Flotilla
	23rd U-Flotilla (shooting instruction)
	Testing of new boats (Erprobungsgruppe)
Hela (Peninsula near Danzig)	Agru Front
Memel (now Klaip da, Lithuania)	24th U-Flotilla (submerged torpedo firing)
Libau (now Liep ja, Lithuania)	25th U-Flotilla (shooting instruction)
Stettin (now Szczecin, Poland)	4th U-Flotilla (completion of boats before assigned to front-line unit)

Gotenhafen (now Gydnia)   24th U-Flotilla (submerged torpedo firing)
                                 27th U-Flotilla (tactical training).

Whilst some of the training units carried their own complement of U-boats, including
the majority of the Type II boats that had spearheaded the opening offensive against
British forces in 1939 and 1940, others were for the sharpening of new crews aboard
newly-commissioned U-boats. Ancillary units such as torpedo-recovery vessels and
torpedo targets were attached where required, and the strength of any particular training
units could fluctuate dramatically. For example, the 25th U-Training Flotilla, which was
primarily concerned with shooting instruction, was periodically based in six separate
locations: Travemünde, Memel, Trondheim, Libau, Gotenhafen and Danzig. The unit's
commander was Korvettenkapitän Georg-Wilhelm Schulz, an 'Ace' of the original U-
boat offensives, and probably most famous for his time aboard *U124*, the 'Edelweiss' boat.
On 2 May he was in Travemünde:

> It was a sad picture; all those brand new U-boats were being scuttled one by one.
> Motorboats were underway taking the crews away from the area … High Command
> had ordered that myself and my men were to march to Flensburg. After detailed
> discussions with my staff officers we came to the conclusion that the greatest risk and
> reason for such heavy casualties in evacuation shipping was the inability of the target
> ships that we were using to deal with the minefields sown by the English in the Baltic.
> On 3 May at 0500hrs the entire formation departed Travemünde and headed North.
> I was on the 3,000 to 4,000-ton ship *Messina*.[21]

The small convoy that Schulz and his survivors from the 25th U-Training Flotilla
comprised was soon under attack by enemy aircraft, the accompanying ship *Bolkoburg*
suffering sixteen dead and one wounded during the attack. The journey to Flensburg was
broken off and Schulz ordered the vulnerable ships towards land, the *Swakopmund*, *Wega*
and *Bolkoburg* to the south coast of Fehmarn, and *Messina*, *Kürassier* and *Pionier* closer to
the east coast, in sight of the beaches and corresponding defence from land-based flak
emplacements. Schulz aboard *Messina* was acutely aware of the vulnerable situation in
which he found himself:

> Personally I thank my God from the bottom of my heart that he provided me with a
> guardian angel during the voyage from Travemünde to Fehmarn … We gave the air
> raid alarm when we were threatened by enemy aircraft, but there was nothing we
> could do about it – we had given all our flak weapons at Travemünde to the Army
> units, so we had nothing to fire at them.[22]

Eventually Schulz disembarked the entire 2,500 men of his 25th U-Flotilla on Fehrman.
There he learnt of the capitulation of German forces in Italy on 2 May as the radio
room aboard *Messina* was used to keep abreast of the war situation. He also faced
problems within his own staff as the German Reich fragmented. Austria was declared a
Free State, and so Austrian troops were no longer bound to service within the German
Wehrmacht. It was a difficult position that German officers faced throughout the Reich,
and one often only controlled by the force of their will or the close bonds that many
Austrians had forged with their German comrades.[23]

At the end of February, the German Pomeranian front had collapsed, although

A dramatic photograph taken from the attacking Liberator bomber showing *U534* moments before the U-boat was sunk.

beachheads around the ports of Kolberg, Danzig and Gydnia continued to hold. On 15 March 1945, Marshal Ivan Konev launched the four Armies of the 1st Ukrainian Front into the Upper Silesian Offensive, completed by the month's end and marking the beginning of the final push on Berlin. The final defeat and disaster for Hitler's Reich was obviously imminent, and on 19 March the Führer issued his infamous 'scorched earth order', seen by most as more a punishment for the German people's unwillingness to fight to the end, and their inability to triumph, than a military plan to deny the enemy of material gain.

U-boats begin to gather under British control: a strange mixture of U-boat crewmen and Royal Navy men aboard the boat at right.

Re: Destruction Measures within Reich Territory

Our nation's struggle for existence forces us to utilize all means, even within Reich territory, to weaken the fighting power of our enemy and to prevent further advances. Any opportunity to inflict lasting damage on the striking power of the enemy must be taken advantage of. It is a mistake to believe that undestroyed or only temporarily paralyzed traffic, communications, industrial, and supply installations will be useful to us again after the recapture of lost territories. During his retreat, the enemy will leave behind only scorched earth and will abandon all concern for the population. I therefore command –

1. All military traffic, communications, industrial and supply installations as well as objects within Reich territory that might be used by the enemy in the continuation of his fight, either now or later, are to be destroyed.
2. It is the responsibility of the military command posts to execute this order to destroy all military objects, including traffic and communications installations.

   The Gauleiters and Commissioners for Reich Defence are responsible for destroying the industrial and supply installations, as well as of other objects of value; the troops must give the Gauleiters and Commissioners for Reich Defence the assistance they need to carry out this task.
3. This command is to be transmitted to all troop commanders as promptly as possible; orders to the contrary are null and void.

Adolf Hitler[24]

Dönitz, like many military leaders, was aghast at this order, and in turn issued commands that although German-held dockyard and harbours could indeed be mined and prepared for demolition, they were only to be destroyed on his express orders. By this means he was able to prevent the destruction of the ports required for the evacuation of German troops and civilians from the east. For example, the available remaining mercantile strength that Germany possessed was controlled by the Gauleiter (Nazi Party Regional Representative) of Hamburg, Karl Kaufmann, a founder member of the Nazi Party. With chaos engulfing the eastern front, Kaufmann handed over the merchant shipping to Dönitz's control, though he appeared still to be involved in the transport of concentration camp inmates, notably from Neuengamme, who had been evacuated and herded to the same ports on which thousands of civilians were now descending. Off Neustadt, thousands of inmates, alongside Russian prisoners-of-war, were put aboard the 27,571-ton liner *Cap Arcona* and the 2,815-ton freighter *Thielbek*, both of which sailed into Lübeck bay. The prisoners were guarded by SS men and held for days in appalling conditions, as the ships lay at anchor in the bay close to shore with constant streams of prisoners being brought aboard by barge.

Unfortunately, on 3 May 1945, British Typhoon fighter bombers from five squadrons of the Second Tactical Air Force attacked shipping in Lübeck Bay, the pilots having been briefed that large ships were due to ferry SS men to Norway from where a final German stand could be made. Squadrons 184, 197 and 263 attacked and sank the target, the 21,046-ton liner *Deutschland*, while aircraft from 198 Squadron sank both ships laden with prisoners. They were both flying white flags, but the British pilots' orders were unequivocal and also, according to the recollections of one pilot, included instructions to machine-gun survivors in the water.

Instrument of Surrender

of

All German armed forces in HOLLAND, in

northwest Germany including all islands,

and in DENMARK.

1. The German Command agrees to the surrender of all German armed
   forces in HOLLAND, in northwest GERMANY including the FRISIAN
   ISLANDS and HELIGOLAND and all other islands, in SCHLESWIG-
   HOLSTEIN, and in DENMARK, to the C.-in-C. 21 Army Group.
   This to include all naval ships in these areas.
   These forces to lay down their arms and to surrender unconditionally.

2. All hostilities on land, on sea, or in the air by German forces
   in the above areas to cease at 0800 hrs. British Double Summer Time
   on Saturday 5 May 1945.

3. The German command to carry out at once, and without argument or
   comment, all further orders that will be issued by the Allied
   Powers on any subject.

4. Disobedience of orders, or failure to comply with them, will be
   regarded as a breach of these surrender terms and will be dealt
   with by the Allied Powers in accordance with the accepted laws
   and usages of war.

5. This instrument of surrender is independent of, without prejudice
   to, and will be superseded by any general instrument of surrender
   imposed by or on behalf of the Allied Powers and applicable to Germany
   and the German armed forces as a whole.

6. This instrument of surrender is written in English and in German.

   The English version is the authentic text.

7. The decision of the Allied Powers will be final if any doubt or
   dispute arises as to the meaning or interpretation of the surrender
   terms.

B. L. Montgomery
Field-Marshal

4 May 1945

1830 hrs

The 'Instrument of Surrender' signed by Admiral von Friedeburg, showing Montgomery's
hasty inclusion of naval forces.

The evacuation from the east: members of the Hitler Youth and civilians are lifted from
the shores of East Prussia.

According to several accounts of the sinking, Fregattenkapitän (Ing.) Heinrich
Schmidt appears to have ordered that no survivors from the concentration camp
inmates aboard the *Cap Arcona* or *Thielbek* be taken, and it was widely reported that men
from the Neustadt U-boat base were responsible for shooting survivors in the water as
they neared the shoreline. Whether that is actually men who were *at* the Neustadt
training base, or men who were *from* there, has never been fully clarified. It would be
quite unlikely for Kriegsmarine men willingly to have opened fire on survivors from this
disaster, although in the highly-charged atmosphere of the collapsing Third Reich,
anything was possible. At around this time, apparently, the Kriegsmarine Field Police,
the Küstenpolizei, were allegedly responsible for their share of 'traitors' hung from
lamp-posts to dissuade retreat in the face of the enemy, a terrible act more often
attributed to SS police and other branches of the Wehrmacht. Nevertheless, British
troops arrived almost as the massacre was taking place, but not in time to bear witness
to what had happened.

Kaufmann, who had been instrumental in allowing the SS to commandeer the two
ships, had, for his part, already tried to arrange the surrender of Hamburg to British
forces as early as the middle of April, to which surrender Dönitz vehemently objected,
as the territory dominated by Hamburg was required to absorb the huge number of
refugees, and the loss of the city could result in the ensuing loss of the Baltic ports of
Schleswig-Holstein from where the evacuation ships were sailing. The terms of the
Unconditional Surrender of which Germany had been made aware meant that, once
Germany capitulated, troops were called upon to surrender their arms wherever they
were, which would leave thousands in the hands of the Russians. The Allied plans to
demarcate a conquered Germany had been known by OKW (Oberkommando der
Wehrmacht), the German Military High Command, since the beginning of 1945, and
Dönitz felt that his path was clear in regard to the evacuation from the east. British

authorities would undoubtedly respect the wishes of their Russian allies, rather than German plans to allow the evacuation to continue, and so resistance must be maintained until the last moment.

According to a summary prepared by the Kriegsmarine's Naval Group East, between 21 January and 8 May, more than a million soldiers and refugees had been thus evacuated from East Prussian ports, whilst another 2,022,000 were taken off the East Prussian coast. Finally the U-boat training bases were lost to the advancing Russians. Memel fell on 28 January, and the other training bases were soon threatened by the Russian advance. Gydnia, northwest of Danzig, fell on Wednesday, 28 March, and two days later the fighting in Danzig ended. The port city fell with forty-five U-boats and ten thousand prisoners-of-war. German troops were trapped in Breslau and Glogau, now totally encircled. Pillau would not surrender until 25 April, by which time 450,000 refugees had managed to be evacuated from the port.

As the Kriegsmarine's surface ships plied the waters of the Baltic, to bring as many as they could to Schleswig-Holstein, U-boat men were also involved, both as auxiliary crew aboard the transport ships, and within their own boats, which also took as many as possible to comparative safety. As the U-boat training bases in the East were evacuated, the westbound boats took as many as they could aboard and transported them west. In fact, the table shows the U-boats that were listed by the U-Boat Archive in Altenbruch as confirmed in taking part in the evacuation missions in 1945 (although there may well have been others, as records are far from complete).

U-Boat Evacuation Missions in 1945

Date (all 1945)	Boat	From/To	Evacuated
13 January	U3002	Unknown/Travemünde	Women and children
25 January	U59	Pillau/Kiel	13 women and children
25 January	U746	Pillau/Stettin	15 severely wounded
25 January	U1306	Pillau/Warnemünde	12 children
26 January	U152	Pillau/Kiel	Led a group of 12 U-boats that carried between them 169 women and children
26 January	U236	Pillau/Kiel	Unknown number of refugees
26 January	U828	Danzig/Swinemünde	Wife and four children of IWO
26 January	U58	Pillau/Kiel	8-10 women and children
27 January	U3522	Hela/Rönne	50 Hitler Youth
27 January	U3524	Danzig/Kiel	Refugees
28 January	U14	Gotenhafen/Kiel	1 woman and her baby
28 January	U17	Gotenhafen/Kiel	20 U-boat men
28 January	U56	Pillau/Kiel	2 women and 4 children
28 January	U57	Pillau/Kiel	8-10 women and children
28 January	U3025	Hela/Rönne	50 Hitler Youth
28 January	U368	Pillau/Kiel	Unknown number of refugees
28 January	U747	Gotenhafen/Kiel	30-40 refugees
28 January	U721	Hela/Warnemünde	21 Hitler Youth

28 January	*U778*	Pillau/Stettin	20 refugees
30 January	*U3501*	Danzig/unknown	Unknown number of refugees
31 January	*U903*	Kolberg/Swinemünde	58 survivors from *Wilhelm Gustloff*
January	*U1065*	Pillau/Warnemünde	16 wounded
January	*UD4*	Königsberg/Eckernförde	Married couple and child
28 February	*U3507*	Gotenhafen/Unknown	60 Hitler Youth
28 February	*U3010*	Hela/Travemünde	50 Naval Hitler Youth
February	*U2507*	Danzig/Warnemünde	Unknown number of refugees
February	*U822*	Hela/Stettin	1 woman
February	*U1197*	Pillau/Kiel	41 refugees
2 March	*U3514*	Hela/Travemünde	30 women and children
2 March	*U3517*	Danzig/Unknown	53 children
10 March	*U1306*	Hela/Warnemünde	1 woman, 3 children and 15 Hitler Youth
14 March	*U999*	Hela/Warnemünde	40 refugees
15 March	*U828*	Swinemünde/Brunsbüttel	6 women and 11 children
16 March	*U1007*	Hela/Rönne	35 Hitler Youth
22 March	*U3505*	Hela/Travemünde	50 Hitler Youth
23 March	*U3528*	Danzig/Kiel	Women and children
23 March	*U3529*	Danzig/Bornholm	Refugees
28 March	*U3012*	Hela/Swinemünde	60 flak troops
29 March	*U3023*	Hela/Swinemünde	120 flak troops
Unknown	*U2524*	Gotenhafen/Warnemünde	25-30 refugees
Unknown	*U721*	Hela/Warnemünde	Refugees
Unknown	*U924*	Hela/Warnemünde	16 children
Unknown	*U2502*	Hela/Travemünde	30 women and children
Unknown	*U1028*	Unknown. Boat sailed though not completed	Refugees
Unknown	*U1110*	Danzig/Kiel	60 refugees
Unknown	*U1205*	Hela/Warnemünde	20 children
Unknown	*U1306*	Hela Swinemünde	30 school children
Unknown	*U2503*	Unknown	Unknown
Unknown	*U2518*	Hela/Swinemünde	3 women and 3 children
Unknown	*U2521*	Unknown	Unknown
Unknown	*U2533*	Hela/Rönne	50 Hitler Youth
Unknown	*U3020*	Hela/Travemünde	50 Hitler Youth
Unknown	*U3013*	Hela/Bornholm	30-40 refugees
Unknown	*U3511*	Hela/Travemünde	50 Hitler Youth

Many of these boats had not even entered active service; others were retired veterans which had served as training vessels for new U-boat crews. Despite their relatively small carrying capacity, every living person who was successfully evacuated, not only from the carnage of the front line, but also from the forthcoming Russian sphere of influence, owed their deliverance to what, in the majority of cases, was a crew as yet untried in battle.

Instrumental in this evacuation using U-boats was the commander of the 22nd U-

Flotilla based in Gotenhafen. The unit's highly decorated commander, Korvettenkapitän Heinrich 'Ajax' Bleichrodt, had been ordered to scuttle the boats under his command and transfer their crews to the infantry defence against the Russians, while he returned to Wilhelmshaven to the remainder of his relocated training command. Successfully arguing that his men had neither the training nor equipment to fight on land, he instead gathered all the boats of his flotilla, cramming them with as many relatives of his crews, and any other available civilians, as possible, and headed west. The flotilla travelled surfaced with flak weapons constantly manned, towing lifeboats full of provisions and more people. It was a remarkable achievement. Maschinengefreiter Alfred Philipp from the 31st U-Flotilla's Type XXI *U2533* remembered their voyage:

> At the end of March we were in harbour at Hela. We lay there for two to three days until the final day we learned that Russian troops had cut off the Hela Peninsula. In the meantime 50 members of the Hitler Youth had arrived and our commander [Oberleutnant zur See Horst Günther, an experienced submariner, ex-IWO from *U275*] gave the order to bring them onboard. We brought them all onboard and accommodated them in the forward compartment. Surprisingly, we were able to sail for some way after departure surfaced until Russian air attack forced us to make an emergency dive. During the dive we momentarily lost control. Our LI had guessed his recalculations with the 50 Hitler Youth in the bow compartment, so when we dived it was with much greater speed and we charged into the depths. At about 98 metres we hit the seafloor hard. But, apart from terrifying us, nothing happened. After a short while we emerged and continued our voyage. Our commander set course for the island of Bornholm and we entered port at Rönne where the kids left the boat. Afterwards, we continued our training.[25]

German troops, here aboard a destroyer, were also evacuated from almost certain annihilation by the Russians. It was a valiant effort by the Kriegsmarine, which saved thousands from an uncertain future within what would become the Russian zone of control.

U541 surrenders to the Royal Navy in Gibraltar.

The curtailment of U-boat training by the overrunning of the Baltic ports was, by May 1945, largely irrelevant. The Wehrmacht had been defeated and there was nothing that could have been furthered by continuing to train men in waters now laced with mines, covered by Russian and British aircraft, and stalked by Russian ships and submarines. Already enough combat-ready U-boats were available in Norway, or at least in preparation for sailing, and the majority of them, too, were fortunate not to be sent into action in what were clearly becoming the last days of the war.

On 30 April Dönitz issued orders that the German fleet should be scuttled to prevent capture, except for those craft that would be required for future fishing, transport or minesweeping. The honour of the Kriegsmarine was at stake, and Dönitz confidently expected his captains to destroy their ships rather than surrender them to the victorious Allies. The code word to instigate the destruction was 'Regenbogen' (rainbow), and on 2 May detailed instructions for Operation Regenbogen were distributed from Flensburg by staff officers of the U-boat fleet to some eighty U-boat commanders whose boats were nearby. Dönitz's original timetable had been for the destruction to be carried out on 4 May, allowing two days for the U-boats to prepare for scuttling. Many U-boats had already been destroyed as the ports were occupied by Allies advancing from both fronts, but the organised scuttling of Regenbogen would allow a final defiance open to the men of the Kriegsmarine: for the end of their vessels to be made on their own terms.

Meanwhile, all U-boats in German waters which were still capable of submerged travel had been ordered to travel to Norway, not only to escape the attention of low-level fighter bombers which were sweeping the Baltic, but also to strengthen the German presence in the last great bastion securely held by the Wehrmacht. Needless to say, this

The crew of *U858* are held aboard US warship guard following
their boat's surrender.

renewed exodus provided Allied aircraft with an almost unparalleled opportunity, and
in the days between 2 May and 6 May, twenty-one U-boats were destroyed in the
Kattegat.

Dönitz, as the Head of the German Government, despatched his newly-appointed
Oberbefehlshaber der Kriegsmarine, or Commander-in-Chief, Generaladmiral Hans
von Friedeburg to negotiate surrender terms with Field Marshal Montgomery at the
latter's headquarters on Lüneburg Heath. Dönitz wished to surrender his forces
piecemeal; those facing the British would be first. While Supreme Allied Command had
forbidden the separate surrender of different German forces, Eisenhower had allowed
Montgomery some leeway to accept such capitulation in Denmark, the Netherlands,
Heligoland and Schleswig-Holstein, as well as any individual troops as a 'tactical matter'.
Thus Montgomery agreed terms with von Friedeburg for the surrender of northern
Germany, but his conditions included the provisos that Holland and Denmark be
included, and that the German fleet also be surrendered: no weapons or vessels were to
be destroyed before being handed over to British authorities. Without these conditions
being met, Montgomery was unable to accept the German surrender.

Dönitz found himself in an impossible quandary. Should he deny the British
conditions, then he faced immediate problems in attempting to continue the mass exodus
of people fleeing from the east away from the Russians. Every day that he could prolong
the evacuation could save thousands as they flocked to the German-held northern
enclave. However, he now faced the fact that to comply with British demands, scheduled
to become effective on 5 May at 0800hrs, he would be forced to cancel Operation

Regenbogen, and hand over the entire German fleet untouched to the victor. It would be a humiliating end to a hard-fought and bitter war which had dragged across the oceans of the world for nearly six long years. Nonetheless, there was far more at stake than his and his navy's pride.

I fully realised that if I handed over our warships I would be acting contrary to the traditions of our navy and of the navies of every other nation. It was in an effort to conform to this code of honour which is accepted by all nations that the German Navy sank the fleet in Scapa Flow at the end of the First World War. But I had no doubt in my own mind that I should have to surrender the ships. This time the situation was very different. This time it was a question of saving countless men, women and children from death just as the war was coming to an end. If I refused on a point of honour to give up the ships, the separate surrender would not go through. The air raids on northern Germany would start afresh and cause yet more loss of life. And that was a thing that I had to prevent at all costs. Accordingly I remained firm in my decision to accept this stipulation as well. The reproach has since been levelled at me that we should still have had time to destroy weapons and sink warships before the surrender came into force. To that I can only retort that such an action would have been against the spirit of our undertakings. Nor must the fact be forgotten that on 3 May, as soon as he heard of our intention to surrender, Montgomery had ordered an immediate cessation of air raids although the surrender had not yet been implemented.[26]

Accordingly, Dönitz issued his ceasefire order, which was transmitted on all wavelengths to the U-boat fleet continuously throughout 4 May. The details of the German

The crew of *U858* are held aboard US warship guard following their boat's surrender.

Thilo Bode, commander of *U858*, officially surrenders his boat to the US Navy.

surrender were then transmitted to all German forces at 1514hrs on 4 May. This, in effect, countermanded the previous instructions that had been given to U-boat commanders that they should scuttle their craft. The Allied insistence that U-boats be handed over intact was emphasised in Dönitz's new transmission.

Meanwhile, von Friedeburg had attempted to repeat the successful surrender terms with American forces, reaching Eisenhower's headquarters at Reims, whereupon the Supreme Allied commander refused to even see him, and vetoed any and all ideas of a separate surrender to American forces. It was unconditional surrender on all fronts or nothing. Despite acquiescing to this American ultimatum, which was backed by the threat of severe penalties if not met, including any separately-surrendering German units to be fired on by American troops, it enabled von Friedeburg and the OKW representative Jodl to secure forty-eight more hours, during which the surrender message would be transmitted to distant and isolated German posts; forty-eight more hours in which to evacuate more people from the east.

In the interim, Dönitz's surrender orders which had been transmitted on 4 May had placed his U-boat captains in something of a quandary. Most boats that were still within the western Baltic Sea had been prepared for scuttling, and their commanders debated the veracity of the new instructions to hand over their boats intact.

> In the meantime we receive news: a ceasefire in northwest Holland; Hamburg, Kiel and Flensburg have been declared open cities; negotiations about an armistice are under way with the British Field Marshal, Sir Bernard Montgomery; northwest Germany and Denmark surrender. But the U-boat war continues until we receive the code word 'Rainbow'. The core of the fleet is being scuttled. Soon thereafter 'Rainbow' is cancelled. The boats of comrades are being bombed and sunk. We are powerless.[27]

Many reasoned that the original instructions had been quite specific, and therefore the order countermanding scuttling must have been issued under duress from the Allies. Therefore its legality was void and they were no longer bound to follow such an order.

It was a point of view not without some foundation and correspondingly, without receiving the code word Regenbogen from BdU, 217 U-boat commanders and crews destroyed their boats, the majority in ports at Kiel, Trevemünde, and within the Gelting Bay. Sixteen further U-boats that had not yet been commissioned were scuttled.

In fact, some boats had already begun to scuttle before the order was countermanded by Dönitz. The first two to do so were Type XXI U-boats, *U3006* and *U3009*. Both attached to the 4th U-Flotilla at Stettin during their working up period, the former was scuttled by Oberleutnant zur See Ernst Fischer at Wilhelmshaven, and the latter by Kapitänleutnant Karl Schimpf in Wesermünde. More followed the next day: *U612*, a training boat of the 31st U-Flotilla captained by Oberleutnant zur See Hans-Peter Dick, and *U1308*, a training boat of the 4th U-Flotilla commanded by Oberleutnant zur See Heinrich Besold. Both were sunk near the port of Warnemünde on 2 May. The following day *U1308* followed suit in the same area. The floodgates had been opened, and by the time of Dönitz's second transmission forbidding the destruction of the German fleet, a total of 136 U-boats, including the serviceable, damaged and incomplete, had already scuttled in the Western Baltic, German Bight, Kaiser Wilhelm Canal, and in Hamburg harbour. Admittedly, those scuttling had been largely in response to imminent capture by Soviet or British forces. The second wave of scuttling that was directly in contravention with Dönitz's instructions involved a further eighty-three U-boats, one of which, *U3516*, was scuttled with five crewmen voluntarily remaining aboard. The scuttling actually continued past Germany's surrender. For example, *U2538* had been en route from Swinemünde to Neustadt when British troops had overrun the Baltic coast. Oberleutnant zur See Heinrich Klapper opted to keep his boat at sea while they decided whether or not to scuttle. Finally, on 9 March, the boat was sunk by its crew off Marstal, Aerø Island, Denmark. Despite the contravention of the Allied instructions, no disciplinary or punitive actions were taken by the Allied forces.

Obermaschinist Kurt Fella remembers the scuttling of the Type XXI *U3027*. 'In the Bremen/Weser AG, while still in training shortly before the commissioning of the Type IXC *U891*, the crew was ordered instead to *U3027*. This boat was sunk by me near Travemünde on 5 March. The crew was sent marching in the direction of Neustadt two days before. At the sinking command, there remained two Unteroffiziere and two enlisted men on board with me.'[28] Another of the boats scuttled in Regenbogen left a unique souvenir behind. *U3513*'s IWO Rolf Schultz remembers:

A new emblem for the boat was designed to our commander's specifications: the coat of arms of the city of Danzig with the lettering 'Peter von Danzig'. Above the Danzig arms there were two eagles drawn. After the boat was commissioned, members of the engineering division aboard made two emblems out of brass, and after they were painted, these were attached to the starboard and port sides of the tower. Several days before the boat was scuttled in the Travemünde roadstead on 3 May 1945, the emblems were unscrewed, and one was saved by our commander despite the turbulent times. The only surviving emblem of a German U-boat.[29]

Despite the widespread destruction of U-boats in contravention of Allied instructions, the remaining U-boats served at least to provide Admiral Sir Max Horton with his formal surrender. Rather than staging this ceremony in one of the conquered ports of Germany, Horton chose Londonderry, the Northern Ireland base from whence dozens

Uwe Kock (in white cap) and the officers of *U249* pictured in Portland, England, after their boat's surrender.

of Allied warships had sailed into the grim battles in the Atlantic. The ceremony itself was held on 14 May 1945, Horton flying into the Royal Naval Air Station at Eglinton, HMS *Gannet*. Opposite him at the ceremony would be a representative flotilla of eight U-boats, manned by skeleton German crews under armed Royal Navy guard. Three warships escorted them into the Foyle, one each from the Royal Navy, the Royal Canadian Navy, and the US Navy. This escort represented the major elements in the naval alliance which had won the Battle of the Atlantic.

Once the U-boats had been secured at Lisahally, their senior officers stepped ashore to salute Horton and make the formal surrender of the U-boat fleet. They were led by Oberleutnant zur See Klaus Hilgendorf. The thirty-three-year-old Hilgendorf had been a veteran of minesweeping operations before being transferred to the U-boat service in 1943. *U1009* had been his sole combat command, and it was from this Type VIIC-41 that he stepped ashore at Lisahally. The surrender was brief in itself, although Horton apparently questioned at least one young U-boat officer in order to get a measure of his erstwhile enemy in person: "'Tell me," he is reputed to have asked, "Are you a regular officer or a reservist?" "Neither, sir," came the reply. "I am a conscript from the Luftwaffe."'[30]

3

To the Victor the Spoils

In the US Naval Yard at Portsmouth the first surrendered U-boat arrived on 15 May 1945 at 1155hrs, when *U805* slipped into harbour under escort by the destroyer USS *Otter*. Three more would follow: *U873* on 16 May, escorted by USS *Vance*; *U1228* on 17 May, escorted by USS *Neal*; and *U234* on 19 May, escorted by USS *Sutton*. A sequence of events would soon unfurl which would end in tragedy for a man from *U873*, and the general maltreatment of men from several of the other boats.

The roots of this debacle could be traced back to the beginning of the year. On 8 January 1945, Admiral Jonas H Ingram, Commander-in-Chief of the US Navy Atlantic Fleet, ignited fresh waves of fear regarding Germany's U-boat threat, when he announced at a crowded press conference that the United States faced the very real danger of a guided missile attack launched from the approaching U-boats of the Seewolf Group. As early as November 1944, the US Navy had been preparing for the possible German deployment of submarine-launched guided missiles. On 29 November, *U1230* landed two spies, an American, William Colepaugh, and a German, Erich Gimpel, during a snowstorm at Crabtree Neck on the edge of Frenchman Bay, Maine, as part of Operation Elster. Colepaugh proved to be the weak link and was soon captured, in turn betraying Gimpel to the FBI, who arrested him in New York. During the exhaustive interrogations that followed, Gimpel boasted that the Kriegsmarine would soon attack mainland United States with missile-firing U-boats currently in development.[31]

Whilst no concrete evidence could be found to substantiate such an idea, the US Navy could ill-afford to ignore the possibility of this new threat. Indeed, in a speech in early 1945, Hitler's Armaments Minister, Albert Speer, alluded to an impending attack using U1 and U2 missiles against New York.[32] V1 unguided flying bombs, and the more sophisticated V2 missile, had already been hammering targets in England and Antwerp, and rumours were circulating about rocket trials aboard submerged U-boats at Peenemünde. Whilst the slow, low altitude V1 Doodlebug could be hit and destroyed either by flak or aircraft, the latter weapon, the V2, was infinitely more troublesome, as not only was its warhead larger and more devastating, but the sole method by which it could be combated was by preventing its launch in the first place.

On 14 April 1945, Dönitz grouped six long-distance boats – *U518*, *U546*, *U805*, *U858*, *U880* and *U1235* – bound for the American coast, into the last group operation within the Atlantic. This Seewolf group was designed to tie down Allied forces within the region by sweeping along the Great Circle convoy route. His rationale, boosted by the

Erich Gimpel pictured at the time of his trial. Sentenced to death for espionage, he would later have his sentence commuted, and was released on the orders of President Harry S Truman, along with some other captured German spies.

erroneous reports of the apparent success of *U1202* within that region, was the likelihood that such convoy traffic would be less heavily defended at this stage of the war, and that any measure of success against these convoys might possibly draw away some of the Royal Navy Hunter groups which were gaining the upper hand against the U-boats involved in the final battles in British coastal waters: 'For almost one and a half years the enemy has experienced no surface attacks on convoys and is prepared for only underwater U-boat operations ... attack ruthlessly and with determination.'[33] In total, during the first five months of 1945, nineteen boats had been despatched to American waters. But it was Seewolf which became the object of American defences, as Ingram's command calculated the likelihood that these were the reputed missile boats bound for the East Coast of the United States.

The US Navy mounted Operation Teardrop in response. This comprised a mid-Atlantic barrier which included four escort groups, in a bid to destroy the U-boats before they were within the predicted launching range. The carriers USS *Mission Bay, Bogue, Core*, and *Croatan*, plus four destroyer escort groups, were ordered to engage and destroy Seewolf. On 16 April, CTG 22.5 (USS *Croatan*) attacked and destroyed two U-boats, *U880* and *U1235*, six days later sinking a third, *U518*. On 24 April, Paul Just's *U546* was destroyed after detection by aircraft from the USS *Bogue*. Just had earlier that day torpedoed and sunk the destroyer USS *Frederick C Davis* after the latter had made contact with the submerged boat. With four of the six boats lost, Seewolf was disbanded that same day:

U858 was ordered to operate independently between Halifax and the Gulf of Maine, and *U805* was directed towards New York.

Of the four that had been destroyed, only *U546* yielded survivors for capture by the Americans. Kapitänleutnant Just and four of his crew were rescued by USS *Flaherty*, and a further twenty-eight men pulled from the frigid waters by other US Navy ships. For Just, however, his ordeal was only just beginning. Landed at the US Navy base at Argentia, Newfoundland, Just, two of his officers and five specialist rating crewmen were segregated from the crew, and each man placed in solitary confinement. While the remaining crewmen were transferred to various American prisoner-of-war camps, the eight remaining men were apparently almost immediately subjected to harsh beatings that continued every day as the Americans attempted to elicit information regarding U-boat missile equipment, and whether the Seewolf boats had been thus equipped.

Just's treatment contravened the Geneva Convention, although Just and the eight other members of his crew were detained as military prisoners, rather than prisoners-of-war, which somewhat circumvented the bureaucratic dictates of the Convention. To an extent, this reflected the later cynical redesignation of German prisoners-of-war already captured and held in European camps, or those who surrendered at end of the war as 'Disarmed Enemy Forces', thus removing them from the protection of the Geneva and Hague Conventions.

The isolated men from *U546* were allegedly subjected to repeated beatings and interrogations, primarily coordinated by Mr Jack Henry Alberti from the Office of Naval Intelligence. It is reported that, on 30 March, Just collapsed during harsh questioning. One such interrogation was witnessed by Lieutenant-Commander Leonard Myhre, captain of USS *Varian*, which had been involved in the hunt and destruction of *U546*. Myhre vigorously protested at the treatment that was being given to the German prisoners, and they were subsequently transferred to Fort Hunt, near Mount Vernon, where it is alleged that the beatings were continued under Alberti's direction. It seems that they only ceased on 9 May 1945, when Just agreed to write a full account of *U546*'s operational existence.[34]

The treatment that Just and his men had received augured ill for other German prisoners about to be taken. Whilst Just had been mishandled in order to elicit any possible information regarding U-boat rocket capabilities while Germany was still at war with the United States, by the time that Alberti once again was able to interrogate fresh prisoners about this topic, the war in Europe had ended. However, Japan remained firmly resisting the Allied advances in Burma and the Pacific, and American fears of this new possible underwater weaponry now encompassed the idea that Japan had been given the technology during one of the many weapon exchanges made with Nazi Germany.

The Type IXD-2 *U873* had sailed from Norway for a planned Caribbean combat patrol on 30 March. Kapitänleutnant Friedrich Steinhoff had been at sea only a matter of days when the end of U-boat hostilities was radioed through on 4 May. In accordance with his instructions, Steinhoff made his way towards the Portsmouth Navy Yard, New Hampshire, to surrender to American forces. Steinhoff was an experienced seaman who had served previously as a merchant navy officer and master, before enlisting in the Navy in 1934. After five months as commander of one of the ships in the 4 Minesweeping Flotilla during 1939 and 1940, he was named commander of the 5

The formidable size of the Type IX U-boat, here seen after surrender in a series of post-war Allied photographs taken to record every possible detail of the boat, inside and out.

Küstensicherungsverband (Coastal Security Unit) Bergen before transferring to U-boat training in March 1941. His first combat U-boat command was *U511*, commissioned on 8 December 1941. He remained in command of this boat until 12 December 1942, and during this period of time, before he could undertake his first war patrol, *U511* was used as the testbed for the rocket trials which had so alarmed the Allies. Seconded to the UAG (U-Boat Acceptance Group), UAK (Unterseeboots Abnahme Kommando) and Agru-Front, the boat was attached to the rocket laboratory at Peenemünde between 31 May and 5 June 1942. There it would be used as a mobile firing platform for rocket projectiles under the code name Project Ursel.

Steinhoff was considered the logical choice for the project as his brother, Dr Ernst Steinhoff, was an integral part of Peenemünde's rocket development team. Ernst, holding three degrees from the Darmstadt Institute of Technology (Bachelor of Science in Aeronautics, Master of Science in Meteorology, and Doctor of Engineering in

Applied Physics), had been appointed Director for Flight Mechanics, Ballistics, Guidance and Control, and Instrumentation at the German Army's Rocket Research Centre at Peenemünde during 1939. A chance conversation between him and his brother had begun the chain of events which culminated in the feasibility study of U-boat fired rockets.

On 4 June 1942 the experiment was ready. *U511* carried an adapted Wehrmacht Werfgerät 41 infantry rocket-launcher, such as those carried on half-tracks in action, which comprised a row of cages inside which the projectile rested. The six cages were angled obliquely at 45 degrees, and after submerging, Steinhoff succeeded in discharging all six rockets. The flight path of the weapons did not exhibit any major ballistic deviations once they had passed through the water surface, even from a depth of up to fifteen metres, and the experiment was considered a success. However, the unguided nature of the weapon rendered them of little use for anything other than blanket shore-bombardment, but the U-boat would have to be in close proximity to the shore to enable any useful deployment of the weapon. Ideas of utilising them against pursuing surface ships were soon deemed beyond the technological limits of the fairly crude weapons system. Instead, emphasis was placed on the development of acoustic torpedoes, which evolved into the T5 Zaunkönig, and even rocket-powered torpedoes, although these were never perfected by the Wehrmacht.

But the principle had been tested successfully, and Dönitz had tacitly approved the idea of using the weapon against the American mainland, particularly the vast shipping facilities in New York harbour. However, like many such German technological advances, development was delayed through technical wrangling and a misallocation of resources. The Kriegsmarine preferred the building of specialised launchers, rather than the utilisation of converted army equipment, but this, coupled with the lack of emphasis placed on the project, conspired to frustrate the scheme. Eventually, the idea of a bombardment of New York was all but scrapped in the face of an increasingly deteriorating U-boat war.

However, the weapon was used in action by three small Type II U-boats of the 30th U-Flotilla which fought against Russian forces in the Black Sea. *U9*, *U19* and *U24* were mounted with various configurations of the rocket-launchers, and fired them against Russian vessels in harbour during the German retreat on the Eastern Front in 1944. There the experiment ended until, also during 1944, discussions were reactivated about the possibility of refining the idea of deck-mounted rockets. Instead, the feasibility of creating a towed container to carry the far more lethal V2 rocket, which could be moved into position by the U-boat before firing, was investigated.

Once again, Ernst Steinhoff had been closely involved in the development of the V2, and after the first successful test launch of a V2 on 3 October 1942, it was Steinhoff who eventually flew the celebrated scientist and project leader, Werner von Braun, as well as Major-General Dornberger, in a Heinkel He-111 to Hitler's Wolfsschanze headquarters to show him a film of the launch.

It was an official from the German Labour Front, Direktor Lafferenz, who had suggested the idea of a watertight container holding a V2. This new plan elicited more attention, and developed into the designing of a 500-ton displacement container, to be towed behind a snorkel-equipped U-boat. Three were planned to be deployed against New York, each carrying a concealed V2. The containers would be towed horizontally until in firing position, whereupon they would be trimmed to bring them to the vertical, whereupon the rockets could be launched. Code named Prufstand XII, the Vulkanwerft began highly-classified work on the three containers, a single version being completed by the end of the war, although the Wehrmacht was never able to test its capability with a live firing. However, it was this technology, and the possibility that it now rested with the Japanese which prompted another flagrant breach of the Geneva Convention in the handling of Friedrich Steinhoff at the conclusion of the war.

After his release from the rocket experiments, Steinhoff carried out two patrols aboard *U511*: the first to the Caribbean Sea which resulted in the sinking of two tankers and damage to a third, and the second aborted prematurely for unspecified health reasons. Following his return he was transferred to a staff post before returning to active duty as captain of the new boat *U873*. After completing trials as part of the Agru front on 1 July 1944, *U873* returned to Bremen's Deschimag-Werft for final adaptation and maintenance, as well as having her keel loaded with mercury and optical glass by Zeiss Jena. This reflected the likelihood of a voyage to the Far East, where the Japanese would unload the valuable cargo to be put into their war effort. The boat's initial departure was delayed when, on 30 July 1944, *U873* suffered a direct hit as it lay in its Bremen shipyard during an air raid. The bomb landed squarely on the conning tower, killing a crewman and injuring three others. Had it exploded, this casualty rate would have been significantly worse, but the bomb proved to be faulty.

On 6 January 1945, *U873* loaded freight and supplies in Kiel before sailing for Norway on 17 February. However, further damage was received there during snorkelling exercises, when *U873* surfaced directly beneath a stationary Type VIIC and suffered collision damage. Finally, Steinhoff sailed for his first war patrol aboard the Type IXD2 on 30 March 1945, alongside another Type IXC boat, and one of the new Type XXIII electro-boats. This initial attempt was thwarted by nature: the weather was so bad that all three boats aborted and returned to harbour. The following day their departure was successful, and *U873* proceeded on snorkel until 5 May 1945, heading via the Denmark route into the Atlantic. The boat's destination had been changed from the Far East to the Caribbean, but as they passed into the Atlantic the radio message that Dönitz had succeeded the now-dead Hitler as Head of State was received. The following day, they received Dönitz's order to cease fire.

On 7 May *U873* received radioed instructions to begin its retreat to Norway and capitulation. However, the officers aboard *U873* were not willing to do so immediately, and they debated their best course of action, keeping *U873* on its original course. Two days later, a radio message transmitted in clear (uncoded) was received, which stated that all U-boats in proximity to the American coastline should head towards American ports in order to surrender. To signal that the boat was indeed intending to surrender, a black flag should be attached to the periscope and flown in clear view. Knowing that surrender was inevitable, Steinhoff ordered the destruction of all secret documents aboard *U873*. On 11 May, the order was given that *U873* should proceed to the closest American port; a few hours later screw noises were detected in the GHG (Gruppen Horch Gerät), the Group Listening Apparatus, or hydrophone, which were immediately identified as enemy destroyers. As *U873* was submerged, Steinhoff faced the reality of his situation: he could be attacked as a hostile U-boat, and thus immediately ordered the boat to surface into the clear night. Once above the waves, Steinhoff ordered unencrypted messages to be transmitted to the approaching Americans, whilst the dark

The wrecks of *U4* and *U10* are examined by victorious Russians in Gotenhafen after the port fell to Soviet forces.

green curtain from Steinhoff's cabin was attached to the periscope to act as the required black flag of surrender.

U873 lay motionless in the water as it was illuminated by searchlight from the approaching destroyer USS *Vance*. A boarding party was swiftly despatched, and *U873* surrendered to the Americans. Radio operator Georg Seitz later recalled a strange event that unfolded after the American Prize Crew had taken control of *U873*.

The prize crew sent over by the US destroyer were quite jumpy because the American sailors were not completely sure whether they were safe or whether our supposed surrender was a trap. First, none of the Americans seemed to speak German, though it soon turned out that there was a German speaker among the boarding party. Instead they just stood and listened as the German crew talked amongst themselves. Only after two days was I astonished when one of the American sailors asked me in a Mannheim dialect: 'Where are you from?' I answered: 'I am from Mannheim.' The American: 'You are from Mannheim itself?' Me: 'No, I am from Seggene.' [Author's note: This refers to Seckenheim, a suburb of Mannheim]. The American replied: 'Do you know the Hartmann's butcher's shop?' Me: 'Naturally I know of that.' The American: 'Every week I rode to that butcher's shop with a bicycle and picked up meat. My parents had, at that time a business with meat in the Seckenheimer Road.' I asked: 'Who are you?' To which he replied: 'My name is Werner Loeb and I emigrated with my parents to the USA before the outbreak of war. My father now works for a meat factory in Chicago and I volunteered for service in the US Navy and was headed for the war in the Pacific.' I asked:

U3503 scuttling within sight of the Swedish coastline.

'Why did you not speak to me until today in German, and why did you not act as interpreter with your good German?' Loeb replied: 'I did not have permission from my officer to speak with you until today, since we were concerned that you might submerge on us again and it may be a trap. Therefore my job was to listen to your conversations during the previous days.'[35]

On 17 May 1945, *U873* entered the American naval base at Portsmouth, New Hampshire, under escort from USS *Vance*. There, the German crew were placed in the Portsmouth naval prison, before transfer to Boston's Charles Street Prison, a normal penitentiary rather than one designated for military use. Here Steinhoff became the centre of renewed attention from Naval Intelligence's Jack H Alberti. After two days of interrogation, during which German eyewitnesses remember seeing him bloody and bruised, Steinhoff committed suicide by severing an artery in his right wrist with a broken piece of his sunglasses and a wire which apparently came from his cap. He bled to death before help could be administered.

Alongside the crew of *U873* were the men from the Type XB minelayer *U234* which had surrendered en route to Japan. The boat's captain, Kapitänleutnant Hein Fehler, later wrote an autobiographical account of his experiences which included his recollections of Charles Street:

The cells of Boston rose in tiers and their doors, made of vertical bars, looked down on a vast and stone-flagged hall. From wall to wall stretched broad canopies of wire mesh to foil suicide jumpers, while armed guards, impressively grim favoured, patrolled the narrow catwalks outside our doors.

The crew of a sister U-boat [*U873*] occupied the rows of cells that backed on to our own and, although we were forbidden to communicate with these comrades, it did not take long for the grapevine to discover that they were in considerable trouble. For some reason or another they had fallen particularly foul of the guard, and the U-boat commander, who occupied the cell behind me, appeared to be bearing the brunt of it. The walls were too thick for spoken words to penetrate and attempts to tap out signal messages also proved abortive. But the uneasiness we felt concerning the fate of our friends was by no means lessened when we heard the wailing, cries, and dull thuds, as though a beating-up was in progress.

Sleeplessness was my companion. Boston by day was bad enough, but at night I found it intolerable ... From out of the silence of the sleeping prison came the sound of men's voices, low-pitched at first and furtive, but rising steadily with an edge of anger in them. Then came a scream, shrill, uncanny, yet somehow familiar for, with a shock that chased all slumber from me, I realised that I'd heard it before ... Another scream and from somewhere behind the wall the doors of a cell clanged open. The U-boat commander![36]

Later Fehler was able to ask the doctor from *U873*, Karl Wilhelm Reinke, what he had seen. Apparently, as the crew of *U873* had been moving to breakfast they noticed their captain's cell door still locked. In view of the noises that they had all heard during the preceding night, they remonstrated with their guards, unwilling to move until they had spoken with Steinhoff. As the Germans and Americans exchanged increasingly heated words, Reinke made it to the cell door to look inside:

I saw a lake of shining moisture under his bed. Blood. I told the guards they must open the door or there would be hell to pay. Eventually they let me go in. I found him ... with his wrist slashed by the sun goggles. He was alive but in a terrible condition ... I pressed the guards quite desperately to get our captain to hospital, but apparently they did not move until it was too late. The jail is in the centre of town and yet two hours elapsed before an ambulance arrived. He was done for.[37]

While German witnesses recounted tales of two guards who appeared to have made a habit of visiting Steinhoff in his cell and beating him up, the US Navy immediately convened a board to investigate what it saw as 'Irregularities Connected with the Handling of Surrendered German Submarines', which covered everything from the wanton theft of personal belongings to the death of Steinhoff. Their findings were numerous, among them the decision that:

... the serious irregularities reported in the handling of German prisoners at the Navy Yard, Portsmouth, were caused by the failure of responsible authorities at the Navy Yard to exercise effective military command in the premises and by the flagrant disregard, by the representatives of Op-16-Z Section of ONI, of the provisions of the Chief of Naval Operations' directive of 19 May 1942, Serial 01227316, which is in conformity with the Geneva Convention, and which particularly prohibits the taking of souvenirs.[38]

The Commandant of the Portsmouth Navy Yard, Rear Admiral Thomas Withers, and Captain of the Yard, Captain Clifford H Roper, were both found to have been derelict in the performance of their duty. Evidence of looting aboard *U805*, the first U-boat to arrive at Portsmouth, by various marines and naval personnel was established. Meanwhile civilian interrogator, Mr Jack Henry Alberti, who had been wearing a naval uniform while performing the duty of an interrogator, greatly exceeded his authority and functions, when he all but took over the examination and processing of prisoners-of-war at the naval prison, and subsequently distributed looted decorations and prisoners' personal property to prison personnel as he saw fit.

Relating to Steinhoff, Alberti was found to have 'caused the Commanding Officer of a surrendered U-boat to be slapped by an enlisted man', in direct violation of the

Geneva Convention and the Chief of Naval Operations' directives. Furthermore the 'supine attitude' of the naval prison's Commanding Officer, Colonel Rossell, USMC, in permitting Mr Alberti to conduct himself in the manner which he did was viewed as 'most reprehensible'.

The US Naval investigation established that the baggage of German prisoners-of-war had been thoroughly looted with the active participation of the Field Officer of the Day, Major Mehrlust, USMCR, as well as other specified naval officers and personnel resulting in the feared loss of important intelligence material. The report recommended that disciplinary action be taken against Rear Admiral Thomas Withers, Captain Clifford H Roper, Colonel J A Rossell, USMC, Captain Clifford G Hines, USN Medical Corps, US Navy (Senior Medical Officer, Naval Prison, Portsmouth), Lieutenant-Commander Walter Bromberg, Medical Corps, USNR (Psychiatrist of the Naval Prison), Major J P Mehrlust, USMC, and Lieutenant-Commander S R Hatton, USNR, of Op-16-Z Section, Office of Naval Intelligence. Furthermore, the Director of Naval Intelligence was directed to take appropriate action in the case of Mr Jack Henry Alberti, Senior Interrogator in the Office of Naval Intelligence, to overhaul the directives under which his special agents were operating, and 'to so indoctrinate and curb them to the end that the activities of his subordinates conform to the directives of the Chief of Naval Operations, and do not discredit the naval uniform.'

On 27 July 1945, Alberti replied to the accusations that appeared to be levelled against him, stating that, in carrying out his duties as a Naval Intelligence interrogator, he had in no way exceeded his authority or function:

> I have been an interrogator since May 1942, and am at present one of the most experienced interrogators in Op-16-Z. Actually, I have been quite active as instructor in interrogation to a number of the officer interrogators in this Branch. Moreover, as early as October 1942, I delivered lectures to the Foreign Intelligence School of ONI on this subject ... In addition, I have operated successfully and favourably with Military Intelligence.
>
> Under the direction of Lt. Comdr. Hatton, USNR, senior interrogation officer present, I assumed the duties of direct interrogation of prisoners at the Naval Prison while Lt. Comdr. Hatton was engaged in matters of interest to the Yard authorities and recovery of documents and equipment of intelligence values plus a detailed check of the reliability of German personnel aboard the captured U-boats, all of which was carried out on the boats themselves.
>
> ... In regard to the Commander of the *U873*, it is true that I caused him to be slapped ONCE by a marine guard. The Commander was of considerable physical proportions, threatening in his attitude and insolent in his demeanour. I was in the uniform of a Lieutenant Commander and his attitude was not in keeping with the terms of the surrender nor was it respectful to the uniform. He alone could furnish the answers to certain questions, replies to which we had been directed to obtain by CNO secret dispatch 151716 of 15 May 1945. In the course of the interrogation of the prisoner which was done by me and at a time when Lieutenant Commander Hatton was engaged in interrogating another prisoner from *U873* in a different part of the prison, the prisoner became extremely menacing and hysterically arrogant. In keeping with well-known psychological principles, I instructed the guard [Private First Class

The huge size of the Type XXI is obvious in this photograph taken in a German port.
Despite design flaws, they would have been a formidable weapon if committed
to battle before Dönitz's cease fire command.

Sol Leventhal] to slap him once. It was done entirely because of his menacing attitude
and arrogance, which ceased after the slapping and I was thereafter treated with the
respect of the Commander.[39]

Alberti recorded that the slap in the face was not hard enough to be called real physical
violence, more for the purpose of insulting and humiliating the German officer. Indeed,
Private Leventhal also stated in sworn testimony that he was part of a specially selected
group of guards picked to be used for the handling of difficult prisoners, doing strictly
what they were told and keeping quiet about it. Steinhoff went into the interrogation
room with Alberti after which Leventhal was called in. At that time, Steinhoff was being
questioned as to the movements of his submarine and Alberti indicated to him that he
was to slap Steinhoff, which he did. Leventhal delivered 'two smart slaps – one with the
palm, the other with the back of his hand', which were not resisted, and after which
Steinhoff gave Alberti the information that he desired. When answering the charge of
looting enemy prisoners, Alberti responded that:

When the Captain of the *U1228* was brought before me for interrogation, I noticed
that he was still wearing an Iron Cross as well as the U-boat badge. These were
ordered to be removed in accordance with the usual custom and because of past
experience; as such decorations have very sharp edges and can readily be used as a
weapon or a means of suicide. I acceded to the request of the Commanding Officer
of the Prison that he be permitted to retain an Iron Cross because there was a plentiful
supply thereof among the captured equipment and it would be possible, therefore,
eventually to return an Iron Cross to the U-boat Commander. Iron Crosses have no
marks of individuality on them and may be freely substituted. Every U-boat carried
a supply of Iron Crosses and decorations generally in their safes which the
Commanding Officer thereof may distribute on authorization, and the plentiful
supply above-mentioned came from such source ... No irregularities of any kind

occurred in the handling of the above mentioned prisoners or their possessions by the personnel of the U.S. Naval Prison at Portsmouth. This comment covers *U805*, *U1228* and *U873*.[40]

Eventually, the matter was settled by the Commander-in-Chief of the US Navy, Fleet Admiral Ernest King, three months before his retirement:

> The report of the Chief of Naval Personnel is a well considered summary of the irregularities which were involved in this case and I concur with the comments of paragraphs 3 and 4 relative to the officers concerned. It is noted that the basic letter has been prepared after conference with the Commandant, U.S. Marine Corps, and I recommend that no U.S. naval or U.S. Marine Corps officer be brought to trial by General Court Martial in this case.
>
> The disciplinary action recommended in paragraph 6 of the basic letter and paragraph 2 of the first endorsement appears adequate in the circumstances of this case and I recommend that the letters of reprimand and admonition be addressed to the officers indicated.
>
> In the cases of Lieutenant Commander S. R. Hatton, USNR, and Mr. Jack Alberti, who were concerned in the irregularities of this incident, I have had an investigation conducted by the Vice Chief of Naval Operations who has taken appropriate action within the Office of Naval Intelligence, and I recommend that no further action be taken insofar as these representatives of the Office of Naval Intelligence are concerned.[41]

Steinhoff was buried in the military graveyard at Fort Devens. His brother's fate in the hands of the Americans was somewhat different. At the end of the war, the US Army instigated Operation Overcast, which involved evacuating captured German rocket scientists and technicians deemed 'important for [the] Pacific war'.[42] Steinhoff was

Norwegian submarine KNM *Kaura*, ex-*U995*, the sole remaining example of a Type VIIC U-boat, later destined for display in Laboe, Germany.

The Wehrmacht Werfgerät 41 infantry rocket-launcher in action in Warsaw. A barely-modified version of this was fitted to *U511*, and successfully launched from the boat while submerged.

amongst those men, and travelled to the United States aboard the troopship SS *Argentina*, arriving on 16 November 1945. There he continued his work as part of the Ballistics Research Laboratories at Aberdeen Proving Ground, Maryland, eventually becoming Chief Scientist at the Air Force Missile Development Center in 1963. He remained there until 1972, when he retired to Alamogordo, New Mexico, dying on 2 December 1987, at the age of 79.

Further scientific material had already been taken from *U234* after the minelayer's surrender to American forces. Kapitänleutnant Fehler had received the surrender message from Dönitz while sailing in the British sector, as outlined in the subsequent orders containing detailed surrender instructions, although he opted to turn his boat and crew over to the Americans rather than British. His reasoning, which soon proved incorrect, was that the latter of the countries would probably hold him and his men captive for an extended period, as they had been 'knocking each other's houses down too enthusiastically'[43] for such a long time, whereas the likelihood was that the

The non-commissioned officers from the crew of *U873* at the boat's commissioning.
Funkmaat Georg Seitz is indicated by the arrow at left.

Americans, whose civilians were relatively untouched by the war, would repatriate them
to a defeated Germany more quickly.

Operating as part of the technological exchange between Japan and Germany, *U234*
carried a valuable cargo and an interesting, and indeed unusual, array of passengers on
its voyage to Japan. At first Fehler had been summoned to OKM (Oberkommando der
Marine), the German Naval Command, in Berlin, and was informed that he would be
taking twenty-seven passengers to Japan, something the commander declared impossible,
given the limited space aboard a combat U-boat. Should they be used to replace crew
members then the efficiency of the boat was in extreme jeopardy. The compromise
reached was that *U234* would transport twelve passengers, with eight crewmen removed.

The passengers comprised two Japanese officers: Air Force Colonel Genzo Shoji, an
aeronautical engineer, and naval Captain Hideo Tomonaga, a submarine construction
specialist; four Luftwaffe men: General Ulrich Kessler, new Air Attaché to Tokyo and a
long-time prominent advocate of establishing a Kriegsmarine air arm, Oberst Fritz
Sandrath, flak specialist, Oberst Erich Menzel, radiocommunications expert, and Oberst-
Leutnant Kai Nieschling, a military judge; four Kriegsmarine men: Kapitänleutnant
Richard Bulla, air-sea co-operation specialist who would also act as the boat's IWO,
Kapitänleutnant Heinrich Hellendorn, Naval flak specialist, Kapitänleutnant (Ing.)
Heinz Schlicke, radar and infrared specialist director of the Naval Test Fields in Kiel,
Kapitän Gerhard Falke, shipbuilding and design specialist; and two civilians: August
Bringewald, senior Messerschmitt engineer, and Franz Ruf, Messerschmitt procurement
specialist, both of whom were specialists in jet and rocket engines and their mass

production. The German contingent were apparently fiercely divided in their loyalties and opinions of German politics, and the conduct of the war, and Fehler was forced to arbitrate in several disputes and arguments amongst his increasingly unwelcome passengers, Kessler frequently venting his frank and negative opinions on the Nazi Party and his superior Hermann Göring, to the shock of his more ardently National Socialist companions.

Additionally, the U-boat was laden with much freight that included two disassembled Messerschmitt 262 fighters, a Henschel Hs293 glide bomb, mercury, optical glass, technical blueprints, cameras, infrared fuses, anti-tank weapons and rockets and 560kg of uranium-235 oxide stored in the boat's mine shafts in 23cm square lead cubes, with 'U235' painted on the exterior of each cube. The U-boat's senior radio operator, Wolfgang Hirschfeld, observed the Japanese officers painting the black characters on the brown paper wrapping of each block, and enquired as to its meaning. They replied that the cargo had originally been for the boat *U235*, which was no longer heading to Japan. His curiosity piqued, Hirschfeld was confused to learn that *U235* was a small Type VIIC training boat which would never have been earmarked for such a mission. After asking his commander about this strange situation, Hirschfeld was told not to speak of it again with the Japanese passengers.

Following Dönitz's orders to cease hostilities and surrender all combat boats, Fehler's two Japanese officers were held under loose guard aboard *U234*, the Germans unsure of how they would react to the news, as Japan had already broken diplomatic ties with Dönitz's government on 5 May. There was considerable debate aboard *U234* as to the

Friedrich Steinhoff (left, in white cap) atop the bridge of *U873* during the boat's working-up trials. The sunglasses that he is wearing are the same that he would later use to commit suicide in his cell in Boston's Charles Street Prison.

best course of action, with ideas ranging from internment in Eire to sailing to South America, or beyond, in the search for sanctuary. Radio operator Wolfgang Hirschfeld remembered:

> Once again there was a long conference involving the officers and some of the passengers. General Kessler and Oberst von Sandrath wanted to proceed with the mission to Tokyo, but in any case not to surrender; if necessary they could suggest places in Argentina where we would be sheltered once we got ashore. Bull and Pfaff wanted to sail to an island in the South Pacific. Dr Walter, the boat's medical officer, and Judge Nieschling, who were the most fervent Nazis aboard, were both adamant for surrender. My personal feeling was that we should obey the last order that had been Kapitän zur See Rösing's signal of 8 May ordering us to continue with the voyage or put back into Bergen.[44]

With continued Allied broadcasts to unaccounted-for U-boats stating that those that failed to comply with surrender instructions would be treated as pirates, Fehler eventually accepted the inevitable and opted to hand his boat over. Unwilling to surrender, the two Japanese officers committed suicide by overdosing on the barbiturate Luminal, which took thirty-six hours to kill them. Fehler surfaced to bury the two men at sea, along with a three-hundred-year-old Samurai sword which had been entrusted to him for the duration of the journey. For the aforementioned reasons, Fehler decided to surrender to American forces, but radioed on 12 May that he would

Steinhoff is marched ashore following his surrendered boat's arrival in the United States.

The crew of *U873* stand under American guard, as they await instructions from their captors. The treatment which would ultimately lead to Steinhoff's suicide has never been fully disclosed by American authorities.

sail for Halifax, Nova Scotia, in order to prevent Canadian forces reaching the boat first. In fact, he set course for Newport, Virginia, American authorities soon realising his deception and despatching two destroyers to intercept the boat. It was USS *Sutton* which found *U234* south of the Grand Banks, a Prize Crew being placed aboard shortly thereafter.

Disaster nearly overtook them during the American seizure. *U234* was stationary, wallowing in the swell as the Prize Crew made her secure by the usual method of looping a chain around the periscope, and dropping it into the control room. There they affixed the other end to the hydroplane wheels, watched by a bemused German crew, who were aware that the wheels were not the primary method used to dive the boat, merely an emergency backup to the push buttons operated by the planesmen. Eventually, American sailors warily took their positions inside the boat, and prepared to get the boat underway. However, what the man operating the rudder failed to realise was that, when the button was depressed to move the rudder to port or starboard, the other had to be depressed to bring it back to centre. *U234* had already drifted broadside to the swell, her bow pointing directly at USS *Sutton*'s amidships, the destroyer starting to move rather than remain in what seemed a vulnerable position. All guns were trained on *U234*, with the American crew jumpily expecting some form of trap.

Suddenly, as the boat began moving, the rudder, which was fully turned to port, locked into its position because the American helmsman had not moved it back to amidships. *U234* rapidly gained speed on what appeared a direct ramming course. Aware that they were only seconds away from destruction at the guns of USS *Sutton*, which was unaware

Another view of the surrendered crew from *U873*.

that the U-boat was experiencing rudder failure, the American Prize Officer ordered Fehler to disengage the rudder.

> Since he was not allowed to use the loudspeakers or the internal microphone, he had to send a messenger to the stern [and the auxiliary manual steering wheel] from the control room. The messenger made his way through the circular communications doorways by seizing the upper coaming in both hands and swinging his legs through and forwards. When the American sentry in the stern torpedo room saw this German coming towards him at speed and in full flight he dropped his machine gun and raised his hands. This type of panic was incomprehensible to us until we saw American propaganda films later during our captivity. U-boat men were rated on a par with Mafia gangsters by Hollywood.[45]

The dangerous position was resolved in the nick of time, and the Stars and Stripes flag was hoisted on the U-boat's conning tower. Later that day, an American sailor was shot in the kidneys as he fooled about with the German service pistols found aboard the boat, later dying, despite Dr Walter operating on the mortally-wounded man. *U234* was taken to Portsmouth Naval Shipyard, where the press, who had already heard of the captured boat and its high-ranking passengers, descended on the harbour in droves. As a typical example, radio reporter Charlie Gray of the WHEB evening news observed the disembarkation of the crew and passengers, Kessler apparently standing out as 'a typical Hollywood version of a German general. He wore a long leather greatcoat, which reached to his ankles, highly polished leather boots and an Iron Cross which hung tightly about his neck. He posed for newsreel cameramen and seemed to be enjoying the publicity he was receiving. He was tall and wore white gloves.' Kessler spoke to the assembled throng of journalists in fluent English with a 'decidedly Oxford accent', and when asked how he felt about Germany's surrender replied, '"I was in the last World War. I've been through it before. I'll probably go through it again."'[46]

Once the men aboard U234 had disembarked, the folly of Fehler's hopes was soon discovered. Like those three other U-boats which had already entered harbour, the boat and its crew were both looted of personal belongings and military documents, so much so that much of military value was lost.

However, an interesting and much-debated postscript remains from the American seizure of U234's cargo. The exact characteristics of the uranium carried aboard the boat remain unknown, the most common school of thought being that it was not weapons-grade material and was intended for use as a catalyst in the production of synthetic methanol to be used for aviation fuel. However, following the transfer of the boat's officers to Washington, DC, for further interrogation after the tragedies in Boston's Charles Street jail, the boat's IIWO Leutnant zur See Karl Ernst Pfaff was ordered to supervise the opening of the containers holding the uranium from the U-boat's mineshaft. An American welder who operated the cutting torch begged Pfaff not to let them get blown up by a booby trap, to which an exasperated Pfaff replied that not only

Officers from USS *Sutton* hoist the Stars and Stripes aboard a captured *U234*.

did he not wish to die young either, but the cargo was en route to allies in Japan, so why should it be booby-trapped? As the uranium cargo was removed, a civilian in an 'Elliot Ness hat' was present, and Pfaff enquired who he was. 'Oppenheimer,' was the reply, though he has never verified that it was indeed atomic physicist J Robert Oppenheimer, Director of the Los Alamos laboratory in Washington, DC. [47]

Apparently, at that stage of the United States nuclear programme in May 1945, there were considerable problems regarding the development of the atomic bomb. General

U234 is destroyed as a torpedo target for USS *Greenfish* on 20 November 1947.

Leslie Groves, military head of the Manhattan Project, the project to develop the first nuclear weapon, of which Oppenheimer was scientific director, had used some of the sparse American supply of enriched uranium to fuel plutonium reactors at one of the project's three sites at Hanford, Washington. There was a shortage for use within the actual uranium bomb, and this was coupled with the fact that the American scientists had not yet perfected a way to trigger efficiently the second type of atomic device, the plutonium bomb. The United States government had set a deadline of mid-August, and both types of weapon appeared to have stalled.

Within five days of *U234*'s entry into Portsmouth, the infrared fuses were discovered, as the result of Dr Heinz Schlicke's interrogation by Jack Alberti in Washington. A memorandum from Alberti dated 24 May 1945 stated that: 'Dr Schlicke knows about the infrared proximity fuses which are contained in some of these packages ... Dr Schlicke knows how to handle them and is willing to do so.'[48]

The next day Schlicke was placed aboard an aircraft and returned to Portsmouth, where he retrieved the fuses. Schlicke had close ties with several scientists from Germany's own nuclear programme, which had never fully flourished, and his sudden return by the Americans to retrieve the fuses, and transport them back to Washington, betrays something of the eagerness with which the Americans wanted them. He had told Alberti that many of the meetings with German atomic scientists had been for the purpose of imparting information on their technological achievements to the Japanese after *U234* reached there. Indeed, amongst his papers was one that explored the 'investigation of the usability of ultraviolet (invisible) light for transmitting messages or commands and particularly for the remote ignition of warhead fuses.'[49]

American scientists had consistently failed to develop the kind of simultaneously-firing detonation system required to activate a plutonium weapon, and a committee was established in October 1944 specifically to solve that problem. At the head of this committee was the experimental physicist Luis Alvarez. Fehler later identified a 'Lieutenant-Commander Alvarez' as amongst the men who interrogated him regarding his planned voyage to Japan, and later Alvarez was present at a lecture series given by Dr Schlicke to the Navy Department, seemingly acting as the German scientist's 'handler'. Luis Alvarez also finally solved the plutonium bomb detonator timing problem in the last days before the first test firing of such a weapon at the Trinity test site. It is possible, though unproven, that Schlicke's fuses, or derivatives thereof, were utilised in the successful development of the plutonium bomb that was ultimately dropped on Nagasaki, Japan. Furthermore, if, and this remains if, the uranium carried aboard *U234* were of weapons grade, then it could have filled the gap in stocks which would be used in the uranium bomb that was dropped on Hiroshima, Japan.

4

Surrender on Land

By the beginning of 1945 it was obvious that Germany would no longer triumph in its war against the Western Allies and the Soviet Union. And yet the Wehrmacht and Waffen SS continued to resist with a dogmatic tenacity that cannot merely be ascribed to the kind of blind fanaticism often attributed to these fighting units. Indeed, it is difficult even with the value of hindsight to understand the rationale for such a fierce resistance, which persisted as 1945 progressed, other than to believe that Hitler still held considerable sway over the German population. But could blind belief in the Führer, or fear of the all powerful grip of the Gestapo and Allgemeine SS, have resulted in the continuing futile struggle? No, that in itself is the kind of simplistic notion too often used to describe life within the crumbling Third Reich. It is unarguable that Germany was in sheer terror of the Soviet Union, but the Western Allies had also sown the seeds that grew into the pugnacious resistance which they met in their bloody, yet unstoppable, advance into Germany.

Fähnrich Gerhard Both was a trainee U-boat officer, discharged from his curtailed training programme in Pillau at the beginning of 1945, and transferred along with the rest of his fellow cadets and other seamen back to Germany, and the holding area of the Finkenwerder U-boat bunker in Hamburg. His memories of the time provide an insight into the mentality of such young German servicemen.

> A very large measure of optimism was required to believe that a German victory in this war was still possible. It sounds totally illogical today, but at the time most of us still possessed such faith. Maybe the thought of losing this war with all the inhuman tortures that Allies had in store for us, such as the Morgenthau Plan, which was to eliminate all war industries in the Ruhr and Saar basins; ethnic cleansing of half of our German territories on a scale never before seen or since executed anywhere in the world, deliberately starving out what was left of our population, etc, etc, was too horrible to bear. These intentions of the Allies, incidentally, were partially known in Germany even then because of information leaked from enemy propaganda and then spread by people habitually listening to such propaganda. In a way, therefore, this propaganda proved to be an own goal for the Allies in as much as it stiffened the German will to resist.[50]

Indeed, Both was correct in this regard. The Morgenthau Plan, named after its creator Henry Morgenthau, Jr, Secretary of the Treasury of the United States, envisioned harsh

The use of depot ships for Kriegsmarine U-boats was not as widespread as in the submarine service of other navies. Events of 1944/1945 brought the need for such ships in Norway to the fore.

measures inflicted on a defeated Germany, in order to eliminate any capability for Germany to wage war again. Germany was to be partitioned into two independent states, with all heavy industry dismantled, and centres of mining and industry either shared amongst conquering nations, or annexed. This would leave Germany an agricultural nation that would be subject to its more dominant and stronger neighbours. In September 1944, President Roosevelt and Morgenthau persuaded a reluctant Churchill to agree to the plan, although soon afterwards the details of the plan were leaked to the press, leading to strong denials from Roosevelt. To Propaganda Minister Josef Goebbels it was a perfect gift, and he was able to use the plan's details to strengthen German resolve to continue the struggle. Nonetheless, the battles on land and sea could not be won by propaganda alone.

There were two primary German bases for combat U-boats: Kiel and Wilhelmshaven. Both of them had a longstanding military tradition which had been closely allied to the

Infantry training had been part of every enlisted sailor's training period. Men of the U-boat service generally only experienced this as part of their basic training. Relegation to infantry units at the end of the war would see them woefully unprepared for infantry combat, though their ardour for battle was remarked upon by the British Army.

development of German naval power. Kiel lies at the end of a long inlet, the Kielerförde, with the approaches heavily defended until the sea wall of the naval base is reached. Kiel was the home of the 1st U-boat Flotilla, formed using the Type II boats in 1935. A little north of Kiel lies the eastern entrance to the Kaiser Wilhelm Canal, a manmade canal which negates the necessity of circumnavigating Denmark for shipping wishing to travel between the North Sea and the Baltic. The canal also formed a defensive barrier for the northern portion of Schleswig-Holstein, although in 1945, as the British advanced along this part of Germany, it was rendered redundant by German military command ordering no resistance on this line. The canal also provided a choke-point in Kriegsmarine shipping, which the Royal Air Force could exploit by liberal use of mines.

From the North Sea end of the canal at Brunsbüttel, German shipping could head west, following the shoreline in channels swept clear of mines, and protected by flak ships and shore batteries on the North German Plain. Water from the mouth of the Elbe, and the approach to Hamburg's expansive U-boat yards, swirled around Cuxhaven, the home of the Kriegsmarine's minesweeper service. Further east lies Wilhelmshaven in the estuarine mouth of the Jade River, the military harbour dominating what was essentially a naval town. The 2nd U-Flotilla had made this its base before the outbreak of the Second World War, and U-boats continued to frequent the harbour until the capture of the town by Polish forces in 1945. During March, the light cruiser *Köln* was sunk at Wilhelmshaven by Allied bombing, the harbour installations hammered repeatedly by the almost constant attention from Allied aircraft. As the Poles approached, Wilhelmshaven would see its share of scuttled U-boats clogging the harbour, with the stores of the naval base being thrown open for the local population to plunder at will, rather than be given over to the enemy.

The third and final port city that hosted a combat flotilla was Flensburg, home to the 33rd U-Flotilla. This flotilla also encompassed the boats that were based in the Far East, although their logistical needs were obviously far easier to handle *in situ* by Dommes, rather than by remote control from Germany. Flensburg also became the site of Dönitz's government in the final days of the war.

The cities of Bremen and Hamburg, which also dominated the North German Plain, were both major centres of construction. There the Organisation Todt had erected monumental concrete shelters for boats under construction, as well as the crews who were undergoing the familiarisation routines that were a staple part of the evolution of a U-boat crew from raw recruits to men familiar with the inner working of their sophisticated weapon of war. In earlier days, when the war had still hung in the balance, crews would spend weeks in the company of the boat while still under construction, learning from the shipyard workers the details of the boat's systems and components. This intimate knowledge would serve many crews well when in action, under pressure, and sustaining damage. The knowledge that could make the difference between survival and death had often been gleaned from this period of boat familiarisation. However, by May 1945, the yards were in chaos and the luxury of familiarisation time had long since gone. The majority of U-boat men who found themselves in the Bremen or Hamburg shipyards in the final weeks of the conflict were soon clutching Panzerfaust and rifles in the trenches facing the advancing Allies. Many Kriegsmarine men who were no longer

Carl Emmermann, the U-boat 'Ace' who had found fame as commander of *U172*. In May 1945 he was involved in the infantry battles around Hamburg as part of the 2nd Naval Infantry Division.

able to serve aboard either the capital ships, or who had finished their U-boat training with no boats available, as well as those others whose training was incomplete, were instead transferred to the reserve pool of naval forces that would soon be assigned to land units.

> It became clear that the U-boat arm, in spite of the new weapons which had restored its superiority over the defence, would not again be engaged in large-scale operations. The U-boat campaign was no longer the Navy's most important task and I therefore transferred large portions of the fleet to assist in the defence of the Eastern Front and to rescue German nationals from the Russians.
>
> Naval personnel who had been earmarked for U-boats and surface ships under construction, or who could be spared from other duties, were either transferred to the Army or were formed into naval divisions and sent to the Eastern Front. During the last months of the war some 50,000 naval ratings in this way took part in the defence of Germany's eastern provinces.[51]

While some Kriegsmarine men may have been comfortable with the idea of continuing the fight against the enemy on land, there were others who were less so. Marinestabsarzt H G Schütze had served as medical officer aboard *U382*, *U221* and *U358*, as well as acting as Flotilla Medical Officer for the 29th U-Flotilla in Toulon. Transferred to Hamburg before Toulon fell, Schütze was stationed at Finkenwerder with the 31st U-Flotilla as the war neared its end:

> The escape of my family and parents from the Festung Breslau had been successful! … My wife and both babies were accommodated in my medical station in Finkenwerder … my parents were able to stay with my parent in law in Altona, hoping to soon be able to resettle in Schleswig-Holstein.
>
> The war is lost! Depressing news comes from the radio. Berlin, the Reich's capital, is under attack by Soviet troops. The war is nearing its end. In the West Allied troops have occupied the Ruhr region. A British Army pushes through Lüneburger Heath towards Hamburg.
>
> Then a new order reaches us: all available U-boat crews in the Heath region are to march to the front and stop the enemy armoured columns with Panzerfaust. I am to provide a headquarters for the medical personnel in my area where the wounded can be cared for.
>
> Sailors, U-boat men as infantrymen? That can only go wrong! But an order is an order.[52]

At the beginning of February, five thousand naval men of all grades were released to the Commander of the Replacement Army, Reichsführer SS Heinrich Himmler, primarily to be used to bring under-strength Waffen SS units back to fighting readiness. The 20th Panzer Grenadier Division certainly received several thousand untried Kriegsmarine men as replacements, going so far as to send them into action still wearing their naval blue uniforms, as there was no time or supply to do otherwise. More Kriegsmarine men were transferred to the 32nd SS Grenadier Division while others appeared in small battle groups, fighting alongside Volkssturm and police units that had been thrown into the cauldron. The 1st Naval Infantry Division was formed in February and transferred into action against the Russians, but it was to the next division that the majority of unemployed U-boat men were sent.[53]

The 2nd Naval Infantry Division was created in Schleswig-Holstein during March 1945 and reached the frontlines in April. The term 'Marines' has often been applied to these troops, although this is actually far from the reality of the troops committed into ground action in 1945. During the late nineteenth and early twentieth centuries, Imperial Germany had raised marine units that fought in Germany's brief attempt at empire-building, most notably in South-West Africa. However, during the First World War marines had formed the majority of the 1st, 2nd and 3rd Naval Divisions, which were of relatively low combat value, primarily composed of men surplus to Imperial Germany Navy requirements. They had been used as security for German naval installations, and were generally unable to tackle the task of infantry assault and defence. This characteristic was continued into the closing months of the Second World War. The constituent units for the 2nd Naval Infantry Division look impressive on paper:

Marine-Grenadier-Regiment 5 commanded by Kapitän zur See Hermann Jordan, a Seekadet during the previous war, former Oberst in the Luftwaffe before transfer to the Kriegsmarine during September 1944. Jordan was killed in action on 20 April 1945.

Marine-Grenadier-Regiment 6 commanded by the U-boat 'Ace', Kapitän zur See Werner Hartmann, who, after departing combat U-boats, had commanded FdU (Führer der Unterseeboote) South and units of the Kleinkampfverbände before being transferred to organise and lead the Danzig and West Prussian Volkssturm. Beneath Hartmann's command were two battalions, one led by another 'Ace', U-boat commander, Reinhard Hardegen.

Marine-Grenadier-Regiment 7, commanded by Kapitän zur See Karl Neitzel, commander of the Gotenhafen's 2nd Ubootslehrdivision (U-boat Training Division) until its disbandment in February 1945 following evacuation.

Marine-Füsilier-Bataillon 2 (Korvettenkapitän Josef Gördes, Kriegsmarine Artillery officer)

Marine-Artillerie-Regiment 2

Marine-Panzjäger-Abteilung 2

Marine-Pionier-Bataillon 2

Marine-Nachrichten-Abteilung 2

Marine-Feldersatz-Bataillon 2

Marine-Versorgungs-Regiment 200.

Unfortunately, those unit designations do little to reflect the genuine fighting strength or abilities of the units. Although commanded by some of the most illustrious names in the Kriegsmarine's U-boat service, men who had trained in the intricacies of U-boat operational warfare were about to be pitted against veteran infantry and armoured units which had successfully fought across continental Europe, and often for years previously elsewhere. There are accounts of such last-minute units arriving in the front lines with little more than a Panzerfaust each, expecting to retrieve weapons from the dead or injured in the same manner that the Russians had treated their soldiers years before.

Originally, the 2nd Naval Division had been earmarked for action against the Soviet steamroller, but with a deteriorating situation in the west, its focus was switched and it went into action against British and Canadian forces around Bremen near Celle and Braunschweig. Ludwig Stöll recalled:

I had been fascinated by U-boats since the last war and as soon as I was old enough I enlisted immediately in the Kriegsmarine, determined to become a U-boat Engineering

Ausweis für den Aufenthalt
in Städten auf Usedom

O. U., den ....

Ausweis Nr.   91175 ✳

Der ....Ltn.(Ing.)........................
(Dienstgrad)

........Helmut   Mörke........
(Vor- und Zuname)

geb. ..5.1o.22.... in: Oberhausen/Sterkr

Größe: ..167........   Gestalt: ..schlank..

Gesicht: ..voll........   Haar: ..hellblond..

Bart: ..keinen........   Augen: ..grau-blau..

Bes. Kennzeichen: ....keine........

ist als Angehöriger der Dienststelle ....

........M 4988o........

berechtigt, sich in ....Swinemünde........
aufzuhalten.

(Dienstsiegel)

(Dienststelle)

Leave Pass for naval personnel, dated April 1945.

Officer. There was, of course, the weeks of infantry training before we actually became officer candidates and began training in the use of the U-boat. Finally I was aboard one! I was transferred to *U148* to train in the Baltic. This was a little Type IID and although I had no political leanings at all – I had even managed to avoid service in the Hitler Youth! – I was ready to go to combat at sea … to sail against England!

Of course, it never happened. The boat was eventually laid up and scuttled. In the meantime we had all been posted and all of a sudden I was back wearing a helmet and

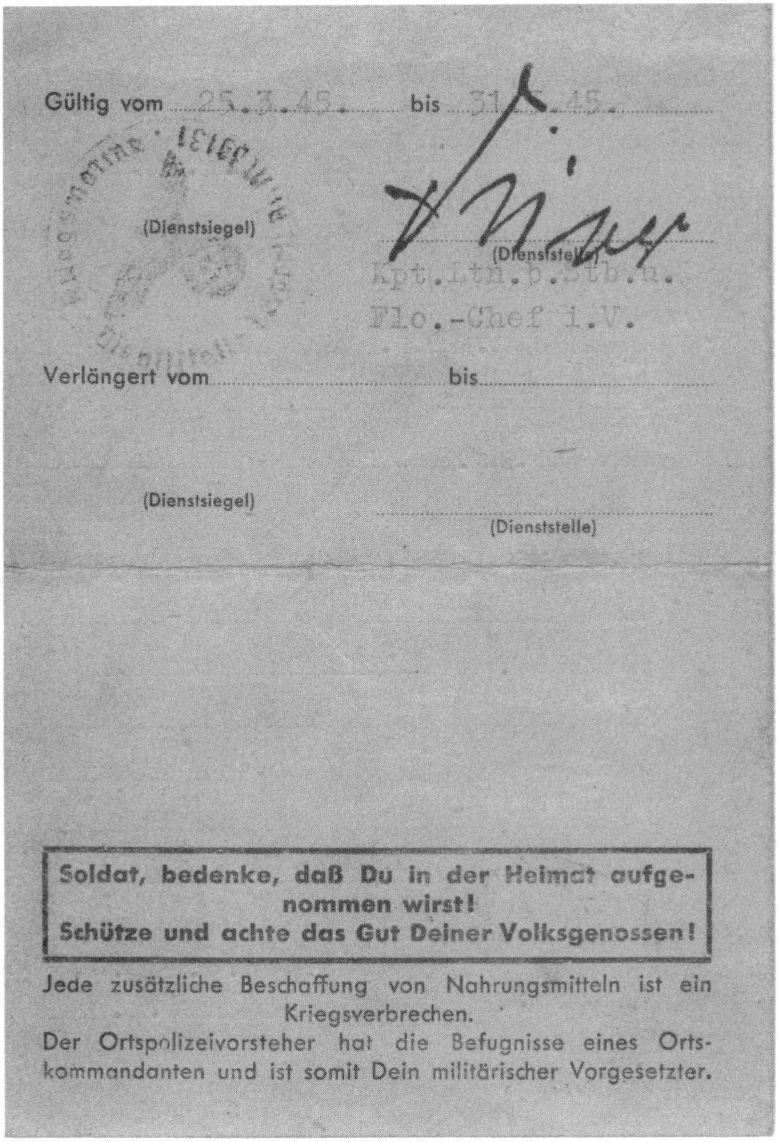

Gültig vom ....25.3.45.... bis ..31.5.45..

(Dienstsiegel)

(Dienststelle)

Kpt.Ltn.b.Stb.u.

Flo.-Chef i.V.

Verlängert vom.................................... bis....................................

(Dienstsiegel)

(Dienststelle)

> **Soldat, bedenke, daß Du in der Heimat aufge-
> nommen wirst!
> Schütze und achte das Gut Deiner Volksgenossen!**

Jede zusätzliche Beschaffung von Nahrungsmitteln ist ein
Kriegsverbrechen.
Der Ortspolizeivorsteher hat die Befugnisse eines Orts-
kommandanten und ist somit Dein militärischer Vorgesetzter.

Leave Pass for naval personnel, dated March 1945.

field grey and marching into action. We had been transferred to the 2nd Naval Infantry Division. Our training had been basic and we were equipped with little by way of heavy weaponry. I remember the basic training using the Panzerfaust anti-tank rocket with which we were expected to destroy enemy tanks. You have to remember that even though we hadn't finished our training, we were sailors. Our war was supposed to be in the engine room of a U-boat, so the idea of charging towards enemy tanks and infantry was totally alien. I must admit to being quite depressed about coming so close to sailing on a combat footing aboard the U-boats before being herded into field grey and fighting in the trenches.

But we still gave it everything that we could. We were quickly trained up and I was assigned to the Regiment commanded by Werner Hartmann, who I had known not only from the newspapers, but from his book that was published in the early days of the war. They threw us into action against British armoured units. It was terrifying but we fought as best we could. We did try but we didn't last long.[54]

In almost identical circumstances, Gerhard Both, who had been on active service aboard destroyers before transferring to the U-boat service in 1944, was also earmarked for the infantry. However, he bitterly believes that there were more underhanded and nefarious methods to dispose of the unassigned Fähnriche that were temporarily housed in Finkenwerder.

There was no further need for such inexperienced junior officers as us. We fell between two stools, so to speak: for a job as a non-commissioned officer one was overqualified and too experienced; for a commissioned rank we were not yet fully qualified, and our training was not quite complete ... Unfortunately, it seems, our fate was left to the discretion of a group of heartless and narrow-minded staff officers who did not bother to seek a solution to this problem but rather opted for off-hand, one-sided quick decisions.

From now on we were subjected to a regular 'ensign annihilation' process. I am not alone in this opinion ... It began with a very unpleasant episode in which the political commissar ... played a leading role. He carpeted a number of our colleagues which later led to their courts martial. Each of these men had thought it a harmless matter to put a bar of chocolate into his pocket, presumably to eat later when we had worked in the holds of the *Venus* stowing cargo. The commissar, Oberleutnant —, had us all searched and then reported the culprits, as mentioned above. A few more colleagues were added to his list when he searched our quarters immediately after our arrival at Finkenwerder and found a few more illicit items. Little became known of what happened to those found guilty – which presumably meant all of them – but since one was a friend and former *Z39* shipmate of mine, I made an effort to find out. He was reduced in rank and sent to a special 'punishment' company on the Eastern Front. We never heard from him again and it is quite easy to imagine his fate.[55]

This willingness to throw inexperienced men into the cauldron of battle against the Russians was manifest throughout Germany and its armed forces. Erich Topp experienced a similar situation while in Germany as temporary commander of *U3030* in April 1945:

Along with a few other experienced sailors on board, I used every available hour to train the new crew ... Throughout these drills we kept up our normal shipboard routines. To simulate realistic conditions we often had to pull switches and levers. We usually turned off the electricity or, if this was impossible, put up warning signs for the men to be especially careful.

One day, the Petty Officer in charge forgot to post these warning signs while we were running our electric motors for underwater propulsion. A young enlisted man got accidentally caught in the machinery and was fatally injured. A court martial followed, and the Petty Officer was sentenced to fight in a penal company at the land front against the advancing Allied troops. The Petty Officer not only admitted his negligence but was deeply shaken by the consequence of his action. To tear him away from our shipboard community at this point would have meant death for him. I protested the finding of the court martial. The Petty Officer stayed with us on board, for here too, he fought at the front.[56]

Indeed, Topp also recounts his general feelings about the deployment of Kriegsmarine men into the grinding battle of infantry attrition after attending a meeting at BdU headquarters.

April 25

We U-boat commanders find ourselves in a heated debate with members of the staff of the U-boat High Command. Should the city of Flensburg on the Danish border, full of refugees and wounded soldiers, be defended or declared an open city? Should the Fähnriche presently training at the Naval Academy in Flensburg be flown to Berlin to form a last line of defence around the Führer? We U-boat men are quite prepared to do our duty to the last, but for such nonsense we will not stand. We left the room in protest.[57]

On 2 March, Hitler decreed that the 2nd Naval Division, forming at Itzehoe and Glückstadt, should receive priority equipping of arms, and be assigned an area of the line near Stettin. The commander, however, balked at the idea and pleaded to be allowed time to train his inexperienced soldiers in infantry-artillery co-operation on a regimental

Veteran U-boat commander KK Heinrich 'Ajax' Bleichrodt addresses his men from the 2nd U-Training Flotilla in Wilhelmshaven on 13 May 1945.

scale. The Führer declared that no time remained for such training and that the men could practise in the area immediately behind the front line, without restriction in their use of weapons.

Although originally earmarked to join the 7th Panzer and 25th Panzer Grenadier Divisions on the suicidal planned counter-attack to break through and relieve Berlin, to be led by SS General Felix Steiner, the division was instead defensively deployed against the British. Attached to the naval troops were a battalion of SS troops who had originally been raised to act as a replacement pool for the 12th SS Panzer Division, Hitler Jugend. Drawn from the fanatical ranks of the Hitler Youth, these troops would prove their worth while attached to Vizeadmiral Ernst Scheurlen's division. Of somewhat more dubious value were two Hungarian units also attached, alongside a tank-hunting unit, flak regiment, and fortress anti-tank detachment.

The division's primary employment seemed to be as a mobile anti-tank unit which could be used to plug the line where it was weakest. The faith that Hitler and his immediate subordinates placed in a unit of former sailors armed with rifles in Panzerfaust seems misguided at best, ridiculous at worst. From this point on, the units of the 2nd Naval Division fought a steady withdrawal, constituent units virtually annihilated if they stood fast for very long against the British advance.

> Our march continued to Helmsbünde where we spent the next night, only to be woken up by murderous machine-gun fire and bombardment by advancing tanks; we managed to extricate ourselves without losses and made it via Hastedt to a forest area along the highway Rotheburg-Scheesel. As we heard the rattles of tanks nearby we explored this forest and, to our surprise, found ourselves face-to-face with a major English armoured unit, with many tanks and other vehicles, camped here overnight. It was very tempting to discharge our Panzerfaust into this lot, but we resisted this temptation as we would have cut off our retreat. Instead we crossed the road in darkness right under the noses of the nearest tanks and marched on to Westerholz and Mulmshorn where we attached ourselves to the divisional headquarters, temporarily housed in a roadside hotel.[58]

The division as a whole had been comprehensively overrun near Bremen, retreating back across the Elbe by ferries of Schnellboote, and returned to Itzehoe and Cuxhaven to reconstitute a useful fighting unit. By this stage the strength of the division had been reduced to 750 officers and men. On 5 May, Itzehoe was due to surrender to the British, and so the 2nd Naval Division marched north toward the Kaiser Wilhelm Canal, arriving at midnight, and heading to the small hamlet of Bunsoh where news of Germany's surrender awaited them. Like their comrades at sea, each man of the division was handed a handwritten piece of paper on which it was recorded that they had been discharged from naval service, though these were utterly worthless. The remainder of the shattered division was eventually surrendered piecemeal to the victorious British forces in Schleswig-Holstein during May. The unit's first commander, Vizeadmiral Ernst Scheurlen, had been killed after his Horch staff car was strafed by British fighter planes on 7 April, dying from his wounds the following day. Werner Hartmann took temporary command, whereupon his place was taken by Army Oberst Graf von Bassewitz, who led the division until the eventual surrender of the remnants of the unit on 8 May.

In the rush to obtain fresh men to throw into the grinder in the face of the Allied onslaughts from east and west, the different arms of the service seemed to bid against each other in an increasingly macabre auction at conferences with Hitler. On 14 April, Dönitz stated that he could release three thousand young Kriegsmarine men, equipped with light packs and Panzerfaust, for operations behind the front line in the west to harass enemy supply lines. Hitler welcomed the offer, but it was never instituted. Dönitz further ordered the establishment of an organisation which would instantly take over the crews of damaged or decommissioned ships and boats, so that they could be trained as infantry without delay. Cornelius Ryan portrayed in his book, *The Last Battle*, the often bizarre, and certainly nightmarish, image of the bartering for infantry strength that took place in Hitler's headquarters when the Führer was faced with concrete information from Generaloberst Gotthard Heinrici, the unfortunate officer charged with the defence of Berlin until his removal in late April.

The time to hammer home the truths of the desperate situation had, to Heinrici's mind, arrived. 'I must tell you,' he said bluntly, 'that since the transfer of the armoured units to Schörner, all my troops – good and bad – must be used as front-line troops. There are no reserves … My Führer, the fact is that, at best, we can hold out for just a few days ... then it must all come to an end.'

There was dead silence. Heinrici knew that his figures were indisputable. The men gathered there were as familiar with casualty statistics as he. The difference was that they would not have spoken of them.

Göring was the first to break the paralysing silence. 'My Führer,' he announced, 'I will place immediately at your disposal 100,000 Luftwaffe men. They will report to the Oder front in a few days.'

Himmler glanced owlishly up at Göring, his arch rival, then at Hitler, as if sampling the Führer's reaction. Then he too made an announcement. 'My Führer,' he said in his high pitched voice, 'the SS has the honour to furnish 25,000 fighters for the Oder front.'

Dönitz was not to be outdone. He had already sent a division of marines to Heinrici; now he declared that he too would subscribe further forces. 'My Führer,' he announced, '12,000 sailors will be released immediately from their ships and rushed to the Oder.'

Heinrici stared at them. They were volunteering untrained, unequipped, unqualified forces from their own private empires, spending lives instead of money in a sort of ghastly auction. They were bidding against one another not to save Germany, but to impress Hitler … Hitler turned to Heinrici. 'There,' he said, 'you have 150,000 men – about twelve divisions. There are your reserves.' The auction was over. Hitler apparently considered the Army Group's problems settled.

Heinrici struggled to preserve his control. 'These men,' he stated flatly, 'are not combat trained. They have been in rear areas and offices or on ships, in maintenance work at Luftwaffe bases …They have never fought at the front. They have never seen a Russian.'

'I tell you,' [Dönitz] snapped at Heinrici, 'the crews of warships are every bit as good as your Wehrmacht troops.' For just a moment Heinrici himself flared. 'Don't you think there's a big difference between fighting at sea and fighting on land? ... I tell *you*, all these men will be slaughtered at the front! Slaughtered!'[59]

Heinrici's appreciation of the combat value of the naval divisions was not incorrect, whether they faced Russian or British forces. The air of unreality that had pervaded Hitler's headquarters and its appreciation of German military strength can be illustrated by Dönitz's own report to the Führer on 14 February regarding the readiness of the 1st Naval Division to be committed to action.

> He gained a very good impression of the troops and their readiness for action. Shortcomings in training are still apparent; however, they can gradually be eliminated. In equipment there is a need above all for heavy weapons, particularly since the assault gun brigade which was allotted them has temporarily been withdrawn. The C-in-C Navy believes the division could well adapt itself to mobile warfare in time.[60]

Dönitz reflected realistically on only one matter: the fact that he doubted the ability of officers in the 'middle ranks', from battalion commanders upwards, to adapt to modern land warfare.

Ultimately, the men of the 2nd Naval Division acquitted themselves as best they could in action. They, and their attached SS unit, had fought a dogged defence that shocked the advancing British. On 11 April, as British troops from 1/5 Welch, of the 53rd Welsh Division, attacked the town of Rethem on the River Aller between Bremen and Hanover, the men of the 2nd Naval Division repulsed the attack in bitter hand-to-hand fighting. The British suffered twenty wounded casualties, and sixty missing believed killed. A sole survivor from one of the units involved, Private Parry, then claimed that his fifteen comrades had been captured and shot by the German defenders, alleging that the murderers were SS men. Six days later, *The Times* newspaper published Parry's very detailed account of the massacre along with an artist's impression of it.

News of the massacre spread quickly, along with information that they were not SS troops, but marines from the naval division. British morale sagged, already battered by the unexpectedly stiff fighting. Veteran Corporal Leslie George of the 1/5 Welch anti-tank platoon had fought from Normandy, earning a DCM in the process. He recalls reaction to the naval troops' defence and news of the massacre.

> I remember it was a total shock, especially for the younger intake who had not until then encountered heavy action … I, myself, was known as a 'bad bastard' as I was the first man in the battalion to gain an award.
>
> I came across a group of about three dozen German POWs who were being searched by a warrant officer of the Field Security Police. He was a cocky little so-and-so who had his lance corporals scattered around the immediate area. The POWs had been some of the defenders of Rethem and quite a few had English cigarettes in their possession. The warrant officer had got to one of the POWs who was about 40 years old and a bit portly. In finding a packet of 'Players' in his pocket, he threw them on the ground then told the German, using sign language, to pick them up. As he bent down to pick them up he kicked him in the backside; as he straightened up he gave him a rabbit punch to make him bend down again. This treatment went on four or five times.
>
> By now, apart from his NCOs, my gun crew and myself, several other soldiers had gathered to the scene and I was becoming very angry. I placed a magazine on my sten gun, cocked it, pointed it at the warrant officer and said to him, 'If you touch that man once more, I will pull this trigger.' He ordered his NCOs to arrest me. My gun

crew looked into my eyes, saw a sign that they now knew and told the NCOs not to go near me or the warrant officer would be a dead man. The warrant officer was by now screaming at his men, but when he looked into my eyes, as I told him to, he realised how close he was to death. I said quietly to him, 'I have been fighting bastards like you (meaning SS and Nazis) and unless you do your job properly, I shall treat you the same way as I would treat them, and if you take it out on the prisoners because of what I have just done to you, I shall find out and will trace you all over Europe and kill you. I have at least three dozen witnesses to what you were doing to that POW.'[61]

It soon transpired that the massacre had never taken place and it is unknown what prompted Parry to make the allegation, other than fatigue and bad light conditions. Indeed, one of the missing men who was supposed to have been shot out of hand was later recaptured by British forces, reporting that the German marines had treated their British prisoners totally correctly.

Rethem proved a tough nut to crack, and the British called in waves of Typhoon fighter bombers and a huge artillery bombardment, which still failed to dislodge the German defenders without severe casualties. To the southeast, British troops finally forced their way over the Aller River near Essel, after commandos mounted a wild bayonet charge on the Kriegsmarine and SS men holding the line that faced the British bridgehead. The commander of the independent Marine-Füsilier-Bataillon 2, Korvettenkapitän Josef Gördes, an artillery officer, was killed by grenade splinters during the battle that finally ended in a German withdrawal, the eastern flank of Rethem now open to attack. To ensure Allied success, a hundred bombers proceeded to flatten what had been an insignificant town of no real strategic value.

The 2nd Naval Division had lost seventy-three men in the fighting, the youngest seventeen years old, the oldest aged fifty-three. British observers after the fighting were

Staff officers of Marine-Grenadier-Regiment 6, 2nd Naval Infantry Division, photographed during the battles in northern Germany, April 1945. Third from left is Kapitän zur See Werner Hartmann.

surprised to see that a great many of the defenders were dead in their foxholes with head wounds, meaning they had died standing up and fighting back, rather than crouching like the demoralised and beaten enemy that the British had expected. Fifteen townspeople were killed and British losses amounted over 230 killed, wounded and missing. Nor was their struggle against the German naval troops over.

Kapitän zur See Neitzel's Marine Grenadier Regiment 7, which was dominated by men from the U-boat training division, was led by the tenacious officer in a series of small-scale night raids against the British troops of 4 Welch, 53rd Welsh Division, on 10 April. Neitzel had exhorted his men to destroy every scrap of enemy equipment they found, moving light with small arms, and no packs or heavy equipment. The Germans infiltrated the British lines and harassed the Welsh troops throughout the night, with confusing hand-to-hand battles flaring up in all areas of the front line near Verden. The Kriegsmarine troops were brave and reckless fighters, but eventually their professional and experienced opponents bested them and the retreat continued. The history of the Guards Armoured Division which faced the 2nd Naval Infantry Division characterised their enemy thus:

> They were nearly all ex-sailors, many of them until lately members of submarine crews. They had had little time for military training and therefore lacked the fighting skill of the paratroops, but their discipline and bravery were exemplary. They were all equipped with bazookas [Panzerfaust], which they used in particularly daring fashion; their tactics often involved them necessarily in annihilation but their aggressive spirit certainly delayed our progress most effectively.[62]

Indeed, a German Corps level strength return of 12 April showed that Marine-Grenadier-Regiment 5 was down to a strength of one officer and 100 men; Marine-Grenadier-Regiment 6, eighteen officers and 365 men, and Marine-Grenadier-Regiment 7 twenty officers and 410 men. The Marine-Fusilier-Bataillon had been whittled down to three officers and 80 men. Their British opponents apparently went as far as to nick-name them the 'Blue SS', which one assumes is a compliment on their combat tenacity more than anything else.

The 2nd Naval Infantry Division, with its strong cadre of U-boat men, acquitted itself better than could be expected in battle, but they were not the sole U-boat personnel fighting the desperate land battles in that area. The great port city of Hamburg was under direct threat from the British. Under the command of Generalmajor Wolz, the city's defences were preparing to hold to the last man under direct orders from Hitler. Dönitz was conducting a desperate evacuation of civilians and military personnel from the east, rather than leave them to the mercy of Russian forces. To surrender Hamburg would be to give away Schleswig-Holstein, from where the shipping conducting the evacuation were operating. Wolz had a largely scratch force that comprised Volkssturm, Hitler Youth, Hamburg's garrison regiment, Luftwaffe flak units, various shattered SS units including the 12th Training Battalion and two small volunteer tank-hunting units. The first, and most famous, was commanded by Korvettenkapitän Peter 'Ali' Cremer, and was comprised of volunteers from the U-boat service. Cremer had recently been in command of the Type XXI *U2519*, but departed the boat in February 1945 to take command of the Marine-Panzervernichtungsbataillon (Naval Tank Destroying Battalion). Another highly-decorated U-boat officer was also involved in the battle around Hamburg. In March 1945, Korvettenkapitän Carl Emmermann was commander of the Type XXI *U3037* before being transferred to take command of the 31st U-training Flotilla in Hamburg. As the British reached the city, he and many of his men took part in the infantry battles that followed as commander of Marine-Bataillon Emmermann.

Like Cremer, Kapitänleutnant Götz von Hartmann, the commander of Panzer-jagdbataillon, was a veteran U-boat commander. Von Hartmann was the former commander of the 1st U-Flotilla's *U563*, and the flak boat *U441*. Badly wounded while leading the second sailing of the ill-fated flak boat, Hartmann was attached to OKM from December 1943 to April 1945 when he was placed in command of the tank-hunting unit that bore his name. Little is known about their activities or successes.

As the British 2nd Army began its attack on Hamburg, the vehemence of the defence they faced surprised them. Cremer's unit of U-boat infantry tank destroyers was mentioned in OKW despatches of 25 April: 'A battle group commanded by Korvetten-kapitän Cremer, including volunteers from a U-boat base, destroyed 24 enemy tanks and other armoured fighting vehicles within two days.'[63] The British reduced their advances to probes, as they prepared for a street-to-street battle against the tenacious defence. However, as the month ended, so too did the evacuation from the east and thus the necessity to hold Hamburg. Wolz was soon authorised by Dönitz to negotiate the surrender of Hamburg and the city was spared yet more destruction. On 3 May, Wolz surrendered the city to British troops of the Second Army. Cremer was not among the troops who surrendered, having been placed in command of Dönitz's bodyguard detachment before the city had fallen. By the close of the war, Cremer's unit was down to a strength of sixteen men.

The city of Berlin was under constant aerial bombardment by the end of 1944, and although during November the threat of Russian troops penetrating far enough into Germany to actually threaten the capital had not yet become real, the danger to records and material from bombing was extreme. At OKM headquarters, Dönitz had long decided to maintain the records of the German Navy, dating back to 1871 and the formation of the German state. There would be no sordid destruction of documents from a military branch which had done nothing to besmirch its honour. Elsewhere, orders to destroy several different military and political archives were issued on 10 April 1945, and among the papers that were then burned were those of the Wehrmachtführungsstab, or Armed Forces Operations Staff, of General Jodl, the Gestapo archives in the Prinz Albrecht Strasse, and the files of the Abwehr (Military Intelligence Service) in Zossen. Dönitz would not countenance such treatment of the naval history that had been entrusted to him. Correspondingly, the entire store of naval records was transferred to the seventeenth-century Castle Tambach, five miles southwest of Coburg in northern Bavaria. This beautiful building, which formed a U-shape around an extensive courtyard, thus became the repository of German naval history from November 1944, including U-boat KTB logs and the BdU KTB.

On the Allied side, moves had been taken to establish an intelligence unit which was charged with collecting just such information, not only in the wake of the advancing Allied armies, but also often in front of them. During Germany's occupation of the Balkans in 1941, the Wehrmacht had achieved considerable success by the use of small self-contained commando-style fighting units, which included Brandenburger men, and accompanied the forward elements of the advance, but whose primary tasks had been the prevention of enemy demolition of harbours and other key installations, the capture of secret documents, and also of important enemy personnel whose interrogation was important to the German advance.

In Britain, Commander Ian Fleming, Personal Assistant to the Director of Naval Intelligence (DNI) (and later creator of James Bond), had reviewed these German achievements and recommended the prompt establishment of a similar unit, an Offensive Naval Intelligence Unit. Overtures were made to the Army and Air Force to develop the kind of specialist multi-branch unit that the Germans had employed, but they were largely rebuffed. Undeterred, the DNI persisted in his efforts and eventually established what became 30 Assault Unit, comprised of naval and army men and marines. The naval contingent tended to be the technical specialists, the soldiers and marines being taken from existing commando units. The unit received its baptism of fire during Operation Torch in 1942, and thereafter became an evolving presence in the front lines in Tunisia, Sicily, Italy and Aegean until the Normandy landings, whereupon 30 Assault Unit was involved in the battle for Brest, before heading east into Germany.

Their brief was broad, although they were furnished with priority lists of people who were hunted for capture. Wernher von Braun (incorrectly listed in Fleming's 'Black Book' of targets as Hans) was the head of the list, because of his role in the rocket research that would later trouble US Naval Intelligence so much when dealing with surrendered U-boats, a hugely important technology not only to be captured from the Germans, but also to be denied to the Russians. To that end, Fleming's operational instructions were stark:

> The customary priorities for documents remain in force. These are:
> First – *Chefsache, Geheime Kommando Sache.*

U-boat men in temporary accommodation at one of the Norwegian concentration points, as they await orders from the British High Command in Norway. The tents were supplied from Finland. Many units were left to fend for themselves for prolonged periods of time until Allied logistics could deal with them.

Second – *Geheime, Nür für den Diestgebrauch.*

Third – Any other documents.

Should any first priority material be discovered, an Officer or Senior NCO should be detailed immediately to break off operations and ensure its safe arrival in the Admiralty.

The necessity of avoiding or eliminating witnesses to successful action and for the demolition of any building or ship's cabin which has yielded results and which is likely to be re-occupied by the enemy is emphasised.

It is important to ensure that every scrap of paper, including ashes, used blotting pads, carbon paper, the contents of waste paper baskets and odd pieces of paper which may be found concealed under furniture, behind maps or mirrors etc, should be collected and forwarded to the Admiralty. It is also necessary to ensure that all code books and ciphers should be kept dry as water causes the text to disappear.[64]

The successes of 30 Assault Unit were almost astounding. They had continually been at the cutting edge of the Allied sweep across Europe, and elements crossed the Rhine with the first wave of troops in March 1945. Once over this last great obstacle before the heart of the German Reich, the various small task forces of 30 Assault Unit were assigned a more advance role by DNI, roving ahead of the main army. SHAEF objected to this, ordering that they were not allowed to advance beyond the leading troops, but local commanders of XXI Army Group chose not to enforce these conditions. By 10 April, 30 Assault Unit was arrayed as follows:

Team 4, attached to Guards Armoured Division headed for Bremen;

Team 5, covering Hanover before heading also to Bremen;

Team 6, attached to Canadian Armoured Division;

Team 7, attached to Polish Armoured Brigade bound for Emden and Wilhelmshaven;

Team 8, covering western Holland;

Team 10, covering Hamburg and the east;

Team 55, covering perceived evacuation areas for key naval personnel in southern Germany. This latter objective was also handled by Team 5, after their discovery in Hanover of the evacuation of naval personnel and scientists to the Harz mountains.

On 26 April, Team 4, led by Lieutenant-Commander Job, and numbering just over thirty men, took the surrender of Bremen, including the Deschimag Shipyards, Job himself leading the advance on a bicycle when one of his few vehicles broke down. Several Type XXI U-boats, completed and under construction, were captured, alongside a Narvik-Class destroyer being rigged for demolition in the harbour. In Kiel, Team 10 combined with the 1st SAS Regiment to take control of the battered city. They crossed the Elbe, attached to 5th Division as 13th Brigade's reconnaissance unit, and were in Lübeck at 0600hrs two days later. Leaving a small detachment to exploit Lübeck, the remainder headed for Kiel arriving at Travemünde at 1130hrs. Within three and a half hours they were at Timmendorfer Strand, and from there reached Neustadt where they found an SS prison ship, SS *Athen*, crammed with six thousand prisoners. Two SS guards were executed.

On 5 May, 30 Assault Unit and the SAS Regiment entered Kiel, whereupon Team 10 immediately occupied the Walterwerke where they captured Dr Helmuth Walter, Professor Kramer and the entire staff of technicians. Despite this success, all secret papers had been destroyed before their arrival. Following the general German surrender, more naval intelligence teams would arrive to exploit the Walterwerke, including the reconstruction by the German engineers of various secret weapons systems, including the XXIIb and XXVI U-boat types, advanced torpedoes, aircraft rocket-propelled bombs and other projects. The Germaniawerft shipyard was neutralised, including the Kilian U-boat bunker, which had taken a direct hit from bombs during the night of 9 April. A bomb impacted on the flak tower which collapsed, large pieces of concrete plummeting onto the boat *U4708* within the bunker. Landing behind the conning tower, water flooded the damaged boat, trapping seven men – two sailors, who were drowned, and five shipyard workers, including engineer Karl Schmidt, who only survived with two others by escaping the tower at the last moment, as the boat was entombed inside the wrecked bunker.

The 30 Assault Unit Team's commander then went to the Flandern bunker to accept the port's surrender from Konteradmiral Joachim von Gerlach. The immediate disarmament of Kriegsmarine forces in the area was arranged, notwithstanding officers and ratings who were allowed to continue carrying small arms while on duty. The official report later stated:

> The Germans, generally speaking, appear to have obeyed these orders implicitly (as well as an injunction, issued over the signature of General [*sic*] Keitel, forbidding the destruction of documents or equipment after 0800 on 5 May). In the circumstances, the party under Commander Curtis showed exemplary tact, since the total of 30 AU 'T Force' and the SAS Regiment amounted to no more than 500 men, while the strength of the German forces in Kiel was at least 25,000. Apart from an incident in which a Royal Marine NCO roughly handled a German Officer (the conduct of the Royal Marine was subsequently held to be justified) the surrender was taken smoothly and efficiently.[65]

Von Gerlach warned Curtis that troops north of the Kiel Canal were preparing a last-ditch stand. These could well have included the men of former U-boat commander Hermann Rasch's Seehund Unit, who had arrived in Flensburg, offering themselves as ready to fight to the last man. Von Gerlach telephoned Dönitz, who personally intervened and guaranteed the 30 Assault Unit team's safety as they crossed the canal. From there they entered the minesweeper base at Friedrichsort and the TVA (Torpedo-Versuchs-Anstalt), or Institution for Torpedo Experiments and Development at Eckenförde, where much of value was recovered. At the end of hostilities on 8 May, Curtis's men were the only Britons north of the Kaiser Wilhelm Canal. They were soon in Flensburg where they were accommodated aboard SS *Patria*, alongside officers of Dönitz's government.

The small British unit was swiftly reinforced by others, who soon found that it was not merely the Wehrmacht which presented problems to the victors, but the masses of displaced persons: former concentration camp inmates, refugees, foreign workers released from German labour, or freed prisoners, who also caused considerable headaches. Corporal Bernard Slack, a Royal Marine from 117 Brigade, remembered:

> Kiel was terrible – there was shipping, railway, warehouses, big cranes, all rolled into one. It was totally demolished. There was a big torpedo shed with all the torpedoes

on cradles waiting for the British experts to check. The torpedo fuel was wood alcohol, which was 98 per cent proof. These DPs (Displaced Persons) had got keys to the shed and were draining the fuel into cups and drinking it.

Hamburg was no better. We were all issued with a little handbook by the Intelligence Corps. You have the honour of being the advance guard of the Army of Occupation. You're ambassadors for Britain. Yet there we were in Hamburg dodging the bricks.[66]

Meanwhile, throughout Germany in the last days of the war, the 30 Assault Unit went from success to success. Team 55, led by Lieutenant-Commander Glanville, was operating in central Germany when Glanville received a report on 12 April that told of a naval intelligence target in Bad Sulza. Immediately they headed for the Stuttgart area, preparing to undertake a meticulous search of the Bad Sulza region, where they hoped to discover the whereabouts of personnel of the German Naval Intelligence Division (III/SKL) and their documents. Their search was partially successful, a boarded-up cellar yielding piles of documents, one of which was a letter which revealed the locations of repositories whence SKL departments had evacuated their documentary material. Most important of all, the SKL/KA (Historical Records and Operational Research) department was revealed to have been taken to Schloss Tambach.

Glanville immediately sought, and obtained, clearance to head directly to Tambach Castle. They arrived at the castle on 25 April, where the garrison, including three junior admirals, handed themselves over. Glanville's outnumbered men then faced a direct threat from a detachment of female Wehrmacht auxiliaries present, who made an attempt at destroying the archive material, until they were arrested and locked in the castle. Overnight, Royal Marines and Wehrmacht guards stood side by side as there were local units of Waffen SS who had not yet admitted defeat.

The archive that had been captured comprised the complete operational history of OKM from 1871 to 1944, which included the war diaries of U-boats and surface vessels, as well as naval planning documents, orders, the minutes of naval and political discussions, and various studies of the problems and nature of naval warfare. Unfortunately, German Constructional Office records had been virtually completely destroyed. This was one of the most important captures made by the 30 Assault Unit, and they were soon reinforced by American troops from a local armoured unit, whereupon Glanville and his men headed south, although they found their path frequently obstructed by French naval intelligence officers on comparable missions.

Men of 30 Assault Unit continued to unearth valuable documents, such as those found by divers at Travemünde: these had been stuffed into torpedo casings and dropped into the harbour. Following a visit to conquered Berlin to attempt to locate those documents that rendered the Tambach archive incomplete, the complete OKM war diaries were later found hidden beneath the doorstep of what was now Royal Navy headquarters in Plön. Secret TVA records were found buried in the forest near Neustadt, and farm buildings around Tambach were scoured for material that had been successfully spirited away by German staff officers who were still present at the castle. Eventually, those German Naval archives were transferred by agreement with SHAEF to the British Admiralty for exploitation. On arrival in London, the records received new file designations according to the British registry system, and there they remain to this day.

In Norway, the Wehrmacht maintained a huge and largely untouched garrison. Suspicions already abounded in Allied circles that Festung Norway would be the site of a fanatical last stand by German troops. While American concerns of that nature largely focussed on a mythical, but potentially real, Bavarian redoubt centred on the Obersalzberg and its lofty Eagle's Nest tea-house, Britain was more preoccupied with German resistance from the formidable units which had entrenched themselves into Norway's often inhospitable landscape. Their fears were not without justification, as operational U-boats continued to sail from the Norwegian bases until the end of the war. Often their missions were the predictable futility that had come to characterise Dönitz's lost Atlantic battle, but they were also involved in the landing of small commando units from various branches of service: the Heer, Kriegsmarine and Waffen SS.

Norway had fallen to German conquerors in May 1940, but not without staunch resistance, particularly in Narvik. During the German invasion the Kriegsmarine bore a heavy toll in lost ships: the cruiser *Blücher* sunk by shore batteries, ten destroyers lost in Narvik to Royal Navy forces, and *U64* sunk by aircraft from HMS *Warspite*. The U-boat screening forces, which included boats captained by many of the most famous names to emerge in U-boat history, such as Günther Prien, were rendered impotent by inoperative weaponry. Torpedo problems became the bane of U-boat crews, due to a combination of faults, most due to insufficient testing before production and commitment to battle. Fighting in the northern latitudes of Norway rendered torpedoes useless, because of the effect of the earth's magnetic field in that area on these increasingly temperamental weapons. In fact the combined problems would not be resolved until 1942. But in Norway in 1940, these problems made the U-boat support of a vulnerable surface fleet useless, resulting in the severe losses suffered in surface combat.

Nonetheless, the campaign was successful, as the invasion of France and the Low Countries required a final Allied abandonment of the fight for Norway, the battle for Narvik being probably the most contentious. Following subjugation by the Wehrmacht, the first U-boat base was established in Bergen. Facilities swiftly brought from Germany allowed U-boats in transit toward the Atlantic to stop off after sailing from German ports, topping up fuel and provisions before breaking through into the North Atlantic. Not until 1942 was the first 'Norwegian' flotilla formed: the 11th U-Flotilla commanded by Fregattenkapitän Hans Cohausz formed in Bergen in May. Operating Type VIICs, the 11th U-Flotilla began to sail primarily against Arctic convoys, coordinated by FdU Norwegen Kapitän zur See Rudolf Peters.

Bergen would also house the first U-boat bunker to be constructed on Norwegian soil. Work on the Bruno bunker was begun in spring 1941 in Laksevåg. The bunker was planned to accommodate nine boats, comprising three dry docks and three wet boxes which could accommodate two boats each. The bunker was not fully completed until 1944, because, as well as materials being diverted to the construction of the French bunkers and ancillary U-boat support structure in the bases that stretched along the Atlantic coast, there were also natural difficulties in getting the construction material to Bergen. The construction infrastructure was beset with problems, the worst being the transport of tons of sand and rock from its location at Masfjord, sixty kilometres north of Bergen. Over one thousand Norwegian workers were employed on the building project, their number swelled by hundreds of Russian prisoners used as slave labour.

Two established Norwegian yards – Bergen's Mekaniske Verksteder and Mjellem &

U318 photographed en route to Hopseidet in northern Norway. Men of the Kleinkampfverbände commando unit MEK35 are pictured alongside the U-boat's crew.

Karlsen – were used initially for boat repairs. Later the Bergen Dampskibsselskab-Werkstatt in Søndrevågen (Laksevåg) dealt with the majority of U-boat repair. The process by which a U-boat was prepared for action in Bergen remained a somewhat difficult logistical undertaking throughout the war. As a typical example, a boat would first be overhauled inside the available space in the bunker if possible. Otherwise it was accommodated in open-air yard facilities, but this entailed vulnerability from air attack. Once completed, the boat would be taken to Byfjorden for its test dives into the deep waters of the fjord. Test-firing of torpedoes and anti-aircraft weaponry would follow, the ammunition transported from German manufacturing plants to a local arms depot at Bakarvågen. Flak practice was made against balloon targets in Hjeltefjord. Once the diving tests were completed, any adjustment in trim would be done in the Bruno bunker before the boat sailed to Knettholmen in Askøy for degaussing: the process of demagnetising the hull by passing it through loops of electric cabling intended to reverse the polarity of the boat's natural magnetic field. Final rust treatment was carried out before the boat was loaded and prepared for sea. Nonetheless, between October 1941 and October 1942, fifty-six U-boats were prepared for action in Bergen. Initially, the facilities in Bergen were able to cope with the boats of the 11th U-Flotilla, as well as transitory U-boats en route to the Atlantic or France. However, following the evacuation of the Atlantic U-boat bases and relocation of all combat boats to Norway, the few available spaces for U-boat repair and docking were immediately pushed beyond their limits.

The newly redeployed U-boats also attracted the attention of the Royal Air Force on a scale which had previously been reserved for Allied bombing raids on the French docks. On 4 October 1944, 136 Lancaster and Halifax bombers attacked both the bunker and Laksevåg shipyard in Bergen, achieving little against the bunker, but severely damaging the yards, and destroying *U228* and *U993*. Another raid a little over three weeks later achieved little, bad weather scattering the bombs throughout Bergen. On 12 January, the third and final attack against Bruno was launched by Royal Air Force 617 Squadron, the unit made famous for its Dambuster raids in Germany. Thirty-two Lancasters and a Mosquito escort/pathfinder hit the bunker with Tallboy bombs, damaging two U-boats. Two Focke-Wulf 190 aircraft were scrambled, claiming three Lancasters shot down. By the end of the war, the Bruno bunker was damaged but still functioning as a viable U-boat base, although unable to sustain the sheer weight of numbers required to maintain the U-boat offensive.

Also in Bergen, the Germans had taken possession of the Norwegian naval base, establishing their own 'Marineholmen' where munitions and provisions required for the combat boats were stored. The Kriegsmarine also established torpedo and artillery work stations. These were located in Melkeplassen, midway between the shipyard in Laksevåg and the Bruno bunker, a small rail system connecting the three.

Within the Marineholmen, there were barracks for officers and enlisted men; the sailors accommodated on the ground floor, whilst the officers occupied the right wing of the first floor, and non-commissioned officers the left. The officer's mess was adorned with photographs of fallen U-boat commanders, and the officers also had their own bathing facilities and sauna. In addition, the complex housed a central telephone exchange, messes and sports hall, garages, provisions store and warehousing for U-boat instruments and ammunition. From May 1942, it also had a full time medical establishment attached, which was commanded by Dr Helmut Wüstekamp at the end of the war. Following what had become a standard U-boat service tradition, this entire complex was named after one of the U-boat men's dead heroes: it was known as Prienlager, named after the commander Günther Prien of *U47*.

The 11th U-Flotilla established its torpedo arsenal in Bakarvågen. As well as the storage and maintenance of the weapons, a 100m quay was built by German engineers, from whence the U-boats could load weapons aboard before heading to sea. These facilities were what kept Bergen as a central despatch area for combat U-boats from all flotillas, and destined for most theatres of action, right through until the conclusion of the war. Housed specifically within Bergen, in total 190 U-boats would pass through the ranks of the 11th U-Flotilla.

In June 1943 a second Norwegian flotilla was formed. Frigattenkapitän Rolf Rüggeberg's 13th U-Flotilla was established: this would see fifty-five U-boats pass through its ranks. The base for this new unit was Trondheim, closer to the polar ocean where U-boats would attempt to intercept the flow of material from Britain to the Soviet Union. Trondheim was also used by the major surface units of the Kriegsmarine and their destroyer escorts: *Tirpitz, Scharnhorst, Admiral Hipper, Admiral Scheer, Prinz Eugen, Admiral Hipper, Lützow* and *Emden* were all based here at some point during the war.

Following the invasion of Norway, the large shipyard A/S Tronhjems Mekaniske Verksted, together with its dock, were commandeered by the Kriegsmarine. With U-boats competing for space with destroyers and S-boats, as well as becoming increasingly vulnerable to air attack, the familiar step of creating a shelter for U-boat repair and refit was undertaken. Work began on what would become the Dora I bunker complex in 1941, and ended on 20 July 1943, the five pens including three dry docks. The work was undertaken by the Organisation Todt's Wiking Einsatzgruppe, comprised primarily of Norwegian workers. Problems in attaining sufficient construction materials hampered the work, much having to be shipped in by rail and sea transport.

Dora I was one of the smallest bunkers built by the Germans for the U-boat service. Dora I attracted the one and only air attack on Trondheim on 24 July 1943 when American 8th Air Force aircraft bombed the town, focussing on the shipyard and bunker. The bunker suffered only minor damage, but *U622* was sunk while taking fuel from the tanker *Munkholm*. This bunker also housed a torpedo storage facility in its own box between the dry docks and wet pens. The huge logistical problem involved in shipping torpedoes from Germany was circumvented by the establishment of a Torpedo Arsenal at Trondheim, in Rønningsbakken, one kilometre southeast of Nyhavna. Eventually, a torpedo manufacturing plant was established at Munkvoll.

In the last year of war, Dora I was also used to help absorb the number of U-boats transferring from the defunct French bases. But, like Bergen, the facilities were insufficient for demand, which thus required more U-boats to make the journey back to German shipyards. Correspondingly, work had already begun on Dora II at Nyhavna, this containing two dry docks and three wet pens, each capable of holding two boats. Construction had begun as early as 1942, but the same construction difficulties meant that by end of the war the bunker was only sixty-five per cent complete. A third bunker had been planned, but never proceeded past the blueprint stage.

The last major combat U-boat base in Norway was Narvik. This was the most northerly base established by the Kriegsmarine, and eventually hosted boats of the 14th

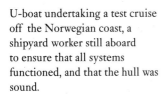

U-boat undertaking a test cruise off the Norwegian coast, a shipyard worker still aboard to ensure that all systems functioned, and that the hull was sound.

U-Flotilla, which was established in December 1944. Narvik boasted no Organisation Todt-built bunker to house the boats. Instead, the harbour was heavily defended by flak weaponry of all calibres, and the boats were often distributed further afield into outlying fjords and harbours. In Narvik itself, a small city centred firmly on iron-ore exports, the U-boats moored a command ship, the *Aviso Grille*, which had been Hitler's state yacht, an escort vessel, a depot ship containing workshops, and a tanker. The city boasted a naval hospital and the usual ancillary Kriegsmarine units of harbour protection and escort. In the narrow approaches to Narvik, at Bogen on the north side of Ofotfjords, the Kriegsmarine established yards. These would not only be used by the U-boats, but also periodically to host such surface ships as *Tirpitz*, *Admiral Hipper*, *Admiral Scheer* and *Lützow*, which occasionally moved there to avoid air attacks in Bergen harbour.

Both Kirkenes and Hammerfest also had small U-boat bases established. Depot ships were moored there to support those boats assigned to the interception of Arctic convoys which required replenishment. These depot ships would supply limited amounts of everything that was needed for basic maintenance of the boats and crews. Machine shops were provided, and ammunition storage, as well as facilities such as cinemas and accommodation, in conditions infinitely preferable to life aboard a combat boat. Hammerfest, in turn, attracted the attention of the Russian air force, and on 14 February 1944 was severely firebombed. South of Hammerfest in Altafjord, the workstation ship *Neumark* was moored. The crew of this vessel specialised in torpedo maintenance, as well as all aspects of electric motors and engines. As well as servicing U-boats, the *Neumark* was frequently used for maintenance aboard the *Tirpitz* and other surface units.

During the final year of the war, the U-boat service established bases in the south, the most prominent being at Horten. This Norwegian port, which also played host to various large surface ships, came under increasing pressure from the Royal Air Force as the war progressed. On 23 February 1945, the largest attack on the city took place, when seventy-two Lancaster bombers and ten Mosquito pathfinders bombed the docks, although they did not manage to damage the vital, and unprotected, dry docks that the U-boats were using. When the war ended, there were still five U-boats using those same docks. Elsewhere, the smaller bases at Kristiansand, Egersund, Stavanger and Haugesund were increasingly used by the U-boats in their attempts to disperse under the threat of concentrated Allied air and naval attack. At these smaller satellite bases only basic repairs could be undertaken, anything major requiring the berths at Bergen or Trondheim. Nonetheless, in August 1944 a new flotilla was formed at Kristiansand. Kapitänleutnant Konstantin von Rappard, who would later command the Type XXIII *U2324*, was placed in command of the 15th U-Flotilla at Kristiansand. It appears that this flotilla never achieved fully operational status, von Rappard having been the former head of shooting instruction at the 23rd U-Training Flotilla in Danzig. In April 1945, the 'Ace' commander Korvettenkapitän Ernst Mengersen succeeded von Rappard, who was sailing into the waters off the British Isles. Mengersen had formerly been in charge of tactical instruction at Travemünde for the 25th U-Flotilla. Stavanger's U-boat installation was controlled by Oberleutnant zur See Heinrich Mürl, former commander of the Type XXIII *U2327* before being transferred to instructional duties.

As was the case in all spheres of Atlantic U-boat operations, the flotilla infrastructure was purely of a logistical nature. Flotilla commanders had no operational control over the boats beneath their command. All of the U-boats which sailed for operational regions within the Atlantic were controlled directly by BdU, first from Germany, then France, and then once more from Germany as the tide of war turned. Regionally, flotillas were grouped under the administrative control of more localised intermediate commands: the FdU system. These were divided into FdU West (Atlantic), FdU North (Norway and Arctic) and FdU Mediterranean. The U-boats that were assigned to the bases in Japanese-held Malaya and Singapore were controlled to a certain degree locally, although instructions were still radioed by arduous links to Fregattenkapitän Dommes who was the local commander. The boats within the Black Sea also operated semi-independently, six small Type IIs controlled by the flotilla commander of the 30th U-Flotilla Kapitänleutnant Helmut Rosenbaum.

By the beginning of 1945, FdU West had already relocated to Norway and taken charge of the boats that operated below Narvik. FdU North was relegated to the Arctic boats based in Narvik as its sole concern. These regional commands coordinated the rotations of crews, maintenance of the boats, and the general logistical supply needs of the combat flotillas within their sphere of operations. They also coordinated closely the activities of the flotillas of surface security vessels which would provide minesweeping and escort duties for the U-boats in transit to and from the ports. However, their roles stopped short of operational control, except in the north. FdU North, Korvettenkapitän Reinhard Suhren, was allowed far more latitude in issuing operational instructions to his boats than was FdU West. Suhren became responsible for the operations of the Arctic boats, and was able to issue independent mission instructions for the Narvik flotilla.

During the first week of May, two U-boats were involved in a savage and unusual incident for the Kriegsmarine that served to illustrate the fact that the war was not yet over. Oberleutnant zur See Josef Will's *U318* and Oberleutnant zur See Hans Falke's *U992* of the 14th and 13th U-Flotillas respectively arrived near the small fishing village of Hopseidet in eastern Finnmark, a barren and windswept region at the northern tip of Norway. Hopseidet occupied a narrow isthmus of land between two fjords which approached from east and west. Only eighty kilometres from the Finnish border, it had become a transit point for Norwegian and Russian forces who were occupying areas recently evacuated by the Wehrmacht. The latter, aware of the imminent surrender, had begun to gather in several collection points. Finland had withdrawn from the war in the autumn of 1944, and Soviet troops had begun their Murmansk offensive, with the

German 20th and 21st Mountain Armies withdrawing into northern Norway during January 1945, operating a scorched earth retreat. By May 1945 the region was relatively untroubled by the war. However, on 5 May the two U-boats surfaced on opposite sides of the small fishing village. Aboard were men of Kapitänleutnant Wolfgang Woerdemann's MEK35 (Marine Einsatz Kommando), the Kriegsmarine's commando service. Men of the MEKs had been active on all fronts during the war, but this is one of the few mentions of MEK35 that this author has found.

Approximately ten kilometres from the village, thirty men came ashore in small rubber dinghies and succeeded in taking prisoner a local fisherman named Ivar Øye, whom they questioned intensively, and then used as a guide for a return to the village. Ashore, the U-boats had been seen during their approach by the local Norwegians, three policemen making up the entire garrison on that day. One of their number informed the nearest Norwegian military unit, news of the U-boats' presence reaching Colonel Arne Dagfin Dahl, commander of Norwegian Northern District, with some three thousand troops scattered throughout the region. Dahl had returned to Norway from Scotland on 11 November 1944 with three hundred soldiers of the 2nd Norwegian Mountain Company. They had been transported by ship to Murmansk, and from there joined the Russian advance in Finnmark. The Norwegian civilians who had remained in Finnmark during the German occupation were disappointed that Dahl had returned with so few troops, but later that winter further Norwegian soldiers arrived from Sweden, designated 'Police' troops rather than mountain soldiers. Since 1943, the Norwegian Government in exile in London had obtained permission from Swedish authorities to raise military formations from Norwegian refugees who were still on Swedish territory, designated as 'Police' in order to disguise their formal military training. Eventually numbering some twelve thousand men, they were largely equipped with Swedish weapons and equipment and trained by combined Norwegian and Swedish officers. Such men formed the majority of Dahl's command, three of them being resident at Hopseidet as the Germans arrived. Dahl was unable to offer reinforcements, despite the prolonged period before the German commando troops returned, and instead the three policemen were told to assemble civilian volunteers and establish a defensive position in Hopseidet. Young boys and local fishermen were gathered together, eyewitnesses later recalling that they had only an old rifle to share between some of them, in addition to the policemen's light weapons.

The following morning at approximately 0230hrs, the Germans returned and the Norwegian defenders opened fire. But as the Germans scattered they returned fire with greater effect, and after the defenders were put under accurate machine gun fire, the Norwegians retreated leaving a single man, Henry Mohr, to cover them. Mohr was soon out of ammunition and raised his arms in surrender. The men of MEK35 approached and apparently badly mishandled Mohr, before sending him back to one of the U-boats with Øye. A second fisherman had been left behind by the Germans. Fisherman Mathis Persen had been shot in the knee during the skirmish, and was lying on a patch of grass near the beach. One of the Germans approached him, looked at his wound, shook his head and pointed his weapon at Persen's head. The fisherman pleaded demonstratively for his life and the German relented, bandaging his knee and leaving him there.

Meanwhile, other members of MEK35 had gathered as many of the village's livestock together as they could and shot them all. All the buildings were either blown up with grenades or burnt to the ground, while many of the men and boys who had fired on them surrendered when they were prevented from running into the mountains, and were rounded up. An eyewitness account from Sigurd Ferman then tells that six of the fishermen were led to the only building still standing, a warehouse. Lined up against the wall with their hands above their heads, Ferman remembers one of the fishermen shouting, 'Are you going to shoot civilians?' before three German soldiers opened fire and killed all six. An officer, possibly Leutnant zur See Ewald Lübben, then moved amongst them administering the *coup de grâce* with a bayonet. Two of the German soldiers then went inside and searched the warehouse, returning with a pair of knives which were placed in the hands of the dead. Elsewhere, in the cellar of a cowshed, villager Caroline Mikalsen was hiding with nine of her eleven children, the youngest of whom was only four months old. Her husband and eldest son were among those who had been shot dead. She was found by one of the attackers, who fired indiscriminately through part of their shelter in an attempt to flush them out of hiding. As Caroline pleaded for mercy, she was then raped in front of her children, the soldier throwing a hand grenade into her shelter as he left. However, the grenade failed to explode.

Eventually the Germans returned to their dinghies and paddled back to the waiting U-boats from which martial music was blaring. Behind them the bodies had had small posters attached to them warning of the consequences of resistance to German occupation. The presence of these posters itself implies that the incident was planned, rather than the kind of knee-jerk reaction reprisals that litter the history of guerrilla warfare involving civilians. *U318* and *U992* then departed the scene and returned to their ports. The following day, at 0500hrs, Norwegian troops finally arrived at the scene and less than an hour later, Germany surrendered. It had been the last German combat

Josef Goebbels visits Georg-Wilhelm Schulz's 25th U-Training Flotilla. Goebbels was one of the few efficient Nazi ministers, and also one of the few who would frequently tour military installations in his own effort to boost sagging German morale.

Peter 'Ali' Cremer and Gerd Thäter
pictured during the fighting around
Hamburg. Cremer, who later captained
Dönitz's bodyguard, wears a curious
mixture of Luftwaffe and Army uniform.

incident in Norway.

It was an extremely unusual event for the Kriegsmarine to be involved in such a massacre, though men of other Marine Einsatz Kommandos had participated in the brutal combat of the Eastern front and war within the Adriatic. Following the end of hostilities, several of the men were questioned by Norwegian authorities about the crime, among them Ewald Lübben. He claimed that he had indeed opened fire on the Norwegians, but that it was simply in a case of self-defence. He claimed that the fishermen had attempted to attack him with knives and he had killed them all with his sub-machine gun. The Norwegians, conscious of the implication of misconduct in ordering civilians to oppose the Germans, allowed the matter to drop.

In 1967, West German authorities arrested six men for the atrocity, again Lübben being one of them. His familiar story of self-defence was again used by all of the accused, and by 1969 they had all been acquitted. More recent Norwegian forensic study of the case has revealed that there are huge inconsistencies between Lübben's version of events and the physical remains. Whilst he claimed to have shot the men as they attacked him, most carry wounds to their sides and backs. Also one long volley from his MP40 could leave thirty-two bullets in the dead men, but more than fifty, of different calibres, were recovered at the time by Norwegian police.

In a war that killed over fifty million people, civilian and military, Hopseidet may seem a minor affair. However, the needless executions, and the lasting effect not only on the relatives of those who were killed or maltreated, but also the Kriegsmarine veterans whose service was besmirched by such a bewilderingly savage raid, will forever be felt. At the scene of the atrocity a simple memorial has been erected. This reads:

> In memory of six unarmed civilian fishermen, mishandled
> and shot on this place by the Germans on 6 May 1945.
> Leonard Eriksen 35 years
> Einar Mikalsen 47 years
> Johan Mikalsen 18 years
> Harald Kristiansen 39 years
> Henry Kristiansen 16 years
> Reidar Karlsen 17 years

By the time of the German surrender, the Wehrmacht's hold on Norway had not relaxed at all. Coupled with the presence of all three service branches in large numbers in most parts of the country, Oberstgruppenführer Wilhelm Rediess, commander of SS forces in Norway, had forces numbering some six thousand men at his disposal. With a National Socialist government installed by the German conquerors, Norway had actually mustered many adherents to this cause, including thousands of troops who enlisted in the Waffen SS, as well as the three services of the Wehrmacht. That is not to say that Norway embraced the Quisling government, but it would be ingenuous to pretend that all Norwegians were opposed to them, in much the same way that the other occupied countries of Europe behaved. Indeed, fifteen thousand Norwegians volunteered for service in the Wehrmacht or Waffen SS, and as late as April 1945 recruiting was begun for the fourth SS og Politikompani, composed of police troops who would be largely used in combating Russian forces in northern Norway, or for anti-partisan warfare. The unit was not fully formed by the time of the German surrender.

Rediess' SS troops were directly subordinate to Josef Terboven, the Nazi Reichskommisar of Norway. Terboven was the real political power in Norway, using Vidkun Quisling, the former army officer who had led the Norwegian fascist party before hostilities, and who seized the post of Prime Minister during the German invasion in 1940, as a figurehead political leader. Terboven had joined the NSDAP (National-sozialistiche Deutsche Arbeiter Partei) in 1923, and reported directly to Hitler from his Norwegian empire, remaining a staunchly-devoted acolyte of the Führer to the end of his life. He had made no secret of his desire to establish Festung Norwegen (Fortress Norway), where the indisputably powerful Wehrmacht and SS forces that remained intact and firmly entrenched would have to be fought for every inch of territory before they would surrender. However, he exercised no military control over the 360,000 Wehrmacht forces within the country. His heavy-handed tactics in subduing the Norwegian populace had even earned displeasure from Josef Goebbels, who in his diary railed against Terboven's 'bullying tactics'. Goebbels made no secret of his displeasure with Terboven , once labelling him a 'bull in a china shop' within his diaries. Another example of this was written by Goebbels on 27 January 1942, when he recorded:

Terboven intends to deliver a radio address bitterly attacking the Bishop of Norway, who has acquired notoriety because of a number of stupid remarks. I advised him most urgently to keep hands off. I consider it beneath our dignity and harmful to our authority for a Reich commissioner in an area occupied by us to attack a public personage without, at the same time, saying how we will punish him. You attack without punishing only when you have no power. If you have power, you arrest and punish and give the reason why.[67]

Nonetheless, Allied fears that Festung Norwegen would become a reality were amply justified. Couple with Terboven's fanatical dedication to the Third Reich, the military forces were dominated by men of great combat experience. There were numerous units which had seen extensive action on the eastern and northern fronts against Russian troops. Kriegsmarine forces were commanded by Admiral Theodor Krancke, former commander of Marineoberkommando West, appointed Marineoberkommando Norwegen in April 1945. Units of the Heer answered to General der Gebirgstruppe Franz-Friedrich Böhme, as Armed Forces Commander, Norway, and Chief of the 20th Mountain Army. Böhme was a man who had proven his military capabilities since the First World War, but who had also created some controversy for his use of retaliatory strikes against Serbs, while serving as Army Commander in Serbia. He ordered the taking of one hundred hostages, who would be executed for every German soldier killed by Serbian partisans, and fifty for every German wounded.[68]

Ironically, whilst Terboven's tenacious hold on the political will, so often alluded to in Nazi rhetoric, was the primary concern of Allied observers, it was Heinrich Himmler who opened dialogue with the Allies to resolve the issue of German troops in Norway. The fear of last-ditch German defence caused great consternation among all Allied leaders, including the Norwegian Government in exile in London. They believed, furthermore, that should the Germans attempt to go down fighting, there was a strong likelihood that Sweden would be drawn into the battle, something that the Swedish government wished to avoid at all costs. Correspondingly, at a meeting in Stockholm of the Swedish count, Folke Bernadotte, with Brigadeführer Walter Schellenberg, Reichsführer SS Heinrich Himmler's representative, where Schellenberg was unsuccessfully attempting to negotiate the surrender of Germany on his superior's behalf, it was Bernadotte suggested that German forces in Norway could capitulate to neutral Swedish forces and be swiftly repatriated to Germany. Schellenberg, and Himmler, enthusiastically agreed, and the matter was actively pursued.

Following the death of Hitler, and Dönitz's succession as Head of State, the latter summoned Böhme and Terboven to his headquarters to discuss the impending end of hostilities:

The other question which was a source of particular anxiety was that of the countries … we were still occupying, namely Norway, Denmark and The Netherlands … My primary object was to avoid fighting and bloodshed in these countries, revolts by their populations and countermeasures by the German occupation forces – in other words I wanted to find the best way in which to ensure their peaceful and orderly surrender. On 1 May therefore … I sent for … Reichskommisar Terboven and General Böhme from Norway.

At one of our conferences with Terboven and General Böhme on Norway, Himmler unexpectedly appeared, accompanied by Gruppenführer Schellenberg, the

Chief of the German Foreign Security Service. General Böhme reported that Norway was quiet, that the end of German occupation was expected by the Norwegians to come at any moment, and that they therefore did not wish to risk further and unnecessary bloodshed by rising in revolt.[69]

Schellenberg enthusiastically outlined the scheme that he had managed to establish with Bernadotte. By its very nature, the occupation forces would escape becoming prisoners of war of the Allies and be permitted a swift return home, while Norway was quietly evacuated. Dönitz was unconvinced:

> I viewed with suspicion both the motives that had actuated these unofficial negotiations and the success that had attended them. Apart from the dubiousness of the motive, it seemed to me that to take such a step would, of itself, be a mistake. How, in our present state of impotence, could we 'try and pull a swift one' on the Allies by offering the surrender of Norway not to them but to a neutral country! Nor was I at all sure that to be interned in Sweden would ultimately prove to be of advantage to the German troops themselves. Who would be prepared to guarantee that Sweden would not under pressure hand them over to the Russians! (This is exactly what happened, later, to those Germans who were landed at Malmö).[70]

Dönitz authorised Schellenberg to establish whether the Swedish offer was made with any concurrence on behalf of the Allied countries, but he never heard from the SS man again. In the meantime, Böhme and Terboven returned to Norway, fully aware that they were to adhere strictly to instructions and directives issued by Dönitz in his capacity as Head of State and thus de facto head of the Armed Forces. In a secret directive to his military commanders, Böhme ordered 'unconditional military obedience' enforced with 'iron discipline'.[71] The end was drawing rapidly near: it was not the time for the German occupation forces in Norway either to lose their collective nerve, or to crack under the strain of impending surrender.

On the Kriegsmarine side, U-boats had begun to disperse away from the primary bases into isolated fjords, safe havens from Allied bombers and fighter bombers which constantly harassed the known gathering points of Kriegsmarine vessels. Depot ships were used here more extensively than in most other theatres in which the U-boats operated in a combat capacity. Nonetheless, there still existed several U-boat bases that were both fully-armed and equipped, and able to maintain a state of combat readiness right up to, and beyond, the German surrender. The primary locations were Narvik, Trondheim, Bergen, Horten, Kristiansand Süd, and Harstad, target of Operation Judgement which had sunk *U711*.

With the capitulation of Denmark's occupation forces on 5 May, the likelihood of a peaceful resolution inched nearer to Norway. That evening General Dwight D Eisenhower sent a telegram to the resistance headquarters in Norway, which was passed to Böhme. Within the carefully worded text were practical instructions as to how Böhme could make direct contact with Allied headquarters. Within two days Germany had officially surrendered in Reims, France, and also in a repeat ceremony staged with Russian officers in the ruins of Berlin. On 7 May, Böhme announced the unconditional surrender of German troops in Norway. With implementation scheduled for midnight on 8 May, Dönitz aided the easing of tension in Norway by dismissing Terboven as

Reichskommissar, transferring all of his ministerial and political powers, including command of the SS, to Böhme. Shortly thereafter, Terboven committed suicide by detonating 50kg of dynamite in a bunker on the Skaugum compound where he resided; he was alongside the body of SS Obergruppenführer Wilhelm Rediess, who had shot himself earlier. Meanwhile, Dönitz had stressed once again that General Böhme was to follow the plan for capitulation very closely, Böhme in turn making a radio broadcast in which he declared that all German troops in Norway would obey orders.

While the Wehrmacht waited for developments, the Norwegian underground resistance, the Milorg, mobilised, some forty thousand armed Norwegians taking station opposite fully armed and alert German units. The Milorg occupied the Royal Palace, the central police station in Oslo, as well as a number of other public buildings and strategic places. By 10 May, the Milorg had guards in Lillehammer, location of Böhme's headquarters. But by this stage, the surrender had already begun. During the afternoon of 8 May, the Allied military mission arrived in Oslo.

This was headed by General Sir Andrew Thorne, a Scottish officer who had been military attaché both in Washington and Berlin during the 1930s, and had visited Norway in 1932, meeting Quisling, amongst other political luminaries. Thorne had experience in dealing with both Norwegian and German National Socialists, and had been preparing for his role as the Liberator of Norway since 1943. When he finally arrived with his military mission, which included Crown Prince Olav, his primary task was the disarming of over 360,000 German troops with only 30,000 of his own, augmented by 40,000 Milorg men. There were also over 100,000 concentration camp inmates from nations throughout Europe and elsewhere, who needed to be cared for and repatriated, while attempting to avoid the hordes of displaced persons who roamed Europe after Germany's surrender. Another of his priority tasks was the assembly of German arms and equipment which was scheduled for destruction. Norway's returning government protested strongly that they could use the surrendered weapons to rearm their own military, but Thorne followed his instructions. Somewhat cynically, one of the motivating forces for such disposal of German weaponry was to enable British arms manufacturers to make future exports to Norway, who remained in need of their materials.

Once in the Norwegian capital, the mission delivered its conditions for capitulation to the German authorities. These included the arrest and internment of all German and Norwegian Nazis who were on a list compiled by the Allies. All SS troops were to be disarmed, and Wehrmacht formations were to be directed to concentration areas specified by the Allies. The German forces were also instructed to respect men of the Milorg as armed combatants, rather than partisans and to obey all instructions delivered by any Norwegian authority. During the course of that night Böhme's office agreed to the terms and the surrender was agreed. Erich Topp remembered:

May 8.

We solemnly lower our flag. I assemble the crew and inform them of the latest developments. Then we move out into deeper water and jettison all secret materials as well as our torpedoes.

May 10.

The U-boat basin is well guarded on all sides. In the evening the boat next to ours

Photograph purporting to show men of the MEK35 and victims of the Hopseidet massacre.
The reasons for this attack are unclear, and it is unusual for the U-boat service
to be so closely involved in such an event.

flies a German flag suspended from a balloon. Bad taste. Also a question of proper
leadership. I decide to retreat with my boat to Smörstein. Our own good discipline is
endangered by being too close to the other boats. Once bad habits are formed, they
are difficult to overcome. In Smörstein we live ashore in rural surroundings ... The
corps of engineers supplies us with electricity and a landing craft. Long discussions
whether we should send a part of the crew home on the landing craft. We decide
against it for disciplinary reasons. The crew must stay together. We must obey the
Allied instructions in all their ramifications, no matter where that might lead us. Deep
down I feel, however, that our behaviour will make no difference with regard to the
treatment we Germans will receive. It will be degrading in any case.[72]

As the Wehrmacht troops withdrew into their existing protective enclaves, Norwegian,
British and American troops were despatched to Norway, many to directly assist in the
disarmament of Wehrmacht units. Lieutenant Jack Whitton, DSC, had been commander
of the submarine HMS *Unbending* until 30 April 1945.

I was sent to Bergen on VE Day plus one, to take the surrender of and organise the
sailing of the U-boats to the UK. In addition to *U2511* there were two other Type XXIs
and about 46 other types, mostly Type VIICs. I relieved Schnee and his crew as there
was a rumour that they might try to scuttle her. I took command and with a scratch
crew of Royal Navy submarine personnel sailed her to Northern Ireland. The
German crew were marched seven miles (Norwegian miles) escorted by Milorg
(Norwegian Underground) personnel to a prisoner of war camp recently vacated by
Russian slave labourers.[73]

On 12 May, Topp's choices were rapidly being removed. The Allied Armistice
Commission announced that all non-essential personnel aboard the U-boats in port be

removed, leaving only the engine room crew aboard. The following day, this decision was modified, further instructions stating that all men except the commander, IWO, Chief Engineer, two Obermaschinisten, and twenty-nine others, primarily engine room personnel, were to remain aboard *U2513*. With his reduced complement, Topp awaited the arrival of the British in Smörstein, which finally happened at 1400hrs on 16 May. Captain Mervyn Wingfield, DSO, DSC and Bar, arrived in the company of several other officers, and what was fast becoming the standard complement of Milorg troops. Wingfield had commanded submarines with great dash and courage in action with the Royal Navy, and had been placed in charge of the U-boats stationed in Norway, tasked with bringing them back to the United Kingdom. Wingfield and Topp found a natural rapport, the British Captain impressed with his tour of the Type XXI, and later commenting that Britain had won the war 'just in time'. Wingfield was also tasked with bringing the scattered U-boats into their concentration points, where they could be more easily controlled by the British naval contingents that were now in Norway. *U2513* was one of many boats ordered to sail once more, heading first to Holm and then onwards to Holmestrand.

British destroyers HMS *Venomous* and *Valorous* were despatched to Norway on 14 May to undertake clearance operations prior to the entry of Allied personnel into Kristiansand South as part of the reoccupation of Norway. German officers performed the official handover ceremony aboard HMS *Venomous* during the following day.

The withdrawal of Kriegsmarine units was ordered on 16 May. Even as far as the Lofoten Islands, locals remembered the departure of the U-boat men. During the German retreat of 1944 and 1945, the Lofoten Islands had swelled with German troops, though there existed no bona fide U-boat facilities. Men of the Kriegsmarine who had taken refuge on Lofoten held a party aboard the aged Norwegian battleship *Tordenskjold* to celebrate leaving Svolvär. Apparently, amongst the passengers was an unruly, but unidentified, U-boat crew, who seemed hell-bent on making trouble for the Milorg men in the area, not to mention the local inhabitants. The Norwegians breathed a huge sigh of relief when the ship with its crew and 180 German prisoners set out from the harbour towards Bogen where a large U-boat repair yard had been established. However, their joy was short-lived. The *Tordenskjold* ran aground ten kilometres from Svolvär, and was forced to return to the town. The Germans, particularly the U-boat crew in question, did not receive a warm welcome, and after a few days they had been moved by any means available to Bogen.

Indeed, as the days in May continued to slip by, tensions within the Norwegian population, based on their fear of German reprisal, began to ease. In place of it came a certain degree of suppressed animosity towards their German former overlords. The British method of gathering German forces into regional concentration points now began to take on the aspect of protecting the Germans themselves, as much as the Norwegians and sparse Allied forces. Oberleutnant zur See Herbert Werner had surrendered at Kristiansand while awaiting the arrival of a new command with which he could sail:

> It was mid-May when I was sent to see the British district commander in a small town east of Kristiansand. My mission was to arrange the evacuation of all naval personnel from the U-boat base. I made the trip by armoured car with two seamen holding

submachine guns at the ready, for we had been warned against an ambush by vengeful members of the Norwegian underground. I found the English commander, one Colonel MacGregor, dressing belatedly in his room in the village hotel.

MacGregor closed the door behind me and offered me a chair … Then [he] poured me a glass of wine – 'It's the best I could find in this damned town.' And as he continued dressing MacGregor told me a little about himself: he had parachuted into the mountains three months ago and had organised the Norwegian resistance. He then explained that his orders called for all nearby German troops to leave Kristiansand within three days and go to the nearby island of Tromoey. I was completely disarmed by MacGregor's informality and I decided that it was neither disgraceful nor dangerous to co-operate with such an officer.[74]

During May, the first U-boats began to depart for the United Kingdom, manned by Royal Navy men, and generally with a skeleton German presence aboard each boat. The remaining boats in Norway were gathered together, Topp's *U2513* sailing into Oslo harbour on 19 May. A little over a week later he was finally removed from his command and taken ashore.

Our boats are now being guarded by British Marines armed with rifles and bayonets. Each boat is being visited by two British officers and several enlisted men. We know what this means. A document is handed to me. The entire crew is to assemble at once on the pier. There will be an opportunity later to gather private belongings.

In the meantime British soldiers ransack the boat. After only four minutes I am missing my Knight's Cross, 500 Norwegian Crowns, and some scarves. Whatever is left of our belongings we pack under the supervision of a British officer. I get the impression that the officers have lost control of their men. Tin cans with food are being opened indiscriminately, our stock of alcoholic beverages plundered. Only after I lodge a formal protest with Captain Wingfield do these excesses stop. When I return to my boat it flies the British flag.

Briefly saluting my boat, I leave the last piece of German soil in Norway … The train trip lasts twenty hours … A harsh and cold night. The Norwegians refuse to give us water even though they have plenty of it. We are defamed, slandered, despised, hated. The enemy's propaganda has done its job.[75]

Indeed, as the last Germans were herded off their U-boats they faced an uncertain fate, much of which would depend on blind luck. In general, the U-boat crews were imprisoned wherever was convenient for the British to keep them as isolated as possible from the Norwegian population. Their boats were taken from their harbours, and sailed to the United Kingdom for later disposal or distribution between the victorious Allies. Often the Germans were then left almost to their own devices before sufficient Allied strength was on hand to provide transport.

Some were not so fortunate as to be left alone, however. After hostilities had ended, the Norwegian government forced German prisoners-of-war to clear minefields on land that had been planted as part of Hitler's coastal defensive line that had stretched from Norway to the French border with Spain. By the time that the clearance had been completed in September 1946, 392 German prisoners had been injured and 275 killed. By contrast, only two Norwegians and four British mine disposal experts had sustained any

Extremely unusual photograph
taken at the end of the war
showing a U-boat NCO
sporting a tank destruction badge
issued to infantry units.

injuries at all. Allegedly contributing to this disproportionate casualty rate was an Allied
practice of chasing German prisoners across fields recently deemed clear, in order to
ensure that no mines had been missed. The Geneva Convention of 27 July 1929
specifically states in Article 32 that: 'It is forbidden to use prisoners of war at unhealthful
or dangerous work.'

Like several of the other victorious nations, the Norwegians claimed that, due to the
time spent in Norway since their surrender, the German prisoners were now to be
considered 'Disarmed Enemy Forces', thereby circumventing that specific clause of the
Geneva Convention, which was solely relative to the treatment of prisoners-of-war. The
Norwegian breach of the spirit of the Geneva Convention, if not the actual word of
law, was not the most major violation that the majority of U-boat men suffered. When
they were finally shipped from Norwegian ports to Germany, many found the stop in
their Fatherland only transitory. The Allied powers had not finished with them yet.

5

The End in France

The U-boat bases at Lorient, Saint-Nazaire and La Pallice were still held by German forces at the end of the war, as were installations on the Gironde and Dunkirk. Many U-boat personnel and men of the Kleinkampfverbände had been isolated in these German fortresses, where they had endured months of siege warfare. Some of the last places to surrender on mainland Europe were the besieged U-boat bases along the Atlantic coast. In September 1944, the Americans had mounted a direct assault on Brest, which resulted in an epic battle against German paratroopers, infantry and naval personnel within the debris of the city itself, culminating in ten thousand American, and a similar number of German, casualties. The city was nearly completely destroyed, and the deep water harbour which had been the primary objective had been rendered unusable by the Germans, requiring months to clear away the six hundred wrecks, of everything from merchant ships to cars, that clogged the waterway. Ironically, the battle had eventually become one of prestige for the Allies, as Cherbourg had already been liberated more quickly than anticipated, which provided the necessary port infrastructure that the Allies needed to supply their drive toward Germany. Therefore, following the evacuation of operational U-boats from France at the tail-end of 1944, the Allies had been content merely to blockade the remaining U-boat fortress cities still held by the Germans. Once again, the defending German forces were made up of a variety of units from the three armed services, and included non-Germans.

The port city of Brest, which had hosted a French naval presence for as long as the navy had existed, had been used by the German Kriegsmarine as the home of the 1st and 9th U-Flotillas. From the shelter of an expansive U-boat pen which lay at the western fringe of the military harbour, boats from these two flotillas had sailed regularly into the battle of the Atlantic. Primarily composed of Type VIICs, they also ranged as far as the Caribbean Sea, and into the Mediterranean, where they would have passed over to the local flotillas for further operations. Spies were landed on the coast of the United States by boats of the 1st U-Flotilla, which formed a second wave of attack boats involved in Operation Paukenschlag. The city's incomplete Morvan Hospital had been requisitioned by the 9th U-Flotilla as its headquarters, and the ornate buildings of the French Naval Academy by the 1st U-Flotilla.

By 1944, the importance of the capture of Brest by Allied forces landing in Normandy lay in the strategic value of the deep water harbour. Brest was easily defensible against attack from the sea, approached as it was by a narrow channel, the Goulet de Brest. This was covered by batteries of almost every variety in the Kriegsmarine's coastal artillery arsenal, and it was lethal for Allied naval forces who had to contend with harassing U-boats and their support ships once they had entered clearer Biscay waters. Aerial bombing and mining took a steady toll on the ships of the Sicherungsdivision: the minesweepers, patrol boats and flak ships, whilst radar-guided aircraft attack in Biscay inflicted a heavy toll on the U-boats. However, by September 1944, the importance of Brest had waned, replaced by the capture of Cherbourg. The battle that followed broke the back of many American units of Patton's 3rd Army, and gave little by way of compensation to the visitors. The U-boats had departed, both flotillas disbanded, and their survivors transferred to Norway, with the base in Finisterre, Brittany, no longer tenable for the Kriegsmarine.

When Brest surrendered, the variety of troops captured by the Allies reveals the often makeshift nature of the defending units. The backbone of the city's defence had been the troops of the 2nd Fallschirmjäger Division, augmented by the 852nd Regiment of the 343rd Infantry Division and 899th Regiment of the 266th Infantry Division. However, alongside these men were also listed a bewildering array of units, including men from 1st U-Boat Flotilla, 9th U-Boat Flotilla, 7th Vorposten Flotilla, Brest Hafenschutz Flotilla, 6th Minesweeper Flotilla, Russian Wehrmacht troops, Italian artillery units, fortress base companies, security units, service troops, 743rd Butcher Company, and Kriegsmarine and Heer artillery units. A similar kind of defence was to be mounted in the remaining U-boat bases of Lorient, Saint-Nazaire and La Pallice. The base at Bordeaux had been abandoned and occupied by Free French troops on 26 August, although German forces continued to hold out at the entrance to the Gironde River. Elsewhere, the Wehrmacht also held Dunkirk, passed by in the Allied race for Germany. However, although resupplied at least once by Seehund midget submarines, there were no U-boat personnel within Dunkirk.

By the time that German forces capitulated to the Allies, the three surviving Atlantic U-boat bases had endured seven months of siege by combined American and French forces. Interestingly, despite the loss of the Atlantic bases as forward operational centres, Marinegruppenkommando West under Admiral Theodor Krancke continued to exercise control over the ports still in German hands, the area of regional command, Kommandierender Admiral Atlantikküste, being that which encompassed the besieged bases.

Of the 12,800 Kriegsmarine men that were part of Lorient's combat forces (as opposed to 6,300 army troops and 1,100 Luftwaffe), 780 were from the U-boat service. In Lorient, the ground defences were organised into five regiments and three additional battalions. Wehrmachtregiment 1, commanded by Oberst Witt, comprised four battalions each of five companies; Wehrmachtregiment 2, commanded by Fregattenkapitän der Reserve Hillenbrand, only comprised two battalions of similar size; Wehrmachtregiment 3, Oberst Habersang, had five battalions; Wehrmachtregiment 4, Generalmajor der Luftwaffe Kuse, had three battalions of three companies each; and Wehrmachtregiment 5, commanded by Oberst Borst, had two battalions of three companies, as well as a motorised anti-tank company and reconnaissance units. These, along with the four separate battalions (battalions Albrecht, Schaenske battalion der Reserve Gutschke, battalion Böck, made up of independent companies Erzfeld, Schelle, Fahrenkamp, and Plums), were the backbone of the ground defence, the majority of U-boat personnel being grouped together under Hillenbrand's command. But the real Wehrmacht strength lay in the huge artillery emplacements that had once been used for coastal defence, and could now be utilised instead for ground support.

It was the commander of the LXIV Army Corps (Army Group G), General Karl Sachs, who had been charged with the command of Wehrmacht units of the Atlantic garrisons south of the Loire River. Sachs had at his disposal 81,000 men, of whom only 24,000 were actual front-line combat troops. In fact, he had two second line infantry units: 159 Reserve Division in Bordeaux and 6 Infantry Division in the South Loire; the remainder comprised Luftwaffe technicians, occupation garrisons and Kriegsmarine personnel, as well as some ten thousand men of the Organisation Todt. The Wehrmacht began to abandon Bordeaux on 21 August in the face of the Allied advance, and the two fortresses of Gironde North, around Royan, and Gironde South, at the Point de la Grave, were established. The 24,000 men who had held Bordeaux, including 16,000 naval troops, many of whom were from the dissolved 12th U-Flotilla, were organised into ground combat units. Some five thousand men formed Marinebrigade Weber and the Marineregiment Gebauer.

Konteradmiral Carl Weber had been commander of the Bordeaux Arsenal, and his Brigade was made up of three units, the first of which was Marsch-Regiment Badermann, under command of Kapitän Badermann the former Arsenal Chief of Staff; this was formed from four battalions of men from the 12th U-Flotilla, Bordeaux U-boat base, and various Italian support personnel who had been attached to the BETASOM unit. The second, Marsch-Regiment von Pflug-Harttung, was commanded by Kapitän von Pflug-Harttung, and was made up of surviving men from the 8th Minesweeping Flotilla and 10th Marine Flak Abteilung, augmented with survivors from the destroyer Z37 scuttled in Bordeaux. The last, Marsch-Regiment Kühnemann, commanded by Kapitän Kühnemann, comprised five battalions of similar composition, primarily men of the harbour defence. A final reserve unit, Kapitän Gebauer's Marineregiment Gebauer, completed the strength available for Weber's brigade. However, they were

Kriegsmarine troops muster for parade in Saint-Nazaire, 1945.

Workers from the Saint-Nazaire U-boat base, photographed with the base commander
at Christmas 1944 during the siege.

intercepted by American troops of the US 83rd Infantry Division, whilst retreating to
Royan, and surrendered en masse on 15 September 1944.

Though the Fortress Commander in Lorient was General der Artillerie Fahrmbacher,
the Kriegsmarine units were commanded by Vizeadmiral Matthiae in his role as the,
inaptly named, Seekommandant. Beneath him, his Chief of Staff was Kapitän zur See
Ernst Kals, Chief of the 2nd U-Flotilla, and responsible for command of the U-boat
base and security detachments. Kals remained in titular command of the 2nd U-Flotilla
until the conclusion of the war, although he was injured in a landmine explosion during
December 1944 as he toured the front lines.

Similarly, the Fortress of Saint-Nazaire was commanded by Army Generalleutnant
Hans Junck, former commander of the 265th Infantry Division, whilst the naval portion
fell beneath Seekommandant Konteradmiral Mirow's control. There were various naval
infantry formations within the Saint-Nazaire defensive perimeter, although none have
been identified as specifically comprised of U-boat personnel, and each was named after
its commanding officer. The primary naval ground units identified were: Marine-
Grenadier-Battaillon Emminger, commanded by Korvettenkapitän Wilhelm Emminger,
a former artillery officer; Marine-Grenadier-Battaillon Haackert, commanded by
Kapitänleutnant Heinrich Haackert, former chief of the 6th Vorpostenflottille; Marine-
Grenadier-Battaillon Josephi, commanded by Korvettenkapitän Walter Josephi, chief of
the 10th Minesweeping Flotilla and killed in action on 20 March 1945; Marine-
Grenadier-Battaillon Lieser, commanded by Kapitänleutnant Wilhelm Lieser from the
6th Vorpostenflottille; and Marine-Grenadier-Battaillon Würffel under Kapitänleutnant
der Reserve Bernard Würffel, the captain of Sperrbrecher 122 from the 2nd
Sperrbrecherflottille.

La Rochelle was the sole Atlantic port in which the naval commander, Vizeadmiral Schirlitz (also Kommandierender Admiral Atlantikküste) was also the Fortress Commandant. Beneath his command in the besieged town was the Marine-Regiment Zapp, commanded by Fregattenkapitän Richard Zapp, erstwhile commander of the 3rd U-Flotilla. Two of the unit's battalions (the 3rd and 4th) were comprised of men from the 3rd U-Flotilla, stiffened with a cadre of Heer troops. Their sister unit was Marine-Regiment John, commanded by Kapitän zur See Hans John, commander of the 4th Sicherungsdivision, previously responsible for harbour defence and mine clearance, though now largely reduced to a scattering of armed trawlers sheltered within the U-boat bunker. John's unit was composed mainly of men from his command, two battalions made up of personnel from 4th Sicherungsdivision and 8th Minesweeping Flotilla.

The Gironde Nord Fortress was also commanded by a naval officer, Konteradmiral Michahelles, also responsible for the region's Kriegsmarine forces as Seekommandant Gascogne. There, too, Kriegsmarine forces were utilised in the infantry role, although the majority of men from 12th U-Flotilla in Bordeaux had already been captured during the retreat from the city. However, scattered remnants remained within the Kriegsmarine troops that comprised the Marine-Battaillon Tirpitz, primarily composed of men from the 2nd Sperrbrecherflottille. On the south bank of the river, in Festung Gironde Süd, stragglers from the U-boat base were folded into Marine-Battaillon Narvik made up of men primarily from the destroyers of 8th Destroyer Flotilla Narvik.

The issue of fortress command had been debated in Berlin in conference between

German prisoners are marched into the fortress that guards the entrance to Lorient after the city's surrender in 1945. The captives of the French suffered the worst conditions inflicted on them by any of the western Allies following the end of the Second World War. Hard labour, mine-clearing and systematic starvation accounted for thousands of deaths amongst the prisoners, many of whom had survived the U-boat war only to die in peacetime.

American and French forces enter Lorient after the ceasefire, watched by men from the mixed service German garrison.

Dönitz and Hitler. The Führer ordered an investigation into the officers who occupied the posts of Fortress Commandant, after news of a difference of opinion amongst the troops holding the Channel Islands as to the validity of their continued occupation reached Berlin. Hitler remarked that he felt the Commandant positions should be held by naval officers as 'many fortresses have been given up, but no ships were ever lost without fighting to the last man.'[76] Dönitz replied that the Channel Islands situation had been remedied, and that naval officers had been assigned as Fortress Commandants in the west, in all but Lorient and Saint-Nazaire. He went further and requested that Generalleutnant Junck be replaced in his post at Saint-Nazaire by the previous Commandant, infantry Generalmajor Maximillian Hünten, as the former was handicapped by illness and there was 'no guarantee that he can provide the necessary resistance.'[77]

The more southerly Atlantic ports had come under direct threat from the Allied landings in Provence on 15 August 1944, as well as the breakout from the Normandy bridgehead that Patton achieved that same month with his 3rd Army. In Angers, the FdU West, Kapitän zur See Hans-Rudolf Rösing ordered all combat U-boats to evacuate the French bases and travel to Norway, where he himself was destined. With Bordeaux summarily abandoned by the Germans, the garrisons at Royan, Lorient, La Rochelle and Saint-Nazaire braced themselves for what they believed was the inevitable assault that would follow, but never came. Instead, months of siege warfare and a grim battle of attrition would ensue. Once it became apparent that American forces would not attempt to attack the garrison towns directly, the isolated German forces prepared thick lines of defence, often hinged on existing artillery emplacements and bunker complexes established during four years of occupation. The 265th Infantry Division was split between Lorient and Saint-Nazaire, as the Kriegsmarine men who had not been

Oberst Borst meets American officers to negotiate the surrender of the Lorient garrison.

accommodated aboard the last U-boats leaving for their new bases in Norway exchanged their naval blue for the field grey of the Army. Alongside the regular infantry and naval troops were elements of the 2nd Fallschirmjäger Division, the majority of whom were lost in Brest. Foreign garrison troops such as Russians and Georgians were present as well, though many succeeded in deserting, before the remainder were disarmed and used as labourers in constructing defensive fortifications.

The constructors of the bunkers which constituted the centre point of the U-boat bases themselves had allowed for the provision of defence against ground attack as much as they had provided for flak weaponry. In Saint-Nazaire, for example, two mortar positions were constructed on the bunker itself. One raised emplacement, on the rear of the bunker, housed a small 5cm M19 emplacement while the other, a simple Tobruk located between the M19 and the flak positions, accommodated a 12cm weapon. Two casemates were constructed at the bunker rear, housing a 47mm Skoda Pak36 and a pair of heavy machine guns. A further three heavy machine gun emplacements covered the flanks of the harbour basin. Finally, rows of dragon-teeth anti-tank obstacles blocked all approaches overland to the U-boat base. Elsewhere, the Organisation Todt had

An ad hoc armoured vehicle, created in the workshops of the U-boat base at La Pallice, pictured here during the surrender of the fortress to French forces.

constructed many strong points for use against any possible infantry attack, should a defensive battle for Saint-Nazaire ever get as far as the inner city itself near the harbour.

Saint-Nazaire had hosted the 6th and 7th U-Flotillas, the latter probably one of the most successful units of the U-boat service. Flotillas were little more than administrative groupings of boats, all controlled directly by BdU, and the flotilla commands themselves were occupied with the logistical coordination that kept the boats maintained and protected, and the crews accommodated and cared for. However, amongst the boats of the 7th U-Flotilla were those captained by such luminaries of the U-boat service as Günther Prien and Otto Kretschmer.

The U-boat bunker complex at Saint-Nazaire was reached by traversing a bunkered lock gate, allowing the U-boats to sail in and out of the military harbour regardless of the tidal state. The muddy waters of the Loire River mixed with the seawater of Biscay that flowed past the enclosed harbour. In 1942, British commandos and Royal Navy forces had attacked the harbour at Saint-Nazaire in a bid to destroy the lock gates to the only dry dock capable of accommodating the capital ships such as *Tirpitz*. Their raid was successful: the aged HMS *Campbeltown* rammed into the lock with timed explosives later detonating on cue. However, operations of the U-boat bases were never impeded, except by the terrible rate of attrition of U-boats under aerial threat in Biscay. The fourteen dry and wet pens (eight and six respectively) of the Saint-Nazaire bunker were protected, as elsewhere, by large armoured doors, and remained impregnable until their eventual surrender.

With the slaughter at Brest uppermost in Allied thinking, there was never to be a serious attempt to take the encircled U-boat bases. Instead, American troops, reinforced by Free French forces and FFI (Free French Interior) irregulars, hemmed in the German positions and began months of raiding, as well as defending themselves against similar tactics from the Wehrmacht positions. Initially, Lorient was the scene of violent combat between the 895th and 896th Battalions of the Wehrmacht's 265th Infantry Division, which had seen combat in Normandy. But as Allied plans to bypass the U-boat bases became clear, entrenchment took the place of full-scale combat.

The isolated pocket at Lorient was centred on, and dominated by, the extensive harbour basin on the Scorff River. To the west, the front stretched along the Laïte River, to the east the more expansive Etel River. These impassable barriers were natural defensive positions which the Wehrmacht defenders exploited. Between them stretched extensive minefields and anti-tank ditches, the few remaining entry points heavily defended with artillery. The Lorient garrison numbered some twenty-five thousand men, a mixture of all three services and including many members of the now-defunct 2nd U-boat flotilla. Lorient was also within easy reach of the German-held island Belle-Île, with its rich and fertile agricultural land. There, the garrison of a thousand Kriegsmarine men were in a considerably superior state with regard to both physical condition and morale, than their counterparts on the mainland, due primarily to the much better supply of food. The smaller Île de Groix held another thousand men, though these were mainly Russian, Polish and Armenian troops of doubtful military value, who had been shifted to the isolated post in order to dissuade desertion.

During the peak of U-boat success, Lorient had been considered the most important of the French harbours. The first bunkers created for the U-boats were two arched cathedral-like creations in the fishing port, aptly named Dom Bunkers. These were fed

General Fahrmbacher prepares to surrender Lorient to General Kramer of the US 66th Infantry Division.

by a slipway and turntable, but could only accommodate the small Type II U-boats with which the 1st U-Flotilla had begun the war. Completed in 1941, they were also augmented with a small two-pen bunker further along the Scorff River. Both pens were wet berths, and a total of four boats could be accommodated at once. Clearly, these were insufficient for the needs of two combat flotillas of large oceangoing U-boats. By 1943, three huge U-boat bunkers had been built next to the French fishing port at Keroman. These three were the most sophisticated that the Kriegsmarine had created. Keroman I and II were ashore, functioning as dry docks for the boats of the 2nd and 10th U-Flotillas, the majority of which were the Type IXB and C. It had been the 2nd U-Flotilla that spearheaded Operation Paukenschlag, whilst boats of the 10th were among the first to sail against shipping off South Africa and into the Indian Ocean. The U-boats were lifted from the water at an oblique angle onto a slipway beneath the thick concrete canopy. Once the boat was clear of the water it was fed by rails onto a transverse system of slipways that each led into a bunkered dry dock, a total of twelve available between the mouths of Keroman I and Keroman II, which faced each other. Once inside, the boats were safe from air attack as they underwent complete overhaul. Keroman III, the last bunker to be added to the installation, comprised seven docks, five of which could be pumped dry, the entrance to them guarded by the sunken hulks of two elderly French warships to which were tethered barrage balloons to dissuade low-level Allied air attack. An extension, Keroman IV, was planned and begun, but amounted to little more than portions of a shell which housed offices, before work was abandoned.

Facing the huge bunker complex was the headland at Kerneval. It was here that BdU and his staff occupied three chateaux, from which the U-boat campaigns were directed. The entire area was heavily defended by bunkered machine guns and artillery pieces, anti-tank obstacles and ditches and various infantry strong points. Men of the 10th U-Flotilla were accommodated in large bunker barracks within Lorient, whilst those of the 2nd U-Flotilla had at first been housed within the French naval base that existed on the Scorff River. However, with increased Allied air attack rendering the town virtually uninhabitable, the camp named Lager Lemp had been established inland, where the crews were shuttled between patrols. Whilst working on their boats or preparing for patrol, they would often live within the Keroman bunker complex, which housed barracks and all of the necessary administrative spaces that the flotillas required.

By May 1945, the Keroman complex had become the administrative centre of the defence of the Lorient pocket. While Lorient itself lay in ruins, after some of the most concentrated aerial bombardment of the war in France, the bunkers stood as supposed testament to the Thousand Year Reich. Frequent supply trips were mounted by a small flotilla of motor boats, formed for the task, and sheltered within the U-boat bunkers. These small vessels also distributed collected supplies to various points inside the Lorient garrison, as well as venturing to Saint-Nazaire, alleviating at least some of the debilitating effects of hunger that were being experienced. As Lorient possessed no land suitable for aircraft landing, mail destined for Lorient, which was delivered by bomber to Saint-Nazaire, was also returned via this hardy flotilla. In the last months of 1944, one or two seaplanes managed to make the Lorient harbour on such mail and supply runs, but they were soon unable to reach the port as the German lines contracted further west. Regular sorties were mounted by German troops from Lorient into no-man's-land between the opposing forces to gather whatever food could be found, particularly potatoes and wheat. The survival rations available per day for the German garrison comprised: coffee without sugar in the morning; 200g bread; lunch of carrot and cabbage soup; dinner of 50g sausage and 20g butter. Twice a week, 50g of a tomato-based vitamin supplement was distributed, and the men were issued two cigarettes per day. Locally-produced apples continued to be made into cider, and six hundred cows on the also German-held Île de Groix were available.

Lorient's defenders even had a small armoured unit which was made up of a captured French B1, three Renault R35s, five Panzer IVs, one captured Sherman, and four armoured Sdkfz 251 half tracks. But their strongest asset was artillery. More than one hundred and forty large calibre cannons were within German territory, and they were used to good effect against the besieging Allies.

The Saint-Nazaire pocket covered an area of nearly fifteen hundred square kilometres, fringed to the north and northeast by the natural obstacles of the wide La Vilaine River and the Nantes Canal. The primary approach roads to the east were heavily mined and demolitions placed on major bridges, those on the La Roche-Bernard bridge over La Vilaine detonating accidentally after being struck by lightning during a storm on 15 April. Alongside the 28,000 men of the German garrison, 130,000 French civilians were also trapped by the rapidity of the American advance. As Brest came under attack, Saint-Nazaire's German commanders were ordered to hold the city to the last man on 17 August 1944. Festung Saint-Nazaire was born.

Men who had been employed as workmen by the Kriegsmarine Werft, and had not managed to leave the cities before they were isolated, were either drafted into military units or employed in manufacturing mobile mounts for attaching to the large naval guns, which were now largely impotent as they pointed seawards, as well as those removed from the various Kriegsmarine craft hemmed into the ports. Eventually, the thirty thousand men of the garrison were arranged into twenty battalions north of the Loire, and a further five to the south. Once again, like Lorient, artillery was a major asset to the Germans. Rumours circulated within the besieging French that seven or eight Tiger

Artillery General Fahrmbacher arrives at the field of surrender near Caudan in a camouflaged staff car on 10 May 1945.

tanks were present within the pocket, but they were false. Small craft of the 7th, 10th and 42nd Minesweeping Flotillas plied the Loire, distributing men and equipment, whilst also scouring nearby islands for any available supplies.

By May 1945, the besieging troops primarily comprised men of the US 66th Infantry Division, named the Black Panthers after their divisional insignia, and French naval infantry of the 2nd Battalion, 4th Regiment. FFI irregulars bolstered the Allied forces. The 66th Infantry had been placed there following the loss of 784 of their number when the troopship SS *Leopoldville* was sunk by *U486* near Cherbourg on Christmas Eve 1944. The division had been en route to the Ardennes battle when its morale was severely shaken by the sinking, and the decision was taken to redeploy the remains of the unit to a quieter sector of the front.

Also in Saint-Nazaire was the last functioning U-boat to be based in France in 1945. The 7th U-Flotilla's *U255* had been decommissioned in August 1944 following damage to the snorkel installation. However, following the investiture of Saint-Nazaire by the Americans, the boat was repaired by Kriegsmarine Werft workers within the besieged base to a state of operational readiness, after a Heinkel 115 floatplane brought essential spare parts. During February 1945 the boat received fuel from *U868*, which had sailed a supply mission from Norway carrying stores and ammunition. Further fuel was taken in March from *U878*, which had also arrived from Norway. Finally fully equipped, the boat was manned by U-boat men who had been unable to leave on the last boats in August 1944. *U255* was put under the command of Oberleutnant zur See Helmuth Heinrich, previous commander of *U299*, who arrived in the port as a passenger aboard *U878*. He finally sailed into action, without a First Officer, on 17 April 1945 for four days, whereupon the boat laid eight TMC mines, which had been stored at the base, in the waters of Les Sables d'Olonne. The boat was constantly in need of repair, the starboard forward hydroplane was missing, and the keel fractured toward the stern, and yet it continued to operate as best it could. Following the mining mission, the boat was used as a transport vessel between La Pallice and Saint-Nazaire, the former in possession of more food supplies than the other. Two return trips were made, one to collect more fuel from the recently arrived *U510*, the final one ending in its home port on 7 May 1945.

Festung La Rochelle covered nearly four hundred square kilometres of land that once again made the most of natural defences, such as the thick swamp land to the northeast and south. It was actually the best supplied of the French garrisons, small Kriegsmarine ships maintaining transport links between the offshore islands of Île de Ré and Île d'Oléron, as well as the other fortresses of Lorient, Saint-Nazaire and Royan. They even managed to reach Spain using fishing boats to retrieve supplies of fresh fruit. Correspondingly, rations were greater, the daily allowance being 400g bread, 15g fat, 100g potatoes, 60-100g meat, and 15g butter.

However, the fighting units of the fifteen thousand strong garrison, including some thirty per cent foreign troops, were inferior, with only the naval troops being equipped with German Mauser rifles, and the remainder generally holding captured French weapons, of which many dated back to the previous world war. Artillery was as numerous as in the other port cities, and once again there was some armour within the La Rochelle pocket. This time, though, it was constituted by civilian vehicles adapted within the U-boat base's workshops into armoured Panzerjäger.

The actual U-boat base lay outside of the medieval town of La Rochelle at the dock

German defenders of Lorient await incarceration after the German surrender.

area of La Pallice. There the Organisation Todt had constructed a ten-box U-boat bunker, which was approached through a bunkered lock. The seven dry docks and three wet pens could handle a total of thirteen boats at once, the 3rd U-Flotilla the sole unit to be assigned to this port. The bunker would even be used for the repairs on the stern of a destroyer, which had been battered by Coastal Command aircraft as they attempted to clear the Germans from the waters of the Bay of Biscay.

Inside the fortresses there were periods of great privation and near starvation, but also a curious normality which settled over everything. Although morale had plummeted in August 1944, when the bases had first come under siege, a combination of intensive propaganda and harsh discipline gradually lifted the spirits of the defenders. Wehrmacht mail was maintained as best as it possibly could be, both into and out of the trapped garrison. The majority of mail transfers into the besieged areas were done by the He111s of Transportfliegergruppe 30, who were also responsible for ammunition, medicine, and other supply drops. They flew these missions primarily by night, beginning in September 1944, during which month six of the aircraft were lost. Ten more were brought down in October 1944, either shot down or crashing during operational flights to the Atlantic fortresses. Crashes were regular as the aircraft would land on darkened runways between midnight and 0100hrs, departing by 0300hrs to allow escape again in darkness. Through November and December the aircraft moved home to Zellhausen, and suffered another nineteen He111s lost to various causes, while engaged on night flights to the Atlantic fortresses, and also to the Channel Islands. This grim tally would continue until the final missions were flown at the end of the war. The idea of supplying the besieged fortresses by U-boat was largely discounted. In a meeting between Dönitz and Hitler which began on 31 October Dönitz elaborated:

The C-in-C Navy rejects the proposal for supplying the fortifications in the West by submarines, because such a measure would be ineffective. Fortifications must in the future acquire their own additional provisions by means of sorties. He suggests simultaneous sorties from Lorient and Saint-Nazaire in order to occupy and to exploit the area in

American forces pass the surrendering German garrison of Lorient.

between. Especially important supplies could, however, in exceptional cases be brought by submarine.[78]

However, the Commanding Admiral West, Admiral Krancke, requested that a monthly U-boat patrol be assigned the task, as not only would the ability of the fortresses to hold out against the enemy be strengthened even with only small quantities of supply, but the effect on morale would be extremely positive. Four U-boats would have been required to mount the operations, and Dönitz refused to commit to the idea when it was initially raised by Krancke in January 1945. Eventually he would relent, and sporadic supply missions were made. In November 1944, *U722* and *U773* both bought essential supplies to the base, sailing with only a solitary torpedo for defence, the remainder of the boat given over to cargo. During early February, *U275* entered the port, but it was to obtain repairs to the boat's defective snorkel, departing after two weeks; it was lost in action on 10 March after striking a mine south of Seaford. On 1 January 1945, the BdU War Diary recorded the progress of such supply missions:

> Two VIIC type boats put in with supplies to St. Nazaire which had been cut off. They did not come up against any enemy defences. We cannot comply with a request that such support be carried out continuously, as the small supplies (maximum 25 tons per boat) would have no effective influence on conditions in the fortress, and the removal

of boats from operations would have a very bad effect on the fighting strength.

Supreme Command of the Navy has received the right to make decisions on supplies, so they can concentrate on transporting those things which are most needed. At the beginning of January, therefore, a third submarine (type IXC) put out, to take fuel to *U255*, the last boat which had been made clear to put out from western France and also to take weapons and other things which were needed at St. Nazaire.[79]

Thus *U868* brought supplies of stores and ammunition to Saint-Nazaire in February, spending nearly a month in the port before returning to Norway, torpedoing and sinking the Canadian minesweeper HMCS *Guysborough* off Brest during the return voyage. *U878* also transported supplies and ammunition, as well as Oberleutnant zur See Heinrich, who was due to take command of *U255*, to Saint-Nazaire, arriving in March. The boat departed for Norway again on 6 April, and was sunk with all hands by British escort ships four days later, while attempting to attack convoy ON295 west-southwest of Brest. The 11th U-Flotilla's *U485* sailed from Trondheim to La Pallice, docking there on 24 April and departing five days later. Although the cargo space was indeed limited, one such U-boat could carry fuel, two million cigarettes, eleven hundred pairs of shoes, fifteen hundred pairs of socks, medicines, Panzerfaust anti-tank weapons, and other such supplies.

A system of agricultural requisitions was established by the German commanders, centred on the various town halls within each enclave. The enclave of Saint-Nazaire was relatively poor agriculturally, except in the south, the sector demarcated by the wide Loire River, where some thirty tons of wheat, twenty tons of potatoes, and two and a half tons of meat could be spared and sent to the northern sector. La Rochelle fared even worse, with an increased reliance on supplies from Germany either by aircraft or U-boat. Despite the relative success of such measures that allowed for survival, there were still severe shortages of everything, particularly for the thousands of French civilians. Electricity supplies to Saint-Nazaire were cut at Nantes, although the Germans utilised generators within the U-boat base and aboard two steam ships to augment supply. Heating was another issue, as there was no means by which fresh supplies of coal could be received, and winter 1944/45 turned bitterly cold. The French administration stayed active within the areas still occupied, with the local Mairies and gendarmes maintaining what order and control they could, in the face of an increasingly uncertain future. In October 1944, German authorities in Saint-Nazaire reached agreement with their Allied counterparts to evacuate as many civilians as possible and some twenty thousand were removed by train. Members of the International Red Cross in turn entered the fortress to estimate the amount of food necessary to sustain the remaining civilians, and this was later shipped in on specially organised trains.

While artillery duels and infantry raiding parties became the norm in terms of combat, everything was done inside German lines to keep troops occupied and their morale as high as possible. For example, at the beginning of April 1945, the Director of the Kriegsmarine Werft in Saint-Nazaire, Vizeadmiral Witold Rother, organised an exhibition of various homemade objects by and for the troops of the U-boat base. The exhibition was formally announced in the German force's newspaper *Die Festung* on 30 March under the title, 'Here, we show what we can do!'. The exhibition was eventually held in boxes 12 and 13 of the U-boat bunker and contained many different items which ranged from customised weapons to art. Opened on 5 April in the presence of the three Fortress commanders, men flocked to see the displays, Rother's morale-boosting effort not being in vain. In Lorient, a cinema continued to screen films two or three times a week.

In La Rochelle an unusual calm had fallen on the front lines. This was largely the result of an agreement which had been reached in secret between Schirlitz and a French naval officer named Hubert Meyer. The French commander, General Edgard de Larminat, ordered Meyer to attempt to broker an agreement, which would save the medieval town and obtain a peaceful solution to the siege stalemate. In secret meetings that were held in an abandoned casino between September 1944 and May 1945, Schirlitz and Meyer concluded a deal that would prevent the destruction of the U-boat base and its surrounding town. The Allies were also allowed by Schirlitz to supply La Rochelle's civilian residents with food and medicine, the German commander giving his guarantee that neither would be used by the Wehrmacht forces. On 18 October the two men reached an agreement, whereby the French would neither cross the anti-tank ditch that demarcated the front lines, nor ask for air support against La Rochelle, and the Germans would not destroy the port's infrastructure. However, the agreement would not last as long as the siege, and on 10 February the port was mined for demolition by the Wehrmacht.

On 30 April, French forces at La Rochelle launched Operation Mousquetaire (Musketeer) with three infantry regiments, armoured units, and artillery. By this stage the German forces at Royan had finally surrendered to French troops after an attack by 50,000 men supported by strong armoured units. The 10,000 defenders had been swiftly overwhelmed, despite fierce resistance. The goal of Mousquetaire was the destruction of the German pocket at La Rochelle. Initial resistance was relatively weak, the Kriegsmarine troops fighting a delaying action as they slowly retreated, giving up five kilometres of land to the French on the first day alone. The Île d'Oléron was also attacked in Operation Jupiter, as tanks and infantry landed on the south coast.

The defenders of La Rochelle were forced steadily back, as German artillery pieces that had been captured on Oléron were turned against the retreating Wehrmacht troops. The suicide of Adolf Hitler brought to an end what, in effect, was an unnecessary battle, as the attacking French forces paused after the announcement of Dönitz's accession to power in the crumbling remnants of the Third Reich. Dönitz radioed to Schirlitz that further resistance was futile, and fresh negotiations were held between Schirlitz and Meyer on 4 May, which ultimately safeguarded the port from destruction, unlike Royan which had been devastated by the combat in April. Schirlitz announced that he would release French prisoners-of-war and surrender the port intact. In turn, Meyer ordered French units of gendarmes and armed firemen into the German lines, where they were given Wehrmacht weapons, enabling them to maintain order as the garrison prepared to surrender. On 7 May, the radio announcement of Germany's unconditional surrender, to become effective on 9 May, was received. Events teetered on the brink of ugly, with several Germans manhandled by celebrating French civilians as Schirlitz surrendered his men, who marched into captivity without their small arms, but equipped with hand grenades to dissuade any opportunistic French patriots.[80]

As French troops entered the U-boat bunker at La Pallice, they found U766 in good condition still, the boat having been decommissioned there after escaping Brest with

General Fahrmbacher surrenders Lorient to the 66th Infantry Division in a field near Caudan.

fourteen additional personnel aboard in August 1944. The attacks against Royan, La Rochelle, and the islands had cost the lives of nearly six hundred French soldiers, and an estimated fifteen hundred Germans. At least three thousand men were wounded in the last days of the war, on a front that had remained relatively peaceful since September 1944. The German naval troops in Lorient too had made one final defiant sortie. On 3 May, infantrymen were taken from the port aboard vessels of the Hafenschutzflottille and landed on the small islands of Houat and Hoëdic, near Belle-Île, which had been recaptured by Free French troops during December, reoccupying them and shuttling captured food supplies back to Lorient itself.

Lorient surrendered to American forces on 10 May. Fahrmbacher had finally decided to surrender his troops, as by that stage there was only five days' supply of bread, two weeks' worth of fat, and at most two months' worth of meat. Resistance had already ended in Berlin, and the further loss of life by continuing the fight in Lorient would be pointless. He had already refused one offer to capitulate by American officers on 4 May, when delegates from the opposing sides met in Plouhinec to attempt to create a secure zone for civilians to inhabit in the event of massed American bombing raids on Lorient. He had not yet managed to make contact with Dönitz, his new head of state, at that point, and would not surrender without authorisation. Finally, on 7 May, Fahrmbacher accepted the inevitable, and despatched emissaries to surrender his command.

Fahrmbacher's Adjutant, Oberst Borst, crossed the river on the afternoon of 7 May in a small motor launch, along with a fellow infantry officer and one from the Kriegsmarine, and met with American officers. There was a brief moment of extreme awkwardness as Borst was greeted by his opposite number, and delivered a stiff-armed salute characterised by the Americans as a Nazi salute, but it was more from habit than any attempt by Borst to goad his erstwhile enemy. The officers retired to the Le Carour café in Magouër, where they discussed the conditions of surrender. Borst had initially hesitated to sign the document without further consultation with his commander, but Keating's repeat of the threat to bombard Lorient by air served to accelerate proceedings. Returning to Fahrmbacher to discuss the American ultimatum, Borst was back a little past 2000hrs that evening and signed the document in the presence of Colonel Keating, Chief of Staff of the US 66th Infantry Division, and Colonel Joppé of the 19th French Infantry Division, within the Café Breton. The conditions of the surrender included a ceasefire to begin at one minute past midnight on 9 May, German mine clearance of the road approaches to Lorient, destruction of all barricades and obstructions, the constitution of an arms dump for surrendered weapons, cancellation of any plans to destroy any intact port facilities, and the provision of a surrender ceremony. The ceremony took place on 10 May at 1600hrs in a field near Caudan to the east of Lorient. Fahrmbacher arrived in a camouflaged car, and symbolically surrendered his pistol to General Kramer of the 66th Infantry Division.

The German defenders of Lorient carried out the stipulated conditions of the surrender document, as well as incinerating all military records that were held by Fahrmbacher and other fortress commands. Thus much was lost which could have allowed closer study of life inside the fortress. German military justice did not end with the capitulation. On 8 May, twenty-one-year-old Kriegsmarine man Herbert Heppkes was shot by firing squad after being condemned to death for a crime unknown. He was buried the following day in the French cemetery of Kérentrech in Lorient. During 1945, five German servicemen had been condemned to death, and summarily executed by firing squad and interred within the same cemetery.

In total 24,441 prisoners-of-war were taken in Lorient. These included 614 officers (including Fahrmbacher, Admiral Matthiae, Luftwaffe Generalmajor Julius Kuse, who had been in charge of the Luftwaffe Kampfgruppe in the southern section of the Lorient pocket, and Kapitän zur See Ernst Kals of the 2nd U-Flotilla), and 21,636 non-commissioned officers and enlisted men. Amongst the naval vessels captured there were also two U-boats, both of which were out of service: *U123* and *U129*. The former was in reasonable shape in box K3, but the latter had been scuttled in front of the U-boat pens.

The garrison at Saint-Nazaire made first contact with the Allies to discuss surrender on 7 May, at Cordemais on the enclave's eastern front. Another meeting followed at 1000hrs the following day, during which final terms were agreed, and Generalleutnant Junck's chief of staff signed the official surrender document at 1700hrs that day. The ceasefire was not to be in effect until midnight, and skirmishes and sporadic bursts of gunfire along the front lines were heard almost to the last moment. A surrender ceremony was scheduled for 11 May, which had the dual effect of allowing the Wehrmacht administration to organise its forces, and also to disarm mines blocking the main accesses to the fortress.

In Bouvron on 11 May, General Junck handed his sidearm over to General Kramer, commander of the 6th Infantry Division, in the presence of French General Chomel, as Allied troops entered the pocket. The final operational U-boat from the port, Heinrich's *U255*, had departed on 8 May bound for Norway, but surrendered at sea once the capitulation was announced, docking at Loch Alsh where it was handed over to the Royal Navy.

French marines arrive at La Pallice following the German surrender. La Pallice and La Rochelle were the least damaged of the French U-boat bases held by the Wehrmacht until the end of the war.

As Allied troops entered the shattered remnants of the town, the German bunkers which comprised the U-boat base, centred on the enormous shelters themselves, were among the few buildings still intact. Inside the dry dock within box number 4, *U510* still lay where it had been awaiting maintenance, and the completion of its snorkel installation which had begun following arrival in the battered port on 24 April 1945 after its epic voyage to Europe from Batavia in the Far East.

For the surrendered garrisons of France's U-boat installations there was nothing but captivity ahead, their conditions dependent on the nation which held them and their physical location. For those held by the French, it was a difficult and uncertain future that they now faced.

6

Military Justice

It perhaps appears curious now, but the victorious Allied armies in northern Germany opted to keep many German units armed, and assigned to them the task of keeping order in a country whose infrastructure had comprehensively collapsed, and where roving bands of troops, from all armies, were dangerously free of restraint. For example, in Flensburg, Wolfgang Lüth, one of the two most highly-decorated officers in the U-boat service, was named area commander. He had been in command of the Naval Academy to which Dönitz had retreated with his new governmental responsibilities only a short time before. After the armistice had come into effect, Lüth was allowed to continue to post armed German sentries around the perimeter of the academy, drawn mainly from the ranks of Dönitz's guard battalion. This, in turn, incorporated Korvettenkapitän Cremer and his anti-tank unit, who had extracted such a heavy toll on the British near Hamburg. Ironically, it was this very detachment of sentries which would end Lüth's life on 13 May. Conditions outside the academy were near anarchic, with bursts of machine-gun fire and explosions periodically heard reverberating through the countryside. Lüth had ordered Cremer's men to issue a single challenge and then shoot. At 0300hrs, eighteen-year-old sentry Matthias Gottlob heard approaching footsteps. After a single challenge, the footsteps halted, but no reply was received. Twice more Gottlob shouted his challenge, the young man growing increasingly nervous. Once his third attempt at eliciting a response failed, he fired a single shot from the hip, striking

Effective U-boat crews became a tightly-knit community and strongly identified themselves with their boat. The unfortunate few who graduated to ground combat in one of the Atlantic fortresses or in northern Germany were often kept in units which bore the closest possible resemblance to their previous crew.

Wolfgang Lüth, one of the most highly decorated U-boat 'Aces' of the war. Tragically killed after hostilities in a freak accident in Flensburg.

Wolfgang Lüth in the head and killing him instantly. It was a curious and futile way for Lüth to die after years of front-line service in U-boats. But despite several conspiracy theories and the idea that it was a form of military suicide, the likelihood is that it was little more than a tragic accident played out between men whose nerves and endurance had been worn thin by war.

Lüth had been attending to Dönitz and his government duties in the Academy's Sports Hall before his death. Dönitz continued to operate in his role as Germany's new leader whilst he awaited developments among the Allies as to his ultimate fate. He was even granted special permission to bury Lüth with full military honours, including a coffin draped in the Kriegsmarine ensign, accompanied by an honour guard of six U-boat officers. A detachment of armed naval troops fired three volleys over the coffin, and Dönitz provided the last words in the service as Lüth was laid to rest in the grounds of the Academy. Lüth was not only a veteran commander, but also a complex person in terms of his leadership role. His dedication to his men was as fierce as the loyalty that he felt toward his wife and children at home. The last primary motivating force appeared to be an ardent belief in a National Socialist Germany. In this he was not alone: Knight's Cross holder Korvettenkapitän Ernst Mengersen is remembered as being fiercely devoted to the ideals of National Socialism, like Lüth. Mengersen was a veteran of the

Dönitz addresses his U-boat men. The apparent level of informality that Dönitz had with
his U-boat crews was no affectation, and bred a loyalty which transcended the ordinary
relationship between servicemen and their Commander-in-Chief.

Spanish civil war as well as commander of *U18*, *U101* and *U607*, and had been promoted
to a staff post in June 1943, becoming chief of the 15th U-Flotilla.

During the days following Hitler's death a bizarre normality apparently prevailed in
the U-boat enclaves. FdU West had been ordered to prepare U-boats for operations up
until the moment of Dönitz's ceasefire order. On 4 May, Oberleutnant zur See Herbert
Werner arrived in Kristiansand to take command of a new U-boat. Werner later wrote
of his experiences in a book which has become at once famous and infamous in the
pantheon of U-boat literature. His book, *Iron Coffins*, provides a great insight into his
wartime experiences which stretched from 1941 through to the end of the war. However,
Werner's criticism of U-boat operational planning, which continued to send obsolete
boats out against increasingly overwhelming odds is fierce and plainly expressed. Also,
many of his technical facts, involving U-boat numbers, sinkings and the like, have been
proven incorrect. But does this undermine the book in its entirety? I, personally, do not
believe so. With that in mind, it is interesting to relate the tale of Werner's reception by
his new flotilla commander in Norway. The latter is referred to in the book as 'Kapitän
Jürgensen', but it appears that Werner is referring to Korvettenkapitän Mengersen
behind the pseudonym.

I arrived in Kristiansand around 0700. A blue sky spanned the city … A youthful Adjutant showed me into the Commanding Officer's elaborate room. Before me rose a decorated officer in blues who had been a U-boat commander when hunting and shooting had been a pleasure. Kapitän Jürgensen was one of the lucky few who had been withdrawn from the front line just in time to escape the holocaust.

'I beg to report for duty, sir,' I saluted.

'Oh yes, naturally, I've been informed of your arrival. You're supposed to take a new command. Your boat hasn't arrived yet. I assume she'll sail into port any time. Why don't you accommodate yourself in the meantime? I'll let you know. That's all for now.'

This short, cool reception gave me a strange premonition. Something was odd about Jürgensen's behaviour, something that went beyond the strain that had signed his face. He seemed to be absent minded and flustered. I walked out of his office convinced that he knew of some calamity that he had been unwilling to divulge.[81]

Werner, like most of his comrades, was under little real illusion as to the real position that the U-boat had reached in the war against the Allies. His book reveals the constant litany of messages from boats sinking at sea and, like the accounts of many other veterans, relates tales of too many missing friends from other boats for any illusions to be retained regarding the possibility of attaining a successful outcome in this losing battle. By May 1945, it would have been sheer folly for any of the surviving U-boat crews to continue to believe in the prospect of any kind of final victory. Hitler was dead, Germany invaded and in ruins. The front-line crews had been denied those potential wonder weapons, the electro-boats, with their tantalising promise of victory. Despite a large number under training, or having reached the Norwegian enclaves, it was obviously too little, and too late. Even if a last-minute bloodbath had been made possible at sea, using those boats ready or near-ready for action, it would have had no effect on the eventual outcome of the conflict. Instead, there would have been a needless waste of the lives of both Allied seamen and German civilians, as the Allies would, no doubt, have remorselessly increased the intensity of air and land attacks on German soil, until the will to fight was completely extinguished. The Norwegian redoubt, had it continued to fight using the boats available, would also have been in direct violation of orders from the recognised German government in Flensburg. There would be no Wagnerian-style 'Götterdämmerung' for the U-boat service: no final death ride to be immortalised into the legend of the Kriegsmarine, and its devotion to the battle.

However, as men and women continued to die on the barricades of a shattered Berlin, the sting of military defeat, together with the death of the country's leader, in what many imagined was action against the Russians, rather than the reality of his inglorious suicide, no doubt cut to the very core of the more politically-motivated German military officers. Dönitz's recent harsh admonishments delivered to his officers implied that those who accepted defeat were traitors worthy only of a traitor's death: these also undoubtedly continued to ring in the heads of the men facing the complete collapse of their country, and its expected subjugation under the harshest Allied terms. Discipline is the bedrock of any military formation, and with such a confused chaos of emotions in existence regarding the fate that was rapidly overtaking the Wehrmacht, it appears that many lost their sense when they were in most need of it. In his book, Werner recounts how he and a fellow officer had begun to plan to escape to South America, rather than meekly to submit to the Allied victors. This, of course, would have been desertion, as they were not at sea in the ambiguous situation in which both *U977* and *U530* found themselves initially, where they sincerely doubted the veracity of instructions to surrender. If Werner had managed to slip away from a German base, having reclaimed use of a functioning U-boat with a hand-picked crew, and then set off on a trip to South America, his actions would have branded him and his men as deserters, no matter how much his fellow U-boat men might have applauded his defiance.

However, Werner's plans appeared to have been affected profoundly by a spectacle that he witnessed in the final moments of the war. The men of the Kristiansand base had been called together to the docks where their commander 'Jürgensen' wished to make a demonstration for their benefit:

Fred and I recoiled in horror when we entered the dimly lighted square where the U-boat crews had formed a human horseshoe facing the white-walled shop. There, suspended from a makeshift scaffold, hung three nooses. Below stood a large table, with three high stools lined up on top. In front of the gallows was a crude bench, covered with a huge Navy war flag. A ship's lantern, placed on the red cloth, cast an eerie light on a Navy sabre and a copy of Hitler's book *Mein Kampf.* A band of armed marines took up position behind the stage. Staff officers rushed back and forth. Leutnant Lange, Jürgensen's young Adjutant, shouted frantic orders.

As the crowd stirred uneasily Jürgensen began speaking: 'Soldiers, I have called you together to demonstrate how we will avoid another 1918. I am going to make an example of these three deserters – an example that will strike fear into the hearts of any men with revolutionary tendencies. We will protect and nourish these ideals instilled in us by our martyred Führer. Guards, bring these men to justice.'

What followed was a perfect nightmare come to life. The captives, their hands tied behind their backs, were led into the square. Momentarily they were paralysed by the sight of the nooses; then they broke away and fled. Lange shot one man repeatedly in the back. As the fugitive fell on his face, the two others surrendered. Then all three were brutally dragged back to the scaffold.

Lange shouted a long list of trumped up charges. He then demanded the severest punishment: death by hanging. No one in the crowd dared to protest in the face of so many rifles.

Jürgensen pronounced the three men guilty on all counts and condemned them 'to be hanged by the neck until death has separated body and soul.'

The guards were then ordered to execute the sentence. But before the three doomed men reached the platform, they broke free again and began fighting desperately for their lives. Shots were fired. There was struggling, trampling; dust rose in the lantern's gloomy light. The three were recaptured, but with superhuman force they broke free once again. They fought, kicked, and punched until they were surrounded and again overwhelmed.

Now Jürgensen cried, 'Shoot these men dead, don't hang them, shoot them!'

The marines heard the call and all went very fast. One man raised his rifle and fired point blank. The mate's face flew off like a pancake. The two other prisoners collapsed and were riddled with bullets. The marines dragged the three bodies against the wall

Karl Dönitz and Alfred Jodl at the time of their arrest in Flensburg. Ultimately, Jodl would be hanged after numerous guilty verdicts from the Nuremberg trials, while Dönitz would receive a stiff prison sentence.

of the repair shop and left them there. The crews were dismissed; the guards marched away; everyone vanished.

Long after midnight, two petty officers helped me lift the bodies into a rowboat. We fastened heavy weights to their feet and neck, then rowed out into the middle of the fjord. Three splashes – and the dead seamen had at least received a sailor's burial.[82]

The truth of this event has long been debated, not helped by Werner's apparent use of pseudonyms, whilst he had previously stated in his own foreword that all the names were real and of actual people. The confusion of the final days of the war masked the summary execution of many military personnel, as well as civilians who had been deemed not to have withstood the Allied advance sufficiently. This in itself is not an unusual situation. The chaos that succeeded the liberation of many occupied countries in 1944 and 1945 often led to mass hysterical reprisals by both the retreating occupiers and recently emboldened 'patriots'. Nonetheless, a few cases of Kriegsmarine summary executions have been recorded. On 5 May 1945, eleven sailors from the minesweeper *M612* were executed aboard their ship a little north of Sønderborg, Denmark. The day before their death, the minesweeper had been ordered to sail into the Eastern Baltic to participate in the final evacuation of German troops still fighting in isolated pockets against the Russians. However, on receipt of this order the eleven men mutinied, and took control of their ship in a short-lived bid for freedom. Unfortunately for them, their actions were detected by men from another ship, who promptly boarded the minesweeper, arrested them, and speedily tried and condemned them. The eleven were sentenced to death and shot the following evening. Their bodies were dumped into the sea, and four of them never recovered, whilst the other seven were not given a proper burial until they had drifted ashore some days later.

More prominent in the pantheon of Kriegsmarine history was the execution of three sailors from the Schnellboote. At the German capitulation, the three men were being held aboard the S-boat tender *Buea*. At the beginning of May, they had been assigned to one of the naval infantry units that was being raised, in order to be thrown into the cauldron of fighting in Berlin. On 6 May, the three deserted, rather than face the likelihood of a pointless death on a battlefield for which they had not been trained, and for a cause that was already lost. However, as they fled towards their German homes they were captured by armed Danes, and returned to the S-boat base from which they had absconded. The three were swiftly tried, and found guilty. Their death sentence was carried out on 10 May, after it had been confirmed by the leader of the Schnellboote service, FdS (Führer der Schnellboote) Kommodore Petersen.

The difficulty of confirming this sentence, on three men who had narrowly avoided death in the most catastrophic conflict the world had ever seen, must have been an incredible burden for Petersen. The FdS, like BdU, was renowned for his absolute dedication to the welfare of the men beneath his command. During the war, he had clashed with other Wehrmacht branch leaders, for what they considered almost an unwillingness to send his men into battles that he felt were either unjustified militarily, or from which they stood little chance of survival. A devout Christian, Petersen was always unwilling to risk his men's lives needlessly. He embodied most of the qualities required to be an effective and popular commander of troops, but following the end of hostilities, it seems that he considered the need to maintain military discipline within the ranks of his defeated men required that they should not perceive any diminishment of military law and authority. Petersen was pilloried by German courts after the war for this action and, to his eternal credit, he never once shifted responsibility for the confirmation of the three death sentences to anybody else, nor did he deign to plea that circumstances were beyond his control.

The motivation for Petersen's actions in this case may well have mirrored those in

FdU West Hand Rudolf Rösing (second from right), pictured here in company with commander of the 11th U-Flotilla Lehmann-Willenbrock (second from left), at the presentation of the Oak Leaves to the Knight's Cross to Rolf Thomsen (right) on 29 April 1945.

the events described by Herbert Werner. If, indeed, Mengersen is to be identified with the fictional Jürgensen, he was a highly politically-motivated officer, and the necessity of controlling what, in effect, could amount to thousands of discontented, and potentially rebellious, armed military personnel may well have needed the full weight of martial law to be used. However, the evident hysteria, together with the drumhead nature of the 'court' which condemned these men, more closely resembled the thousands of summary executions carried out by police and military units throughout Germany, as they attempted to stiffen flagging resolve in the face of defeat. The methodical methods of a military court martial do not seem to have been followed, although once again the circumstances may well have prompted expediency as a replacement for justice.

The advantage of hindsight allows us to view the passing and carrying out of capital punishment verdicts at such a late stage in the war as acts that seem unduly harsh, almost cruel. However, both the Wehrmacht and the Allied powers had an equal interest in maintaining discipline. For example, German officers of the Wehrmacht forces retreating from Denmark at the conclusion of hostilities were permitted to keep their side arms and ammunition, their troops under German command but Allied control. The Wehrmacht was responsible for column control, bivouacs during the march, and the feeding of the troops, all maintained under the full co-operation between headquarters units from both sides. Clearly, there were insufficient Allied forces to guard the number of surrendered personnel if they were to be treated as formal prisoners-of-war. In Norway, the problems were even more formidable than those experienced in Denmark, due to the sheer weight of numbers of German troops who had yet to be processed. In Denmark, the retreating Wehrmacht were simply advised to move into Schleswig-Holstein, and find temporary accommodation while the logistical situation was resolved. In Norway it was not so easy, as the border to be crossed was water. Instead, the Germans were concentrated in as few military outposts as possible, where they could be left more or less to their own devices, until the Allies were ready and prepared to deal with them.

The fragile peace that resulted required an iron hand to maintain, one that was seen to be capable of dispensing military justice swiftly against any transgression. The major charge of desertion had always carried a harsh penalty: when faced with the potential mass desertion of discontented Wehrmacht personnel, the potential for disaster was huge. As 'Jürgensen' had said, the spectre of the revolutionary fervour within the surrendered German Fleet, which had followed the end of hostilities in 1918, had left a stain on the honour of the German Navy and this, to an extent, had stigmatised them in the eyes of some German leaders during the Second World War.

In recent times I was present at a meeting of Friends of the U-Boot Archiv in Germany, where Hans-Georg Hess, the former commander of *U995*, was a guest speaker. Hess had long been a somewhat controversial figure, and the Knight's Cross awarded to the young commander towards the end of the war was felt by many veterans to have been unmerited. Additionally, his alleged political leanings, which he had supposedly retained, long after the last echoes of the Second World War had died away, were distasteful to many from that epoch. When challenged by a well-respected U-boat veteran about the death of three U-boat men in Norway who had been tried, condemned, and shot in unseemly haste in Norway at the close of the war, an agitated Hess replied that the men 'had to die'. Apparently, the three had established close relationships with three Norwegian women, and had gone 'over the wire' to see them, in the face of what was a completely unknown fate. As a witness to this exchange I was not fully aware of the circumstances of this event, and the U-Boot Archiv was unwilling to elaborate further on the matter. As a matter of conjecture, I have often wondered if this event that I had heard described vaguely could have been related to the one that many claim was fabricated by Herbert Werner.

Certainly, the Allies recognised the need for the German unit commanders to retain their military powers, until such time as their formations could be completely disbanded. British military headquarters in Norway requested clarification on 24 May 1945 from SHAEF as to the status of German troops serving sentences for the crime of desertion.[83] The reply given was that they were to be returned, either to their own, or to other suitable units, for the execution of their sentences. However, individuals could be retained in Allied detention at the discretion of the British commander.

If the rather summary form of justice which was meted out to the trio of luckless U-boat men, and the three from the S-boat service, appeared to have been motivated by more than purely military considerations, then a similar kind of expedient justice could be said to have been applied to other unfortunate members of the Wehrmacht, including Dönitz, after the conclusion of the war. Tried alongside Hermann Göring, Rudolf Hess, Albert Speer and other luminaries of the Third Reich in Nuremberg, Dönitz was found guilty and sentenced to ten years in prison for 'planning, initiating and waging wars of aggression and other crimes against peace' and 'war crimes'. But was the verdict justified? In this writer's opinion, no. Dönitz was no more guilty of war crimes than any military commander of any nation which had taken part in the war. However, there is the somewhat more difficult area of responsibility for the excesses of the Nazi regime, which included slave labour used in construction, and the kind of profiting from the output of Germany's concentration camp system that ended in U-boat crews being supplied with socks made from the hair of exterminated Jews. Were the U-boat men responsible for this? Were they even aware of it? Again, in this writer's opinion, no. However, the prosecution in Nuremberg persuasively put forward the point of view that, at the very least, Dönitz, due to his high position within the military hierarchy, was at least aware of the concentration camp system in all its myriad operations, including the allocation of twelve thousand concentration camp inmates as forced labour in German shipyards in 1944. Furthermore, Dönitz was found somewhat complicit in the execution of Hitler's infamous Commando Order, whereby Allied commandos were to be summarily shot after interrogation, if captured. While Dönitz's defence argued that no Kriegsmarine unit ever carried out the order, they, in at least one example, handed prisoners over to the SD (Sicherheitsdienst), the Security Service. This order was not cancelled once Dönitz had risen to the post of Oberbefehlshaber der Marine (ObdM) – Commander of the Kriegsmarine.

Dönitz certainly supported Hitler in his capacity as Chief of the Armed Forces and Head of State. That, too, could only tenuously, and incorrectly, be described as criminal with the value of years of hindsight. He did deliver vociferous speeches over the radio, and messages to his U-boat officers in the final days of the war which spoke of the need to 'fly into the face of any German who now becomes the least bit shaky in his loyalty to the National Socialist State and to the Führer. The motives for this are only fear, cowardice and weakness. We are the strong and faithful.' Indeed his message to U-boat officers of 7 April stated that: 'A scoundrel who does not behave so must be hanged and have a placard fastened to him: "Here hangs a traitor who by his low cowardice allows German women and children to die, instead of protecting them like a man."' These, indeed, are the kind of words that could be ascribed to a fanatical, politically- or even racially-motivated leader. However, I believe it is somewhat disingenuous to look at them totally in that light. The mass hysteria that seemed to have permeated the chaotic streets of the crumbling German Reich was nowhere more evident than in the bodies which swung from trees and lamp-posts as warnings to others not to surrender or retreat. But this horror is by no means unique to Germany. It is the final desperate act of a dying nation, amplified if that nation is ruled by the kind of totalitarian regime that Germany was. Dönitz himself was a part of the German machinery of war, and like that machinery, he was as dominated by its leader as were many others. One of Dönitz's immediate subordinates, FdU West Kapitän zur See Hans-Rudolf Rösing, characterised Dönitz to me in these words during an interview at his home in Kiel.

'We all admired him because he had a gift to put himself into the shoes of the commanders in action. I experienced this myself. When you came to him after a patrol to report. All captains went to him after they came back from a mission to make a report. And in France they came to me and gave reports which I took a transcript of and sent to BdU. Then the captain went to Berlin to report to Dönitz personally. So Staff already knew the most important items of the mission and Dönitz was able to put precise questions, and he came to the point, and therefore he could get a lot out of the captains. Of course, other staff officers like Godt were at the meetings, too, and also asked questions but mainly he, yes, you had the feeling that he could put himself

Karl Dönitz posing for a likeness of himself.

into your situation. That was a great gift. He could speak to the submariners. I accompanied him when he saw other parts of the navy, and they were drawn up in ranks, and he stood in the middle with a loudspeaker and spoke to them. Submariners he asked to come around him, very near.

One day in La Rochelle, Dönitz spoke to the U-boat men, the officers sitting around him. He had his Grossadmiral's staff in his hand and he started saying "Well, last evening somebody said to me when he saluted me 'Oh, Herr Grossadmiral, you are again here already,' and he wanted me to salute him, but I tell you I come to see you whenever I can and whoever doesn't believe it I'll give you a kick with this staff!"

He was very direct. When there were two flotillas in the one port he made two separate speeches. He was terrible when on behalf of Hitler he made these speeches … that was quite a different Dönitz than when he was with his own people. I always thought one of the tragedies of his life was becoming Oberbefehlshaber der Marine, if he had remained solely BdU he would have stayed with his people. He had no experience in the way of the Supreme Command, he hadn't been in Berlin before then. Admiral von Friedeberg once told me that I always have to keep Dönitz's back free from the spears of those who were always jealous behind him. But as an officer, he *was* definitely up to the job of commander of the navy.'

Interestingly, Rösing was held in prison at the end of the war, along with Reinhard 'Teddy' Suhren, who had once been his IWO aboard *U48*, and had later risen to the post of FdU Nord, based in Narvik.

'After the surrender I spent more than a year in Allied captivity. It started in the Oslo prison – 'Achenschloss'. There Teddy and I were interned and interrogated. It appears that we were also held as potential witnesses in the trial of Grossadmiral Dönitz. But we were never called. There were other things too, one of which was the apparent moving of members of the SS security service to safety after the end of the war.

When I was finally transferred from Oslo, I gave a small speech to the Director of the jail, and I said to him I appreciate that we were treated well and correctly in your establishment. And he said, "I know you are not all criminals." Teddy remained there for a while longer after I had left.'

The arguments and opinions for and against Dönitz's guilty verdict in Nuremberg will no doubt continue to be stated ad infinitum. The fullest examination, which would include numerous and various arguments about the legal validity of the Nuremberg trials in the first place, is beyond the scope and premise of this book. But the sentencing of Dönitz does serve to illustrate the kind of military justice which continued to prevail within Allied ranks, as well as in Germany, in the first months of 1945.

What can be beyond doubt was that Dönitz's willingness to prolong the war for what amounted to a vital few days was a genuine effort to evacuate German civilians from the path of a vengeful Red Army. His belief in the barbarism of Germany's Communist enemy was absolute, and not without some cause: the excesses of the German occupation of Russia were visited tenfold on a subjugated Germany.

7

Captivity

The end of the war saddled the victorious Allied authorities with a continent of swirling political allegiances, disputed borders, destroyed infrastructures, and millions of displaced persons. On top of those responsibilities were also millions of surrendered enemy military formations. The Kriegsmarine, like most Wehrmacht units, kept its men grouped within its unit formations until they could either be discharged or imprisoned. Dönitz continued to hold power over the men of the U-boat service, alongside all other German military formations, until his arrest on Wednesday 23 May, when he and his government were taken into custody.[84] The loyalty and discipline that largely remained within the surrendered U-boat service was remarkable, and was often used to control other, more lax, groups of men. FdU Nord Korvettenkapitän Reinhard 'Teddy' Suhren later remembered events immediately after the surrender. He and his staff had surrendered in Narvik, and at first remained virtually untroubled by Allied captors.

I resigned myself to a longer stay, and had built for myself outside on the banks of the fjord a head office, containing a living room, a bedroom, a storage room and a shower – and fitted with a searchlight. For it was the wish of the Allies that I should continue as a boss, and be responsible for the five store huts in which the rest of the submariners were accommodated, as well as for the compound of German prisoners who were under interrogation. They were in a barrack compound surrounded by barbed wire, a proper POW camp. It was still there, and what was more the Tommies had no intention of turning the inmates loose. On the contrary: the established regime was to continue. We submariners were commandeered as guards and given the task of maintaining order and discipline, if necessary by force of arms. That was a thankless task, and not without its problems; the offenders didn't want to be ordered about by anyone, no matter where they came from.

One day a few prisoners escaped onto Norwegian soil, which caused a bit of excitement. I explained the situation to the guards. Yes, it was said that they had dug their way out under the wire perimeter fence. Well, I gave orders for them to enforce a strict set of disciplinary measures; but one of the internees was eavesdropping in the next room and overheard the lot. Having nothing more urgent to do, he ran round the huts; 'Suhren has said so and so…'

When I was due to leave, a racket started up behind me. I asked the camp leader, a young Kapitänleutnant, 'What's up now?' 'Well', he replied, 'it's directed at you.'

Unarmed as I was, I got calmly out of the car, and roared, 'Back to your huts; come on, quick march!' This confident approach soon brought them to their senses. I quickly turned to the guards, and gave the order, 'Charge!' When the rabble rousers saw that the guards meant business they dispersed bit by bit until eventually they were all back in their huts. I got hold of five burly NCOs from my own men. In the meantime another two had broken out of the POW compound and were making a nuisance of themselves in the area. The NCOs caught them, tied their arms and legs together and catapulted them back over the two-metre high wire fence. Finally, we got the biggest troublemakers out and brought them into the submariners' compound, where they couldn't get up to any tricks.[85]

Many of the men from within the ranks of the U-boat service would avoid captivity by volunteering for the German Minesweeping Authority, which would continue to sweep the remains of extensive minefields off all German coasts. Serving in their Kriegsmarine uniforms, with swastikas removed, they operated under British control. For the rest, conditions within Allied prisoner-of-war camps for the U-boat men, primarily in France, Canada, United Kingdom and United States, turned out to be hugely variable. It is perhaps as a result of the same loyalty and discipline which had marked the U-boat service as an effective fighting force, willing to carry on the fight long after they had lost the initiative to their enemies, that they would suffer some of the longest internments

A German officer prisoner-of-war is escorted into his new home by his camp commander. Conditions inside British prisoner-of-war camps were very good, though the length of confinement after the end of hostilities violated aspects of the Geneva Convention.

U-boat prisoners are
unloaded by the
Royal Navy.

of Wehrmacht personnel after the war. In the limited view of many of the Allies, such
resolve could only be explained by the crews of the U-boats being dominated by
Nazism, its ideals and methods. Thus they were often viewed as fanatics with all of the
dangers that such men posed. It was a view which had long been espoused in Allied
propaganda and, tragically, is still held to this day by some.

Nevertheless the Geneva Convention is very specific regarding the treatment of
prisoners-of-war, both during and after hostilities, including the duration of potential
imprisonment. It states:

SECTION II. RELEASE AND REPATRIATION UPON CESSATION OF
HOSTILITIES.

Article 75.

When belligerents conclude a convention of armistice, they must, in principle,
have appearing therein stipulations regarding the repatriation of prisoners of war.
If it has not been possible to insert stipulations in this regard in such convention,
belligerents shall nevertheless come to an agreement in this regard as soon as possible.
In any case, repatriation of prisoners shall be effected with the least possible delay
after the conclusion of peace.

Prisoners of war against whom a penal prosecution might be pending for a crime
or an offense of municipal law may, however, be detained until the end of the
proceedings and, if necessary, until the expiration of the punishment. The same shall
be true of those sentenced for a crime or offense of municipal law.

On agreement between the belligerents, commissions may be established for the
purpose of searching for dispersed prisoners and assuring their repatriation.

During the course of the war the majority of U-boat prisoners-of-war had been held in
camps within Canada and the United States. Often they had been processed in the
United Kingdom and held in camps there, but were later moved to camps in North
America. There they were frequently used as labour, particularly in land work, such as

The end of the war in Europe found a number of long-range U-boats stranded in the Far East. These were handed over to the Japanese Navy whilst their crews were interned.

tree felling or the harvesting of cotton in the southern states. Despite what must have been arduous and difficult manual labour, their treatment was almost uniquely fair and just, and there were very few reported complaints of transgressions against their rights as stated in the Geneva Convention. However, following the end of hostilities, the face of their imprisonment was somewhat changed. This was, partially at least, due to the fact that German authorities now no longer held Allied prisoners-of-war and thus could not

German personnel interned by the Japanese in Malaya and Singapore were generally well treated, largely ignored by their erstwhile Allies, but subject to none of the harsh conditions which had befallen Allied prisoners of the Japanese.

Reinhard 'Teddy' Suhren, an 'Ace' from the heady days of U-boat success, photographed here in his later role as FdU North in Narvik.

retaliate in kind, should there be any perceived mistreatment of German prisoners-of-war. This practice had been used throughout the war to ensure the correct treatment of captives held by the enemy, but once that threat had been removed there was little, if anything, that sanctioned German authorities could do to guarantee the fair treatment of their interned troops.

While the actual living conditions of captives held within the United Kingdom and North America never really deteriorated after the conclusion of the war, the manner in which U-boat men were held within Germany, and certainly in France, was often deplorable, sometimes criminal. In France, the desire for revenge against their beaten enemy appeared to take precedence over any humanitarian considerations. Many U-boat men had been transferred to French prison camps in what appeared a largely arbitrary manner, but could sometimes be influenced by the origin of the captured personnel. If, when the Allies eventually began processing its captured U-boat men, their origin was deemed to fall within the French Zone of Occupation, then they would be transferred to French custody. By August 1946 France had nearly 750,000 former German troops in imprisonment, the majority used for slave labour for duties as diverse as mine clearance and coal mining in the Alsace region. These statistics were compiled by the International Red Cross, who also noted that, of those in French captivity, 475,000 had been captured by the Americans, who had transferred them to French control for the express purpose of forced labour. Interestingly, and somewhat indicative of the nature of the work that would await these hapless men, 2,474 German prisoners-of-war were returned to the Americans as they were under-strength.

The unfortunate remainder were described by the foreign correspondents who saw them in captivity as 'a beggar army of pale, thin men clad in vermin-infested tatters.'[86] Eventually, further Red Cross investigations would lead to all them being pronounced as unfit for work, at least three quarters of them due to deliberate and systematic starvation. For example in the prisoner-of-war camp within the Sarthe District, the twenty thousand prisoners received just 900 calories a day: twelve of them dying every day in the camp hospital. Accounts tell of train loads of new prisoners arriving daily, corpses mixed with the living, some of whom had attempted to eat coal in order to survive. On 5 December 1946, the American Government, which had already completed

Surrendered German troops used for labour. Conditions within Allied prisoner-of-war camps varied dramatically following the end of hostilities. The rights guaranteed by the Geneva Convention were circumnavigated to a large degree by the relabelling of German prisoners as 'Disarmed Enemy Personnel', no longer covered by the Convention's clauses.

its own dealings with prisoners within Germany itself, requested the repatriation to Germany of the 674,000 German prisoners-of-war it had handed over to France, Belgium, the Netherlands and Luxemburg, to be completed by October 1947.

France appears to have had a particular disregard for the welfare of German prisoners. The stigma of occupation, and the often brutal methods by which the occupation was enforced, coloured judgement concerning surrendered Wehrmacht prisoners. French authorities reduced captured U-boat men to living outdoors with little shelter or provisions. Often the only way out offered to the German prisoners, with an increase in living standards and human rights, was enlistment in the French Foreign Legion. Many took the offered chance of survival, only to be embroiled in the burgeoning war in French Indo-China. However, it is probable that the lot of the German prisoners in France was preferable to those that had fallen into Russian hands. Despite the miraculous efforts of the Kriegsmarine to evacuate troops and civilians, there were thousands either left behind, or captured in the bitter fighting, U-boat personnel having been seconded to the infantry. At the end of hostilities, Russia herded its German captives into work camps where they were used as slave labour. Churchill noted in his memoirs that, during the Potsdam Conference, when he broached the subject of a lack of labour to work in Britain's rebuilding industry as well as in coal mining, Stalin suggested using the German prisoners-of-war. When Churchill expressed unwillingness to do so, Stalin appears to have been bemused by his squeamishness, stating that there was 'more meat on the German bone' than had been used.

The Supreme Allied Commander in Europe, General Dwight D Eisenhower, applied the letter of the Geneva Convention, if not its spirit, when he prompted the reclassification of German prisoners-of-war as 'Disarmed Enemy Personnel', thus robbing them of the Convention's protection. The infamous camps established near Remagen, in which hundreds of surrendered German troops perished due to starvation and neglect, reflect the ugliest side of this dubious policy. Furthermore, this reclassification enabled the surrendered U-boat men to be used as forced labour, with little or no protection from the International Red Cross. The majority of U-boat prisoners believed that their tenure in Allied prison camps would be brief, before they were repatriated to their homeland. However, many would not see Germany again until as late as 1948: shuttled from North America or Canada, to the United Kingdom or

France before the victors were finished with them. Even men who had surrendered, or had been captured while the war still raged, were held for terms far beyond the end of hostilities. Funkmaat Georg Högel of *U30* and *U110*, captured in May 1941 with the sinking of the latter, had been held prisoner in Canada: 'Following the war's end we were all shipped back to Europe. We had been told that we were going home, to what was left of it, but the ship docked in Britain. I spent some time near Nuneaton in a camp. We were treated very fairly while we worked, but of course we wanted to go home.'[87] Jürgen Oesten, the veteran commander of *U861*, who had only recently completed the arduous and perilous journey from the Far East to Norway, before the German surrender, was more prosaic in his recounting of his incarceration:

> 'I was not released until March 1947. I think the Allies viewed us as Super Nazis as we had kept fighting a lost battle. But we were also the losing side at the behest of the victors. It sometimes did lead to an interesting culture clash. I remember that I was in command of a work detail from a British POW camp. Every day the boys would be loaded on a truck and shipped out for their job. And every day the truck would stop at the same place as the morning coffee took its toll, and all of the boys would be unloaded so that they could relieve themselves by the road. Unfortunately a local woman appeared to have witnessed this every morning and eventually complained to the officer in charge of us. But he was not impressed and in his best Oxford voice he simply replied, "Madam, I'm afraid that these men are from the Continent. This is a German custom you know."'[88]

Indeed, while the story of Germany's U-boats has become synonymous with the Battle of the Atlantic, they also fought tenaciously on several other fronts. The Baltic and Black

A permit issued by the British Naval Authority in Germany allowing this Kriegsmarine radio operator to continue to wear his naval uniform, serving now under British control.

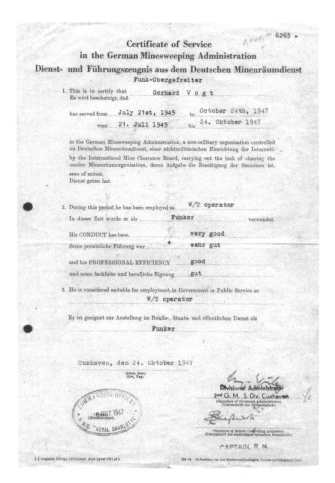

Certificate showing post-war service in the German Minesweeping Administration.

Seas saw their own commitment of fighting U-boats, battling the Russians on two fronts. Dozens of boats operated in the frozen wastes of the Arctic Ocean, the smallest of the five major oceans where British and Russian forces faced the Kriegsmarine, whilst others travelled as far afield as the Indian, and even the Pacific, Ocean. The Kriegsmarine had established U-boat bases in Penang, Jakarta and Singapore, also utilising subsidiary ports, as well as shipyards on the Japanese mainland for maintenance and repair.

The deployment of U-boats to the Far East had primarily been intended for attacking British shipping within the Indian Ocean, perceived as a weak target as Atlantic escort forces grew steadily stronger. Initially, the U-boats experienced some success off Cape Town, where long-range boats made attacks in South African waters, but the planned offensive blow within the Indian Ocean never fully materialised. The expanse of sea was too great, German forces too small, and Japanese-German cooperation difficult at best. Nonetheless, U-boats continued to be despatched to the region, also fulfilling transport requirements. Their military success as offensive attack boats was negligible. The final victory scored by U-boats in the Far East was on 6 February 1945, when Korvettenkapitän Heinrich Timm sank American freighter SS *Peter Silvester* in the Indian

Ocean, while returning from a patrol off Australia and New Zealand.

Whilst based in the east, the U-boats were accommodated primarily in Penang and Singapore. They were also periodically despatched to Batavia, and to Japanese yards for repairs and refitting. The often uneasy relationship of these two nations, Germany and Japan, manifested itself not only on a personal level, but also in that the materials and expertise with which to service a German U-boat were somewhat lacking within Japanese shipyards, which in turn were dominated by the needs of the Imperial Japanese Navy, an integral part of the Japanese struggle in the Pacific.

Upon Germany's surrender, there was great apprehension within the ranks of the German sailors within Japanese territory. Many had seen emaciated Allied prisoners at work around the Malayan U-boat base, and few had any illusions that the Japanese would welcome more Europeans loose within their sphere of influence. The Imperial Japanese forces had been exhorted to fight their European enemy with the same kind of stereotypically-racist propaganda that the Allied nations had used against them. However, the surrendered Germans were treated fairly and responsibly by their erstwhile Allies. At worst, they were left to their own devices, as Japanese forces concentrated on the last days of their floundering war effort. Japanese troops suffered great privation and hardship, as their supplies were either drained away, or intercepted by the American unrestricted submarine warfare campaign that had existed since December 1941. In turn, prisoners of the Japanese would also suffer privation, though not always necessarily through the deliberate torment often meted out to Allied prisoners.

Obermaschinenmaat Josef Dick, from Kapitän zur See Kurt Freiwald's *U181*, later recalled the German crew's internment by the Japanese:

> In mid-October we left [Batavia] for home, but two men had to be left behind because of sickness … We had to turn back south of Cape Town because of a leak in the diesel tanks; 30 cubic metres of fuel were lost and there was no longer enough to get home. We went back into the Singapore yards in mid-January and while we were there the war ended for us. The boats were turned over to the Japanese. We were glad to be free of them, even though half of each crew had to stay on board. The others were taken with trucks by the Japanese to Batu-Baha, which was about 80 miles north of Singapore in Malaysia. But when the Japanese had to surrender we were brought back to Singapore and given to the English as 'surrendered personnel'.
>
> With the English we gutted the two boats and they were later scuttled about sixty miles outside Singapore; we were not there at the time. We then worked for a while at the British base at Selatar and on board the British ships. In July 1946 we were brought back to England and arrived in Liverpool. We were to be shipped from Hull to Bremerhaven, but the ship had already departed and we were told we would have to stay in camp until the next one.[89]

There were accounts of German U-boat personnel who were kept aboard their boats by the Japanese as instructors for the new owners. There they were caught under fire from Allied aircraft attacks against the Japanese harbour installations, manning their U-boats' guns and augmenting the flak barrage. Apparently, at least one American Lightning aircraft was shot down by what were now surrendered German troops. Although the Japanese took control of the U-boats that were within their ports on 8 May 1945, none were ever actually used by their new owners. The U-boats were far smaller than the

Erich Topp (left), the 'Ace' from the 'Red Devil' boat *U552* and later commander of the Type XXI *U2513*.

models operated by the Imperial Japanese Navy, and their refurbishment never received a priority within what was already a beleaguered naval supply system. Although they would all receive new Japanese designations, they were eventually handed over to the Allies and sunk.

In general, the German U-boats that were within Japanese ports were boarded by armed troops, who took official control of them from their German commanders. The exchanges were, without exception, bloodless and formal, and the U-boat crews were marched away into captivity. One of the main concentration centres used for them was the infamous Changi Gaol. This had been built in 1936, designed to accommodate 600 prisoners, of which twenty-four cells were reserved for Europeans. However, by February 1942 over 3,500 civilian men, women and children were jammed within its stinking walls, the 400 women inmates accommodated in a separate female wing. During May 1944, all the interned civilians were transferred to Sime Road, and Changi was filled with prisoners-of-war from Selarang Barracks, and those who returned from the Thai Railways. In total, 12,000 prisoners were despatched to Changi: 5,000 accommodated inside the Gaol itself, and the remainder within the attap sheds built by the prisoners themselves within the prison walls. The German contingent was housed within what had once been guards' barracks. From there they were largely left to fend for themselves, and organised their own routine of work details and forage parties, until the Japanese troops also surrendered, and Allied forces arrived to 'liberate' them. From there, the U-boat men were shipped back to the United Kingdom, and incarcerated with their comrades.

8

Burial at Sea:
Trials and Operation Deadlight

In July 1945, the leaders of the three main victorious Allied countries in the war in Europe met at Cecilienhof, the home of Crown Prince Wilhelm Hohenzollern in Potsdam. Winston Churchill, who was later replaced by Clement Attlee after losing the general election, represented the United Kingdom, the recently-appointed President Harry S Truman represented the United States of America, and Josef Stalin, the Soviet Union. Their purpose was to discuss the administration of surrendered Germany, and one of the topics on which they reached agreement was the need to dispose of Germany's military and mercantile shipping. Included within the myriad clauses of the subsequent agreement was the following: 'The larger part of the German submarine fleet shall be sunk. Not more than thirty submarines shall be preserved and divided equally between the USSR, UK and USA for experimental and technical purposes …

U1023 while on its publicity tour of the United Kingdom in 1945.

The Three Governments agreed that transfers, including those of ships under construction and repair, shall be completed as soon as possible, but not later than 15th February, 1946.'⁹⁰

In fact, twenty-eight U-boats were summarily divided amongst the victorious nations, and not only the three major powers. The Potsdam Conference also specified the establishment of a Tripartite Naval Commission to convene in Berlin between August and December 1945. The three major powers would delegate two officers each to the commission, whose primary task was to divide the remnants of the German Navy between them. In often informal circumstances, the natural difficulties in which the three powers frequently found themselves were successfully surmounted by the Commission.

At the conclusion of the war, the German U-boat Construction Office had destroyed virtually all of its records, rather than let them fall into the hands of the victors. Therefore, there was a premium placed on the ability to operate captured models, in order to gauge their effectiveness, and to test the various German developments which had enabled their U-boats to remain in action until the very last days of the conflict.

Canada received one boat, although it had already begun to use the two which had surrendered in Newfoundland in the closing days of the war. *U889* was commissioned into the Royal Canadian Navy in June 1945, to be used for experimental purposes, largely based around the T5 Zaunkönig torpedoes which had still been aboard the boat, and its GHG (Gruppenhorchgerat) hydrophone array, which was far in advance of anything the Canadians possessed. In January 1946 the boat was discharged from Canadian service, and transferred to the United States, allocated there by the Tripartite Commission. Thus Canada's sole operational U-boat was *U190*, which was actually considered inoperative. The boat undertook a ceremonial tour of the St Lawrence Gulf and River, visiting the very ports which it and its sister boats had attempted to destroy. *U190* continued to function as a training vessel for ASW (anti-submarine warfare) duties until 24 July 1947, when it was decommissioned. Its end was designed to be one of high theatre for the Canadians. *U190* was earmarked for Canadian Operation Scuttled. Having sunk the last Royal Canadian Navy casualty of the war, HMCS *Esquimalt* on 16 April 1945, *U190* was towed to the very spot where it was supposed to be sunk, in a carefully-staged, combined operation involving destroyers, minesweepers, and obsolete aircraft such as Swordfish and Ansons. Twenty-four members of the press were to witness the mock attack, and report the death of the last of Germany's U-boats in Canadian waters, on the same day that the navy celebrated Trafalgar Day, which commemorated Admiral Nelson's triumph over the French in 1805. However, after only a single rocket attack, the uncooperative U-boat sank swiftly, stern first, only nineteen minutes after the operation had begun.

France was allocated six U-boats by the Tripartite Commission, the majority of which were the obsolete diesel-electric designs, which had been in the French ports that Germany had occupied and used as U-boat bases during the war. Nonetheless, they offered the French a shortcut to rebuilding its battered submarine service. The first was the Type IXB U-boat which had begun Operation Paukenschlag in 1942, when it had seemed that Germany might be victorious at sea. *U123* had been decommissioned in Lorient during June 1944 and scuttled on 19 August as the base faced encirclement. At the end of hostilities, she was raised and repaired, and commissioned into the French Navy as *Le Blaison* in April 1948, where the boat served until it was decommissioned once more, and scrapped in August 1957.

The Type IXC *U510* had been found intact within its dry dock inside the Saint-Nazaire bunker, after the garrison had finally surrendered in May 1945. The boat had completed its epic voyage from the Far East, and was awaiting maintenance and fuel when the war ended. It had been found in good condition, the ravages of the sea having done little to the hull, despite the huge distances of ocean that *U510* had crossed. To get the boat back to fighting trim, she was transferred to Lorient, and after little more than a year was considered operational once more. *U510* was commissioned into the French Navy as *Le Bouan* at the beginning of 1947, named after the commander of the torpedo boat *Bison* which had been sunk in Norway during 1940. Originally the boat had kept its wartime configuration of the extended wintergarten, or anti-aircraft platform, but French naval authorities quickly noted the difficulties in diving that this engendered, and *Le Bouan* was gradually altered over the following years to resemble more closely what have come to be seen as modern attack submarines. The submarine served for eighteen years in the French Navy, before being decommissioned and scrapped in 1960.

During August 1944, French forces had liberated the German-held port of Toulon on France's Mediterranean coast. There, at the former home of the 23rd U-Flotilla, were found numerous wrecks, among them several Type VIIC boats, scuttled as the Germans withdrew. *U471* was raised in February 1946 and, after repair, was commissioned into the French Navy as *Le Millé*, before transferring to Lorient where a snorkel was installed. Once again, the boat's superstructure was gradually altered over time, though not as dramatically as that of *U510*. Indeed, when the boat was finally retired from service and scrapped in 1963, it was still instantly recognisable as a Type VIIC.

U766 was the sole Type VIIC that was recovered by the French in the Atlantic ports, except the wreck of *U415*, which had been destroyed before the pens at Brest by a British mine. *U766* was recovered from La Pallice in an extremely poor state. Nonetheless, the

U1305 (centre) and another Type VIIC U-boat after surrender to the Royal Navy in Norway.

The Walter boats were prized trophies, particularly for the Royal Navy, who began trials immediately when they were able to obtain a working version. Here one of the Walter boats undergoes trials in Germany before the end of the war.

boat was repaired and entered French service in February 1946 as *Laubie*. During the 1950s it was attached to a French battle group centred on the battleship *Jean Bart*, simulating the role of an attacking Egyptian Whiskey-class submarine before Operation Mousquetaire, the ill-conceived Anglo-French attempt to invade Egypt and take control of the Suez Canal in 1956. *Laubie* was finally decommissioned in 1961, and scrapped two years later.

The remaining two U-boats that the French Navy took into its possession were of a class which had never been based in France. The French military had shown considerable interest in later German U-boat development, starting an engineering office within its occupied German zone at the end of the war, where tests were carried out on the various design advances made by the Kriegsmarine. The results were, somewhat oddly, shared with Sweden.

The Type XXIII *U2326*, one of the newer boats of which the French Navy had taken charge, was one of the few of its type to see action, sailing on two unsuccessful war patrols before the end of hostilities. Surrendered at Dundee, Scotland, the boat was originally taken into the Royal Navy as *N35*, and used in exercises during the summer of 1945. It was handed over to France under the Tripartite agreement in February 1946 in what became known as Operation Thankful: the transfer of two former U-boats to France. *N36* entered the dry dock at Cherbourg on 13 February for inspection, after which it sailed to Lorient and then La Pallice. The decision was then made to transfer the boat to Toulon, to take advantage of many spare parts for Type XXIII U-boats which had been recovered from the Saint Pierre tunnel in 1944, indicating unfulfilled German plans to designate the small coastal boats to Mediterranean operations. The boat travelled first to Casablanca, and then to Algiers, before setting course for Toulon. However, *U2326* disappeared at sea with all fifteen French crewmen aboard, fifty-four miles from Cape Cepet. The actual cause of its disappearance remains largely speculative, ranging from a diving accident to an onboard battery explosion.

The final boat was *U2326*'s larger cousin, the Type XXI *U2518*. The large boat had surrendered at Horten, Norway, on 8 May, and transferred alongside many others to

British care in Lisahally. In the second part of Operation Thankful, *U2518* reached Cherbourg under tow on 26 February 1946. After being examined at anchor in the harbour, the boat was taken into dry dock, where it remained until August and its first sortie, before heading to the Mediterranean. For an extended period, the boat enjoyed a doubtful experimental status regarding its actual attachment to the French Navy, during which its flak weapons were removed and it was painted black. A diving accident inflicted some damage on 11 November 1946, later repaired in the newly operational Brest harbour. It was definitively entered into the French Navy during April 1947 as the *S12*. As the boat's career continued, it received various changes to its configuration, and on 14 February 1951 was renamed *Roland Morillot*. The boat took part in the Suez invasion, charged with rescuing any downed pilots and continued to serve in the French Navy until 1967, when it was placed in reserve, and then decommissioned and scrapped. It was the final vestige of Kriegsmarine power to be removed from the French Navy.

Norway, the country through which almost every operational U-boat had passed since its invasion by the Wehrmacht in 1940, received four U-boats: *U926*, *U995*, *U1202* and *U4706*. A further boat, *U315*, had been stricken at Trondheim on 1 May 1945 and was broken up by Norwegian authorities in 1947. The first three U-boats were all Type VIICs inducted into the Royal Norwegian Navy to bolster its strength: *U926* became the *KNM Kya*, *U995* the *KNM Kaura*, *U1202* the *KNM Kinn*, and *U4706 KNM Knerten*. The Norwegian authorities received substantial assistance in the post-war rebuilding of their navy. The primary task of the Norwegians, within the context of the burgeoning Cold War, was the denial of their coastline to any possible Soviet transgression, and so they amassed a small fleet of conventional diesel-electric boats. The three Type VIICs were part of this, coupled with five British submarines which were transferred to Norwegian command. *U926* and *U1202* were quite unusual as they did not transfer first to the United Kingdom at the close of the war. Both had surrendered in Bergen and remained there until refitted before entering Norwegian service. *KNM Kya* served until 1962 when it was decommissioned and stricken, *KNM Kinn* was decommissioned and transferred to Hamburg for breaking in 1963. *KMV Kaura*, on the other hand, lived on. Decommissioned from the Royal Norwegian Navy, she was stricken in 1965. Shortly thereafter, the hulk was returned to Germany where extensive restoration was undertaken on the Type VIIC/41

U-boats held in their desolate Scottish anchorage while awaiting disposal in Operation Deadlight. Their exposed position, obvious here, goes some way to explaining their lack of seaworthiness during their final voyages to destruction.

until, in 1971, she was opened as the Museum ship *U995* at Laboe, in the shadow of the naval memorial, and a short distance from the U-boat memorial.

The final Norwegian prize was the Type XXIII *U4706* which had been renamed *KNM Knerten*. The boat, which had made no war patrols and had been surrendered at Kristiansand Süd, had originally been taken to the United Kingdom and given a British pennant number, before being returned to Norway in 1948. The small electro-boat did not enjoy an extensive career: used for storage by the Royal Norwegian Yacht Club from April 1950, it was eventually broken up for scrap four years later.

The United Kingdom was only allocated three more U-boats into its service by the Commission, already having taken far more. Despite the fact that the Royal Navy had operated the captured Type VIIC U-boat *U570* as HMS *Graph* since 1942, they still took four Type VIICs for testing after the war, with the boats being used until 1948.

With the destruction of German constructional records, Britain kept a reduced staff of the German U-boat Construction Office working within its occupational zone, which included the major shipyards Hamburg, Bremen and Kiel, until 1946. Their primary task was the reconstruction of various U-boat types for which no design records existed any longer. Alongside this, working models were used for trials by the Royal Navy.

Two Type XXIs were also allocated to Great Britain, though one was soon turned over to France. The remaining Type XXI, *U3017* was also tested for several years as HMS *N41* before being scrapped in November 1949, and a single Type XXIII *U2348* was used until broken up in Belfast in April 1949. The Royal Navy had considerable interest in Germany's development of the hydrogen peroxide propulsion system which Dr Walter had failed to perfect before the conclusion of the war. At first, British interrogators of German Naval Construction Director Dr Karl Fischer had asked in June 1945 about the feasibility of building ten new Type XXVI U-boats within the Blohm & Voss shipyards at Hamburg. However, in the meantime, other British authorities had begun the complete dismantling and demolition of those same yards.

Undaunted, the Royal Navy raised the scuttled Walter boat *U1407* from the silt of the harbour at Cuxhaven, and transferred it to Britain, where it was used for extensive tests as HMS *Meteorite*. Heinz Ullrich, a colleague of Professor Hellmuth Walter, was used as adviser on the project, and eventually Walter himself was taken to Great Britain with five of his staff, to act as constructional advisers at the Vickers-Armstrong yards in Barrow-in-Furness. Within ten years, two British versions of the Type XXVI had been constructed; *U1407* was scrapped in 1949.

Two U-boats were also used for a tour of the main ports of England to raise money for the King George V Fund for Sailors. The boats were opened for the public, who could take guided tours from members of their Royal Navy crews. At the conclusion of the tour, each member of the public was expected to contribute a small donation to the Fund. *U776* travelled westwards around the United Kingdom, visiting London, Southampton, Dover, Chatham, Harwich, Great Yarmouth, Hull, Grimsby, Middlesbrough, Blyth, Newcastle, Sunderland, Edinburgh, Rosyth, Dundee, Aberdeen, Invergordon, Kirkwall and Lerwick before moving on to Loch Ryan and Operation Deadlight. *U1023*, Heinrich Schroeteler's boat, and one of the last to fire torpedoes in anger, travelled eastward visiting Plymouth, Brixham, Falmouth, Bristol, Cardiff, Swansea, Holyhead, Liverpool, Manchester, Fleetwood, Belfast, Rothesay, Glasgow, Greenock and Oban before heading for Lisahally, also for Operation Deadlight. The tour succeeded: *U776*, for example, attracted 368,065 people to walk through her, and raised over £6,195. In London alone, where the boat was moored for ten days, 166,000 people stepped on board.

The United States were allocated four U-boats by the Tripartite Commission, to add to those that had surrendered in American ports, and thus were already in their hands. While those boats were all studied and then destroyed, others were added from the pool of U-boats in temporary holding in the United Kingdom. The so-called Black Panther, *U1105*, named after the black Alberich anti-sonar panels which covered the hull, was sailed from the United Kingdom, where it had already received the pennant *N16*, to America during 1946. The U-boat was transferred to Portsmouth, New Hampshire, where men from the Naval Research Laboratory in Washington, DC, and the Massachusetts Institute of Technology's Acoustic Laboratory conducted extensive research on the Alberich; the panels had been applied to ten boats during the war, of which this was the sole survivor. Once research was complete, the boat was then towed to Solomon's Island, Maryland, where it was destined for use in testing explosives.

Both USS *Salvager* and *Windlass* towed *U1105* into Chesapeake Bay, where she was temporarily sunk, after which salvage and dragging tests were conducted. After being raised, *U1105* was taken to Point No Point Light, and sunk on 18 November. However, the tests on the boat were not yet over. During 1949, the U-boat was raised once more and towed into the Potomac River, Maryland, where the final demolition would take place. This time the boat was being used to test the effects of a 250lb MK6 depth charge, which was suspended ten metres below the boat's keel and detonated. After being lifted bodily from the water, *U1105* sank upright, the pressure hull cracked open by the blast.

The other Walter Boat, *U1406*, was raised from where it had been scuttled in Cuxhaven harbour, and transported to the United States aboard the freighter SS *Shoemaker*,

Operation Deadlight: a Sunderland flying boat attempts to sink a stationary U-boat.

undergoing extensive trials before being broken up in New York in 1948. Two Type XXIs, *U2513* and *U3008*, were transferred to the United States, both of them still carrying key German personnel, despite American crews having been on the boat while moored at Lisahally, familiarising themselves with its systems and operation. *U3008* arrived in August 1945, and underwent extensive trials until being taken out of service in 1948, and destroyed in explosive tests in May 1954. The wreck was later broken up in Puerto Rico. *U2513* had also arrived in August 1945. This boat had a particular claim to fame: it was the final command of Ace captain Erich Topp. He had left the boat and gone into British captivity on 28 May 1945, the boat taken to the United Kingdom by his Chief Engineer. Some years after the war he met the American officer who would later act as Chief Engineer aboard *U2513* as it underwent testing.

> In 1973 I spent some time as guest in the house of Jim Bradley, who had been the US Liaison Officer at the Military Assistance and Advisory Group ... As it turned out ... Bradley had served as Chief Engineer on the boat when it was being used mainly as a target boat at the anti-submarine warfare school in Key West, Florida.
>
> But one day *U2513* took over a very special task. After the war the Americans experimented with nuclear propulsion systems. To test a novel steering mechanism for those boats, *U2513* was selected as a guinea pig, so to speak, because of all the conventional boats it enjoyed the highest underwater speed. This speed could be boosted for a short time to 24 knots by a special switching arrangement of the batteries. The project was so crucial that one day the President of the United States, Harry Truman, announced a visit to see it work. One day he showed up on board accompanied by the usual number of Secret Service Agents. The boat then got underway, reached deeper waters, dived and began the experiment. The President and his bodyguards stood in the central control room. To demonstrate the steering system in all its effectiveness, the boat's speed was increased to 24 knots. Suddenly, as a result of the heavy demand, the electrical system blacked out and complete darkness enveloped the men in the control room. When the lights came back on they illuminated the following scene. Guns drawn, the Secret Service Agents had completely surrounded the President to protect him from harm. It is not difficult to imagine what had gone through their minds. In fact, this first time on a submarine had allowed their imaginations to run wild. After all, they had heard so much about German U-boats during the war and about mysterious missions after it had ended. It all came together when the lights went out, instilling in them a belief that a *coup d'état* was under way. Thus my boat made history one more time. Later it was sold for scrap.[91]

Topp was incorrect in one factor of his account: his boat was not sold for scrap. *U2513* was hammered into the depths by the guns of destroyer USS *Owen* in October 1951, during tests of new ammunition warheads off the ASW school in Key West, Florida.

The United States showed a keen appreciation of the Kriegsmarine Type XXI design, which was reflected in the development of their own Guppy boats (Greater Underwater Propulsion Power). As well as equipping their boats with snorkels, the idea of an increased battery capacity on a standard diesel-electric boat could be directly attributed to the Type XXI. However, the first submarines that were designed along similar specifications to the German model were those of the Tang Class, six of which entered service between 1951 and 1952.

The small silhouette of a Type XXIII is towed from its anchorage towards its disposal area. The U-boats were in such poor condition that many sank en route, the warships allocated the task of towing not being the most suitable of vessels for the job.

Russia received ten U-boats from the agreement, as well as salvaging the remains of many that had fallen into their possession in occupied harbours. The most curious discovery made by the Russians was a 1:1 scale wooden replica of the Walter Boat *U1407* in the Blankenburg salt mine. The boats *U1057*, *U1058*, *U1064*, *U1231*, *U1305*, *U2353*, *U2529*, *U3035*, *U3041*, and *U3515* were all ceded to the Soviet Union by the agreement. As well as those handed over by Great Britain from the surrendered fleet, the Soviets also took possession of sectional components still lying in the shipyard at Danzig, together with unfinished Type XXIs. The advances made by German U-boat technology would have a profound effect on immediate post-war submarine development, not least of all the new levels of streamlining that the Type XXI represented.

Other nations were able to salvage one or two other U-boats to add to their navies. After the end of hostilities, Argentina handed over both of the boats which had made it to their country to the United States, who scrapped them. Spain refurbished the interned Type VIIC *U573*, which had entered Cartagena Harbour during 1942 after extensive depth-charge damage, and had been sold by the Kriegsmarine to Franco's navy. Later the boat was commissioned as *G7*, later changed to *So1*, and served until 1970. Sweden raised the Type XXI *U3503* which had been scuttled within their territorial waters off Göteborg and the crew interned, although they simply examined the wreck and its technological advances, before scrapping it. Eventually, Germany itself would also utilise scuttled U-boats, raising and refurbishing two Type XXIIIs: *U2365* and *U2367*, the former commissioned as *U-Hai*, the latter as *U-Hecht*, as well as the Type XXI *U2540*.

Among the major decisions which had been formalised by the Tripartite Commission was that while thirty U-boats were to be distributed amongst the victors for trials and experimental purposes, the remaining unallocated submarines were to be 'sunk in the open sea in a depth of not less than one hundred metres by February 15 1946.' This task became the responsibility of the Royal Navy, who still held the surrendered U-boats, rendering quite pointless any distribution amongst the three powers in order for them to share equally in the destruction. The planned destruction of the U-boat fleet was given the designation Operation Deadlight. With the value of hindsight, tempered by the contemporary desire by museums for artefacts that date from the Second World War, Operation Deadlight has come to be characterised as some form of misguided

Burial at sea: a U-boat begins to sink in Operation Deadlight.

destruction, more akin to a large-scale, but essentially futile, vendetta against a potent symbol of Germany's desire to subjugate Europe – the U-boat. However, there are several factors which are readily forgotten with that point of view. Aside from the political machinations which pervaded post-war dealings between erstwhile Allies, who were swiftly becoming more and more polarised as the Cold War approached, there was the fact that the U-boats destroyed by Operation Deadlight, amounting to 110 in all, were largely in a poor state of repair by 1946. They had languished in port while their fate was determined, with little maintenance attempted on them. Moored in the anchorages, they had been exposed to the elements, which allowed them to bump against each other as they were buffeted by winds, thus damaging the hulls, and causing what would in future become difficulties during their disposal. They were also of little military value. The victorious powers had already selected out certain boats, either to examine their technological advances or, in some cases, merely to use to bolster reduced naval strength. The remainder were either superfluous or obsolete, as they had been during the final years of the war.

On 5 November 1945, Commodore J W Farquhar, Chief of Staff of Royal Navy Rosyth Command, chaired a meeting in which the method of disposal of the U-boats was discussed. The decision was that the U-boats would be towed to an area of deep water in the North Atlantic which was approximately 100 miles northwest of Ireland, where they would be sunk. This datum position was codenamed XX. Wherever possible, the U-boats' engines were to used to assist the moving of the vessels, a skeleton German crew used to move the boats downriver from their loch berths until towlines could be attached, whereupon the former Kriegsmarine men were to be removed. Towing would be achieved by means of double bridles at a speed of not more than eight knots, reduced to seven knots for the Type XXIII U-boats. On these smaller boats the conning tower hatches were to be secured, while on all others, including Type II coastal boats, they were to remain open. In the event of a lost tow for any of the unmanned U-boats, they were to be sunk *in situ*, provided that they posed no hazard to shipping. The orders were issued on 14 November.

Thirty-six of the boats were allocated for use as aircraft targets, half for the Fleet Air Arm and half for Coastal Command crews which had not experienced action against the enemy during the previous years of war. The Coastal Command aircraft, Beaufighters, Sunderlands, Mosquitos, Liberators, and Warwicks from 18 and 19 Groups, would be armed mostly with 250lb Mk VI anti-submarine bombs. Their attack position was allocated ten miles to the south of XX, codenamed ZZ (55° 50'N X 10° 05'W). If weather conditions (according to observations aboard the carrier HMS *Nairana* on station and acting as weather ship) permitted the simultaneous operations of naval and air forces in the sinkings, then the main scuttling position would be moved to a new datum point codenamed YY (56° 10'N X 10° 05'W). All towing ships were to stand off three miles from the U-boats as they were attacked. HMS *Blencartha* was also on station nearby to act as safety ship for air-sea rescue duties. The air attacks were scheduled to be finished at 1300hrs each day to allow sufficient daylight for warships to finish off any that had not been sunk.

British submarines of the Third Flotilla undertook elaborate means to prevent any possibility of mistakenly being bombed, should either their, or any aircraft, navigation be faulty. The British submarines were painted on their casing and conning towers with three-foot-wide alternate red and yellow stripes. They were also instructed to burn a red flare from the periscope standard as further means of identifying themselves. The

A Type XXI en route to Great Britain with British officers aboard.

Four U-boats, three Type XXIIIs and a Type IX, in their Scottish anchorage prior to Operation Deadlight.

submarines HMS *Tantivy* and *Templar* were to take part in Deadlight. *Templar* was to make trials using a non-contact pistol. The instructions for *Templar* were clear: the submarine was to attack submerged, go deep after firing, and await either the explosion of the torpedo, or sufficient time for it to have passed out of the firing range.

Operation Deadlight was to be handled in two phases. The idea was to use some of the U-boats for air or submarine targets, the remainder to be disposed of using demolition charges placed aboard by the Royal Navy in both the bow and stern torpedo tubes, and at crucial hatchways within the boats. The fuses were either manually operated, or in the event of the boat being too difficult to board, by electronic fuses attached to the towing ship. Any boat that failed to sink was to be finished off either by use of the Squid weapon, or gunfire: the former was still top secret, so it was not to be used if any members of the press were aboard ship to record the moment. The beginning of the operation was slated as 25 November 1946, and on that date the first 'flight' of U-boats, each with a broad white band painted on its forecastle, was taken under tow from Loch Ryan bound for the designated destruction area. Aircraft of the Fleet Air Arm were planned to fly on D+5 and D+13, whilst the Coastal Command would operate on D+15 and D+23.

One of the most curious assignments that was given during Deadlight was to HMS *Osprey*, which was to make a gramophone recording of the sound of a U-boat sinking and being crushed at depth. To enable this, several boats were fitted with demolition charges in the stern compartment and under the conning tower hatch, but not in the bow compartment. The bulkhead doors were then closed, which would allow the bow torpedo room to remain watertight, so that the sound of it collapsing at depth could be accurately recorded using a Type 147 Sonobuoy.

However, the task proved more difficult than anticipated. The eighty-six boats which had been kept at Loch Ryan were first to go, as they had the furthest to travel to reach the designated scuttling zones. The boats had been moored in an exposed loch, and the wear and tear on them had badly affected their seaworthiness. With the exception of the naval tugs, the warships were totally unsuited to the task, particularly bearing in mind the strong currents at Moville, where the loch meets the open sea. The U-boats were unmanned and difficult to tow. Coupled with this, the weather had deteriorated and conditions were difficult, to say the least. Nonetheless, this first phase of the operation began as scheduled, and ended with the last group, Flight 14, setting sail on 28 December, after a short break for Christmas. The majority were eventually sunk by gunfire, including a large number who had broken their towline but refused to founder under their own power. In total, fifty-six of the U-boats were lost en route to the correct scuttling area.

Boats disposed of in the first phase of Operation Deadlight

Date	U-boat	Type	Sunk by
27 November	*U2322*	XXIII	Towed through the North Channel by the tug HMS *Saucy* and sunk by gunfire in YY.
	U2324	XXIII	Towed through the North Channel by the destroyer HMS *Southdown* and sunk by gunfire in YY.

The stored U-boats at Lisahally, awaiting Operation Deadlight and their somewhat inglorious end.

A Type II U-boat moves from Wilhelmshaven towards the United Kingdom after the end of hostilities.

	U2328	XXIII	Towed through the North Channel by the frigate HMS *Loch Shin*. The towline parted en route to YY and she was sunk by gunfire.
	U2345	XXIII	Towed through the North Channel by the tug HMS *Prosperous* and sunk by demolition charge in YY.
	U2361	XXIII	Towed through the North Channel by the frigate HMS *Cubitt* and sunk by gunfire in YY.
28 November	*U968*	VIIC	Towed through the North Channel by the tug HMS *Prosperous*, but foundered under tow and sank en route to YY.
	U2325	XXIII	Towed through the North Channel by the destroyer HMS *Mendip* and sunk by gunfire in YY.
	U2329	XXIII	Towed through the North Channel by the tug HMS *Masterful* and sunk in YY.
	U2334	XXIII	Towed through the North Channel by the frigate HMS *Rupert* and sunk by gunfire in YY.
	U2335	XXIII	Towed through the North Channel by the tug HMS *Enchanter* and sunk by gunfire in YY.
	U2337	XXIII	Towed through the North Channel by the Polish destroyer *Krakowiak* and sunk by gunfire in YY.
	U2350	XXIII	Towed through the North Channel by the destroyer HMS *Pytchley* and sunk by gunfire in YY.

	U2363	XXIII	Towed through the North Channel by the tug HMS *Saucy* and sunk by gunfire in YY.
29 November	*U298*	VIIC	Towed through the North Channel by the sloop HMS *Fowey* and sunk by gunfire northwest of Malin Head.
	U312	VIIC	Towed through the North Channel by the sloop HMS *Fowey* and foundered under tow north-northwest of Malin Head.
30 November	*U170*	IXC/40	Towed through the North Channel by the tug HMS *Masterful*, though the tow was unsuccessful as boat became unmanageable, and so was sunk by gunfire northwest of Malin Head.
	U281	VIIC	Towed through the North Channel by the Polish destroyer *Blyskawica* and sank under tow northwest of Malin Head.
	U328	VIIC	Towed through the North Channel by the destroyer HMS *Southdown* and sunk by aircraft northwest of Bloody Foreland.
	U369	VIIC	Towed through the North Channel by the destroyer HMS *Rupert* and foundered under tow, sinking off Malin Head.
	U481	VIIC	Towed through the North Channel by the tug HMS *Enforcer*. The towline parted and the boat was sunk by gunfire northwest of Tory Island.
	U868	IXC	Towed through the North Channel by the tug HMS *Saucy* but the towline parted and the boat went into a steep dive off Malin Head en route to YY.
1 December	*U826*	VIIC	Towed through the North Channel by the destroyer HMS *Pytchley* and sunk by gunfire in YY.
	U1004	VIIC	Towed through the North Channel by the tug HMS *Buster* and sunk by gunfire in YY.
	U1061	VIIF	Towed through the North Channel by the tug HMS *Enchanter* and sunk by gunfire in YY.
3 December	*U776*	VIIC	Towed through the North Channel by the tug HMS *Enforcer*, but foundered not far from Loch Ryan.
4 December	*U218*	VIID	Towed through the North Channel by the destroyer HMS *Southdown* and sank under tow northwest of Malin Head.
	U299	VIIC	Towed through the North Channel by the destroyer HMS *Obedient* and sank under tow north of Malin Head.
	U539	IXC/40	Towed through the North Channel by the tug HMS *Saucy* but foundered under tow to YY.

	U778	VIIC	Towed through the North Channel by the frigate HMS *Cubitt* and foundered under tow to YY.
5 December	*U994*	VIIC	Towed through the North Channel by the tug HMS *Prosperous* but foundered under tow while en route to YY.
	U1005	VIIC	Towed through the North Channel by the sloop HMS *Fowey* but foundered under tow to YY while north of Tory Island.
7 December	*U245*	VIIC	Towed through the North Channel by the tug HMS *Enchanter* and sank after the towline parted north-northwest of Rathlin Island.
	U907	VIIC	Towed through the North Channel by the tug HMS *Prosperous* and sank off Fair Head.
	U1019	VIIC	Towed through the North Channel by the destroyer HMS *Pytchley* and sunk by gunfire after the boat began to sink off Malin Head en route to YY.
8 December	*U485*	VIIC	Towed through the North Channel by the tug HMS *Buster* and sunk by gunfire from submarine HMS *Tantivy* northwest of Tory Island.
	U773	VIIC	Towed through the North Channel by the tug HMS *Freedom* and sunk by a torpedo from HMS *Tantivy* in YY.
	U775	VIIC	Towed through the North Channel by the destroyer HMS *Obedient* and sunk by gunfire.
	U1203	VIIC	Towed through the North Channel by the destroyer HMS *Mendip* and sunk by gunfire.
	U1271	VIIC/41	Towed through the North Channel by the destroyer HMS *Southdown* but foundered north of Malin Head.
	U1272	VIIC/41	Towed through the North Channel by the destroyer HMS *Rupert* and sunk by aircraft in ZZ.
9 December	*U532*	IXC/40	Towed through the North Channel by the tug HMS *Masterful* and sunk by a torpedo from HMS *Tantivy* in YY.
	U1052	VIIC	Towed through the North Channel by the frigate HMS *Cubitt* and sunk by rocket-projectile attacks by aircraft of 816 (FAA) Squadron.
	U1307	VIIC	Towed through the North Channel by the sloop HMS *Fowey* and sunk by rocket-projectile attacks by aircraft of 816 (FAA) Squadron.
11 December	*U716*	VIIC	Towed through the North Channel by the destroyer HMS *Rupert* and sunk by aircraft.
	U978		Towed through the North Channel by the tug HMS *Enchanter* and sunk by the submarine HMS *Tantivy* northwest of Bloody Foreland.

Le Millé, ex-*U471*, which sailed under the French flag after being raised from the seabed on the French Mediterranean coast.

	U991	Towed through the North Channel by the tug HMS *Freedom* and sunk by the submarine HMS *Tantivy* northwest of Bloody Foreland.
	U997	Towed through the North Channel by the tug HMS *Buster* and sunk by aircraft west-northwest of Bloody Foreland.
	U1163	Towed through the North Channel by the tug HMS *Emulous* and sunk by aircraft west-northwest of Bloody Foreland.
13 December	*U249*	Towed through the North Channel by the destroyer HMS *Southdown* and sunk by the submarine HMS *Tantivy* northwest of Tory Island.
	U255	Towed through the North Channel by the frigate HMS *Cubitt* and sunk by aircraft northwest of Tory Island.
	U293	Towed through the North Channel by the tug HMS *Masterful*. After used in practice attacks by aircraft the boat was sunk by gunfire northwest of Bloody Foreland.
	U760	Towed through the North Channel by the destroyer HMS *Mendip* and sunk by aircraft northwest of Bloody Foreland.
	U1002	Towed through the North Channel by the tug HMS *Prosperous* and sunk by the submarine HMS *Tantivy* northwest of Bloody Foreland.
15 December	*U1104*	Towed through the North Channel by the frigate HMS *Cawsand Bay*, but lost buoyancy and was

		scuttled with demolition charges northwest of Malin Head.
16 December	*U483*	Towed through the North Channel by the tug HMS *Enchanter* and sunk by gunfire northwest of Tory Island.
	U739	Towed through the North Channel by the tug HMS *Freedom* and sunk by aircraft northwest of Bloody Foreland.
	U928	Towed through the North Channel by the frigate HMS *Rupert* and sunk by aircraft northwest of Bloody Foreland.
	U992	Towed through the North Channel by the sloop HMS *Fowey* and sunk by gunfire northwest of Bloody Foreland.
	U1009	Towed through the North Channel by the frigate HMS *Loch Shin* and sunk by gunfire north of Tory Head.
	U1301	Towed through the North Channel by the tug HMS *Buster* and sunk by gunfire northwest of Bloody Foreland.
17 December	*U293*	Towed through the North Channel by the tug HMS *Masterful*. After used in practice attacks by aircraft the boat was sunk by gunfire northwest of Bloody Foreland.
	U368	Towed through the North Channel by the tug HMS *Masterful* and sunk by gunfire northwest of Bloody Foreland.
	U779	Towed through the North Channel by the

U776 leaving the Westminster Pier where it had become a major tourist attraction.

		destroyer HMS *Southdown* and sunk by gunfire northwest of Bloody Foreland.
	U956	Towed through the North Channel by the tug HMS *Prosperous* and sunk by gunfire northwest of Bloody Foreland.
	U1198	Towed through the North Channel by the destroyer HMS *Orwell* and sunk by gunfire northwest of Bloody Foreland.
	U1230	Towed through the North Channel by the frigate HMS *Cubitt* and sunk by gunfire northwest of Bloody Foreland.
21 December	U149	Towed through the North Channel by the frigate HMS *Cawsand Bay*. After the towline parted in bad weather the boat was sunk by gunfire northwest of Malin Head.
	U150	Towed through the North Channel by the destroyer HMS *Fowey* and was sunk by demolition charge northwest of Bloody Foreland.
	U155	IXC	Towed through the North Channel by the tug HMS *Prosperous*. After the towline parted in bad weather the boat was sunk by gunfire north-northwest of Malin Head.
	U291	VIIC	Towed through the North Channel by the Polish destroyer *Krakowiak*. After the towline parted in bad weather the boat was sunk by gunfire northwest of Tory Island.
	U313	Towed through the North Channel by the destroyer HMS *Blencathra*. The boat foundered and sank northwest of Tory Island after the towline parted.
	U318	VIIC-41	Towed through the North Channel by the tug HMS *Freedom*. The towline parted and the boat was sunk by gunfire north of Bloody Foreland.
	U427	Towed through the North Channel by the tug HMS *Enchanter*. The boat was sunk by gunfire northwest of Tory Island.
	U637	Towed through the North Channel by the tug HMS *Buster* and foundered under tow north-northwest of Malin Head.
	U720	Towed through the North Channel by the destroyer HMS *Quantock* and sunk by gunfire northwest of Bloody Foreland.
	U806	Towed through the North Channel by the tug HMS *Masterful*, became waterlogged and was sunk by gunfire north of Tory Island.
	U1102	Towed through the North Channel by the

		destroyer HMS *Zetland* and sunk by gunfire northwest of Bloody Foreland.
	U1110	Towed through the North Channel by the frigate HMS *Rupert*. The towline parted and she was sunk by gunfire north of Tory Island.
22 December	*U143*	Towed through the North Channel by the frigate HMS *Cubitt*. The towline parted and the boat was sunk by gunfire northwest of Aran Island.
	U145	Towed through the North Channel by the destroyer HMS *Pytchley*. The towline parted and the boat was sunk by gunfire northwest of Aran Island.
	U1194	Towed through the North Channel by the destroyer HMS *Mendip*. The towline parted and the boat was sunk by gunfire northwest of Bloody Foreland.
	U2354	Towed through the North Channel by the frigate HMS *Cosby* and sunk by gunfire northwest of Bloody Foreland.
27 December	*U2321*	Towed through the North Channel by the frigate HMS *Cubitt* and sunk by gunfire northwest of Bloody Foreland.
28 December	*U680*	Towed through the North Channel by the tug HMS *Saucy*. The towline parted and the boat sunk by gunfire north of the Giant's Causeway.
29 December	*U1233*	Towed through the North Channel by the tug HMS *Freedom*. The towline parted and the boat sunk by gunfire northwest of Tory Island.
30 December	*U1103*	Towed through the North Channel by the frigate HMS *Cawsand Bay* and sunk by gunfire northwest of Bloody Foreland.
31 December	*U1165*	Towed from Lisahally by Polish destroyer *Krakowiak* and sunk by gunfire northwest of Fanad Head by destroyer HMS *Offa*.

The second phase of Operation Deadlight was the disposal of those boats that had been grouped at Lisahally on the River Foyle near Londonderry. The U-boats were motored downriver to their final anchorage at Moville where they were abandoned, and subsequently taken under tow. These boats were taken to sea in 'lifts' rather than 'flights'. This operation proved even more difficult than the first, degenerating into a chaotic fiasco with most of the German hulks breaking free of their towing vessels and sinking outside of the designated area. It was not until 6 January that *U901* was the first boat to reach its planned location in YY. Furthermore, the trio of boats which departed on 7 January, accompanied by HMS *Templar*, to be used in the torpedo trial, all foundered in positions far removed from their designated scuttling grounds. The submarine had only managed to mount one successful trial attack – *U1109* on 6 January.

Two further boats were not disposed of until February, *U975* and *U3514* sailing from

Lisahally on 10 February, the latter the final boat sunk during Operation Deadlight. They had been withheld from destruction, the Type XXI pending the safe arrival of a sister boat, *U3515*, which was being handed over to the Soviet Union. The all-clear to scuttle these last two boats was given on 7 February 1946, although this last operation endured one false start, when HMS *Prosperous* and *U3514* both ran aground. Lieutenant Commander P U Sherwood, commander of escort vessel HMS *Loch Arkaig*, recorded the last moments of the Type XXI U-boat in his report of 12 February:

Position XX was reached at 0900hrs on Tuesday 12 February at which time I ordered *Prosperous* to cast off the tow and proceed to Moville.

At 0936hrs opened fire with 4in gun, scoring one hit on the casing forward of the conning tower at 2,000 yards. After five rounds I ceased fire, then strafed *U3514* with

U-boats scuttled inside U-boat pens from Norway to France were often repaired, and entered service in a new navy. Those that were too badly damaged were either scrapped, or in some cases in Germany, left where they were, to be buried beneath the concrete as the bunkers were destroyed by the Royal Engineers.

close range weapons.

At 0958hrs I opened fire with 'Shark' at a range of 800 yards. There was a fair amount of movement on the ship in the westerly swell, but ASDIC conditions were good and contact was firm. Of six projectiles fired, two hits were obtained and exploded amidships on the casing in line with the conning tower. A third 'Shark' hit and ricocheted off the conning tower without exploding ... I had intended to follow this up with a 'Squid' attack, but the range was too short, and before I could open out to gain a reasonable attacking position, the U-boat had plunged nose down with its stern standing vertically in the air. It sank quickly, the stern disappearing at 1004hrs in position 56.00N. 10.05W. Contact was held with 'Q' for a short time, and Type 147B recorded the depth of the U-boat up to 600 feet. After that all contact was lost, and there remained only an oil patch on the surface.[92]

Boats disposed of in the second phase of Operation Deadlight

Date	U-boat	Type	Sunk by
29 December	U930	VIIC-41	Towed from Lisahally by the destroyer HMS *Zetland* and sunk by gunfire by destroyer HMS *Onslow* west of Malin Head.
	U1022		Towed from Lisahally by the destroyer HMS *Quantock* and sunk by gunfire by Polish destroyer *Piorun* after the towline parted.
30 December	U244	VIIC	Towed from Lisahally by the tug HMS *Enchanter* and sunk by gunfire by Polish destroyer *Piorun*.
31 December	U278		Towed from Lisahally by the frigate HMS *Cawsand Bay* and sunk by gunfire by Polish destroyer *Blyskawica*.
	U294		Towed from Lisahally by the frigate HMS *Cubitt* and sunk by gunfire by HMS *Offa* north-northwest of Tory Island.
	U363	VIIC	Towed from Lisahally by the tug HMS *Saucy* and sunk by gunfire northwest of Malin Head.
	U802		Towed from Lisahally by the destroyer HMS *Pytchley*, but foundered north-northwest of Toray Island.
	U861		Towed from Lisahally by the tug HMS *Freedom* and sunk by gunfire by Polish destroyer *Blyskawica* northeast of Malin Head.
	U874		Towed from Lisahally by the destroyer HMS *Mendip*. The towline parted and the boat was sunk by gunfire from destroyer HMS *Offa* northwest of Bloody Foreland.
	U875		Towed from Lisahally by the frigate HMS *Cubitt* and sunk by gunfire from destroyer HMS *Offa* northwest of Malin Head.
	U883		Towed from Lisahally by the frigate HMS *Cosby*

			and sunk by gunfire from destroyer HMS *Offa* north-northwest of Bloody Foreland.
	U1165		Towed from Lisahally by the Polish destroyer *Krakowiak* and sunk by gunfire from destroyer HMS *Offa* northwest of Fanad Head.
	U2341		Towed from Lisahally by the destroyer HMS *Zetland* and sunk by gunfire from Polish destroyer *Blyskawica* north-northwest of Fanad Head.
3 January	*U516*		Towed from Lisahally by the destroyer HMS *Quantock* and sunk by gunfire from Polish destroyer *Piorun* northwest of Malin Head.
	U764		Towed from Lisahally by the Polish destroyer *Krakowiak* and sunk by gunfire from Polish destroyer *Piorun* north-northwest of Tory Island.
	U825		Towed from Lisahally by the destroyer HMS *Mendip*. The towline parted and the boat was sunk by gunfire from Polish destroyer *Blyskawica* north of Malin Head.
	U2336		Towed from Lisahally by the destroyer HMS *Pytchley* and sunk by gunfire northwest of Fanad Head.
	U2351		Towed from Lisahally by the tug HMS *Enchanter* and sunk by gunfire from Polish destroyer *Blyskawica* north-northwest of Fanad Head.
	U2502		Towed from Lisahally by the destroyer HMS *Mendip* and sunk by gunfire northwest of Bloody Foreland.
5 January	*U541*		Towed from Lisahally by the frigate HMS *Cosby* and sunk by gunfire from HMS *Onslaught* north-northwest of Malin Head.
	U2506		Towed from Lisahally by the tug HMS *Saucy* and sunk by gunfire north of Malin Head.
6 January	*U901*		Towed from Lisahally by the frigate HMS *Loch Shin* and sunk by gunfire northwest of Malin Head.
	U1109		Towed from Lisahally by the destroyer HMS *Zetland* and sunk by gunfire from the submarine HMS *Templar* north-northwest of Tory Island.
	U2356		Towed from Lisahally by the destroyer HMS *Blencartha* and sunk by gunfire northwest of Malin Head.
7 January	*U1010*		Towed from Lisahally by the frigate HMS *Loch Shin* and sunk by gunfire from Polish destroyer *Garland* northwest of Malin Head.
	U2511	XXI	Towed from Lisahally by the tug HMS *Enchanter* and sunk by gunfire from the frigate HMS *Sole Bay*

			north-northwest of Malin Head.
9 January	*U1023*	VIIC-41	Towed from Lisahally by the tug HMS *Saucy* and foundered under tow northwest of Malin Head.
10 February	*U975*		Towed from Lisahally by the frigate HMS *Loch Arkaig* and sunk by gunfire northwest of Bloody Foreland.
11 February	*U3514*		Towed from Lisahally by the frigate HMS *Loch Arkaig* and sunk by gunfire northwest of Bloody Foreland.

On land the last vestiges of Dönitz's U-boat fleet remained in the form of the huge, imposing concrete monoliths which had sheltered the boats in Norway, France and Germany. On Sunday, 17 October 1945, Royal Engineers used captured German explosives to blow up the Fink II U-boat pens in Hamburg. These had been constructed between 1941 and 1944 to shelter the building of boats within the expansive Finkenwerder complex. This heralded the first in a coordinated attempt to destroy the German complexes, the final such destruction carried out on the island of Helgoland on 16 April 1947 when the three box Nordsee III complex was obliterated during Operation Big Bang, using 230 tons of explosives.

Destruction of U-boat bunkers

Name	Location	Boxes	Built	Destroyed
Kilian	Kiel	2	1941-1943	25 Oct 1946
Konrad	Kiel	1 (dry-dock)	1943-1944	1945
Elbe II	Hamburg	2	1940-1941	11 Nov 1945
Fink II	Hamburg	5	1941-1944	17 Oct 1945
Nordsee III	Helgoland	3	1940-1941	16 April 1947

The sole remaining bunker is the Valentin complex in Bremen. This huge edifice was built by means which included the use of slave labour, but was incomplete by the end of the war, and was never used in its capacity as a protected construction centre. It remains intact to this day, the sole reminder of the city's close link with Kriegsmarine U-boat building.

Afterword

Thus, more than sixty years later, Dönitz's U-boat service, and indeed the Kriegsmarine as a whole, has passed into history with little physical trace remaining. Only four U-boats have survived to this day: *U505*, captured by the US Navy during the war and now on display in Chicago; *U995*, returned to Germany as a museum piece after service in the Norwegian Navy; *U534*, raised and still displayed as a near-derelict wreck in Great Britain, its future uncertain; and the *Vessikko*, a Type II built by German engineers in pre-war Finland and operated by that country's navy.

Some measure of critical hindsight has railed against the destruction of the surrendered U-boats in Operation Deadlight: to some, this might appear to have been done on an Allied whim. However, this is patently unreasonable: the boats were neglected and barely seaworthy by the time of their destruction and, although as a historian in the twenty-first century, I also mourn the loss of what would have made fascinating museum pieces, the logic of the argument is somewhat nonsensical. The destruction of the U-boats was no more a malicious act of victor's spite than was the scrapping of many famous Allied warships once their practical military lives had come to an end. Other remnants of the Kriegsmarine also met inglorious ends, such as the heavy cruiser *Prinz Eugen*, destroyed near Bikini Atoll, alongside other ships such as the carrier USS *Saratoga*. Once again, its destruction was a practical answer to the disposal of surplus military hardware and nothing more.

On land, Hitler's military machine has left monuments to its power along the entire coastline of Europe from Norway to France, and onwards to Greece. Artillery bunkers and coastal defences are still in existence in various stages of ruin or preservation. The destruction or filling-in of the German U-boat bunkers is a shame for those with an interest in that period of history but, somewhat ironically, the French have gone to considerable lengths to maintain the integrity of the majority of the U-boat bunkers that were built during German occupation. The subject of German occupation, though raw in many ways within France, is rightly remembered as a major part of that country's twentieth-century history.

The surrender of the U-boats was accomplished with very little more drama than that which accompanied the capitulation of other scattered branches of the Wehrmacht. A perpetual fascination remains as to why the U-boats unquestioningly put to sea, in the face of seemingly insurmountable odds, and when the war was obviously lost. Questioning the motivation of the commanders and crew who obeyed orders until the end is, in my opinion, a somewhat redundant activity. The U-boat service was a disciplined body of men in the service of their country. Although by May 1945 the glory days of the U-boats had long since passed, the entire service had been imbued with an almost elite sensibility. The original captains had largely been taken ashore after years in the front line, and yet their strong sense of honour and naval tradition continued to be passed on to newer generations of officers and men who swelled the ranks of the U-boat service.

In 1918, revolution aboard vessels of the Kaiser's Navy had fermented to a state whereby the fleet would not sail into combat. A single battle at Jutland had been fought, after which the High Seas Fleet remained in harbour and ineffectual. Of course, the U-boats continued their battle until the conclusion of that war, but the taint of revolutionary mutiny hung over the Kriegsmarine like an historical shadow. This, too, no doubt inspired them to fight to the last, rather than show any trace of unwillingness for combat.

For many of the younger men of the U-boat service, there was also the issue of National Socialism to inspire them to continue the fight. Many had passed through the ranks of the Hitler Youth, or were simply imbued with a fundamental belief in the rights of Germany to wage war against its enemies. This does not necessarily mean that they conformed to the Nazi stereotype so typical of Hollywood U-boat commanders, but it could help explain the motivation of some of these men. There was also the genuine fear of the enemy. When Hitler attacked Russia in 1941, the war that followed was one of ideologies: a culture clash more profound than anything experienced on the Western Front. That is not to imply that all Germans were motivated by racial ideology, but certainly by May 1945 the fear of the advancing Red Army and its treatment of captured Germans was extreme, and not without some justification. Many Germans saw Communist Russia as the real threat to Europe, some naively clinging to the belief that the Western Allies would recognise this danger, and actually join forces with the beleaguered Wehrmacht and fight the advancing Russians. Dönitz's desperate battle to prolong the combat, and thus lengthen the time available for the evacuation of German troops and civilians from the east, is testament to this attitude towards the Soviet Union, and the likely shape that Europe would take after the end of the war, with subsequent Soviet occupation. This was evident amongst all branches of the German armed forces, and even among foreign volunteers. Indeed, one of the final units to surrender in shattered Berlin were French SS troops, determined to resist the Soviets.

In the minds of many of Dönitz's men, there was also the likely implementation of the Morgenthau Plan to emasculate utterly a defeated Germany. To admit defeat in the face of such dire consequences must have seemed an appalling prospect, and also goes some way to explain the exodus of two boats from a ruined Europe, in the hope of internment in more convivial circumstances. Nowadays, communications technology has advanced to a state quite unimaginable at the time of the Second World War, that it has become too easy to forget that during that conflict both soldiers and civilians were starved of information, other than from what were official sources. The combination of harsh truths and intense propaganda no doubt stiffened German resolve in 1945, making for a resolve which would see them fight to the end and the official surrender of their country.

And once the surrender was declared, the U-boat service obeyed the orders given by their superiors. This, also, is not as unusual as many suppose. When General Percival surrendered the British garrison at Singapore to the Japanese in 1941, his men went into captivity, regardless of their personal opinions on whether the fight could have been continued. This is the nature of military service. The surrender of Dönitz's U-boats follows a standard pattern of military protocol which saw combat-worthy boats, equipment, and trained men handed over to the enemy. The instigation of 'Regenbogen' scuttlings was the sole act of defiance left to many commanders, carried out under a belief that orders issued by Dönitz under Allied pressure were unlawful. But this does not mean that those who handed over their boats to the victors intact were any less dutiful or honourable. Their interpretation of their situation was correct, abiding by the terms of Allied surrender so as to spare their men any possible reprisal.

In captivity, the men of the U-boat service were, like many German prisoners, often held for terms which breached the Hague Convention. Fortunately, very few were captured by Soviet forces, whose brutal internment of German prisoners led to the deaths of so many. French treatment of captured U-boat men was only slightly less harsh, whereas, in general, the other Western Allies provided at least adequate care to their prisoners once the echoes of the war had faded. The prolonged internment of U-boat men in the United States and United Kingdom may have breached the rights of the surrendered U-boat personnel, but they did not suffer unduly during their incarceration. At the end of the war, the horrific excesses of the Nazi regime committed in the concentration camps of occupied Europe became common knowledge, and did little to further the cause of German captives. The German nation was seen as having started two world wars in recent memory, and also as having committed such acts of genocide, that sympathy for prisoners' rights was very sparse within the Allied nations. Additionally, U-boats had been seen as sinister and merciless war machines, their crews worthy of little respect as soldiers, and this is an image that sometimes still lingers in their depiction in film and literature.

Thus when Dönitz's men flew the black flag of surrender they faced an uncertain future at the hands of the victorious Allies. However, their conduct remained worthy of Dönitz's trust in and respect for his men. They had not fought for a national cause, but rather for their nation, as had all soldiers who took part in that terrible conflict. As soldiers they obeyed orders to fight or to stand down. Eventually, in May 1945 the war was lost, and thus the Kriegsmarine U-boat service was ordered to cease its struggle. With few exceptions they did so, and passed into captivity. The strong *esprit de corps* which permeated the ranks of the U-boat service remains visible to this day. The remaining veterans wear their small replica U-boat badges unobtrusively, in a modern-day Germany sometimes still struggling to come to terms with its past, but they carry within them a sense of having belonged to a special branch of the Armed Services. They were Dönitz's men – never fully defeated in battle until ordered to lay down their arms by their Commander-in-Chief, *der Löwe* (the Lion). History should – and will – remember them.

Notes

1. Karl Dönitz, *Ten Years and Twenty Days*, p441.
2. Transcript available at http://www.ibiblio.org/pha/policy/1945/450501a.html.
3. During this patrol *U711* had taken a six man reconnaissance unit (Frontaufklärungstruppe) from *Germanske SS Norge* and landed them covertly at Seglodden, Persfjorden, two miles west of Vardø. The men were Odd Bentzen, Finn Kanderud, Sverre Holmvik, Karl Høgmo, Sverre Jensen and Yrja Nyställe. The men had received special training by the Oslo SD and had been assigned the mission by Sturmbannführer Grønheim. The group were armed with British weapons and equipped with an American radio transmitter, from which they communicated three messages to the German command in Narvik regarding enemy movements. After the end of the war, three of the men surrendered to Norwegian soldiers on 19 May, with the remaining three being captured the following day.
4. Lange survived his sole U-boat command, and was later held in British-Norwegian custody. After the war he enlisted in the German Bundesmarine, and eventually became commander of the German U-boat service.
5. http://web.ukonline.co.uk/gaz/nevs%20story.html. Copyright Sunny Updegrove/Neville Baker/Kremms World 2003.
6. The wreck of *U534* was raised by a Danish treasure-hunting consortium, which was, no doubt, sorely disappointed to discover that all they had salvaged was a combat U-boat. It was temporarily put on display in Birkenhead and has since been moved. The strange claims that the U-boat carried gold, high-ranking Nazis fleeing to South America, or even Heinrich Himmler himself, are the height of fantasy, and even the guide who showed this author around the boat recounted tales of SS intrigue that included the murder of Russian slave labourers used by the SS to load the boat after it had been commandeered by Himmler's staff. Tales such as these, for which there is no convincing evidence, perpetuate the myth of 'U-boat killers' which unfortunately often persists today. For example, the Hollywood film, *U571* (a genuine U-boat number), portrays the murder of a lifeboat full of survivors. In this film U-boat men are characterised as being single-minded, dedicated Nazis, to a man. This simplistic polarisation of good and bad when dealing with the combatants of the Second World War seems unhelpful, whatever one's opinion of the rights and wrongs of history.
7. Norman Franks, *Search, Find and Kill*, p83.
8. *U2365* was later raised and repaired, and recommissioned into the Bundesmarine as *U-Hai* on 15 August 1957 as Germany's first post-war U-boat. Tragically, while on exercise in the North Sea, a welded seam of the prefabricated boat split, and *U-Hai* instantly flooded, killing nineteen men and leaving a sole survivor. Raised once more on 24 September 1966, the wreck was broken up.
9. Franks, p84.

10. Kapitänleutnant Kurt Petersen's Type IXC-40 *U541* was involved in an interesting incident on 26 May 1944. The U-boat sighted and stopped the neutral Portuguese steamer *Serpa Pinto* which was carrying 200 Jewish refugees. After he radioed for instructions regarding the ship, Dönitz personally ordered the Portuguese vessel to be released.

11. Reinhard Kramer and Wolfgang Müller, *Gesunken und Verschollen*, pp171-2.

12. Report on scuttling of *U979*. 'Enclosure No 2 to Flag Officer, Western Germany, No 3/3/4/56 of 23rd June 1945 – Interrogation of First Lieutenant of *U979*'; copy held in U-Boot Archiv, Altenbruch, Germany.

13. Heinz Schäffer, *U-Boat 977*, pp168-9.

14. Schäffer, p170.

15. Schäffer, p199.

16. http://www.bbc.co.uk/ww2peopleswar/stories/23/a4029923.shtml.

17. http://www.bbc.co.uk/ww2peopleswar/stories/08/a4128608.shtml.

18. *Royal Navy News*, 'Commemoration of World War Two – Victory in Europe', May 2005.

19. *Royal Navy News*, 'Commemoration of World War Two – Victory in Europe', May 2005.

20. Pat Godwin, 'The Forgotten Operation', published July 2004 as part of the Destroyer Escort Sailors Association, available online at: http://www.desausa.org/history.htm.

21. Georg-Wilhelm Schulz, *Über dem Nassen Abgrund*, p208.

22. Schulz, p209.

23. Schulz and his entire flotilla eventually surrendered to a Colonel Grey of the British 8 Corps. Grey arrived on Fehrman, unaware that an entire training flotilla had taken refuge there. Once more, the unit was temporarily left to its own devices before transport to captivity was arranged. On 13 May, the 25th U-Training Flotilla was officially disbanded, Schulz facing questions from the victors regarding his order to scuttle boats at Travemünde.

24. Hitler's 'Scorched Earth' Decree (Nero Decree) (March 19, 1945), in *United States Chief Counsel for the Prosecution of Axis Criminality, Nazi Conspiracy and Aggression. Supplement B*, Washington, DC: United States Government Printing Office, 1948; Speer Document 27, pp. 950-1. English translation edited by GHI staff.

25. Reinhard Kramer and Wolfgang Müller, *Gesunken und Verschollen*, pp38-9.

26. Dönitz, pp458-9

27. Erich Topp, *The Odyssey of a U-Boat Commander*, p109.

28. Georg Högel, *U-boat Emblems*, p180.

29. Högel, p182.

30. *Royal Navy News*, 'Commemoration of World War Two – Victory in Europe', May 2005.

31. Gimpel and Colepaugh were both subsequently tried and sentenced to death, though their sentences were commuted by President Truman in September 1945. Gimpel was released in 1955 after ten years incarceration in Alcatraz, Colepaugh paroled in 1960.

32. Opinion remains divided whether Speer was referring to the existing V1 and V2 weapons, and was simply misquoted by the 'U' rather than 'V', or to the possibility of using uranium weapons, ie nuclear weapons. Either way, the idea remained little more than fanciful at that stage of the conflict.

33. 0336/3, April 1945.

34. Paul Kemp, *Strike from the Sea – Submarine Action*, p103.

35. Interview conducted with Georg Seitz by Christian Prag, and now included in Christian's book, *No Ordinary War: The Eventful Career of U-604*, London 2009.

36. A V Sellwood, *The Warring Seas*, pp208-9.

37. Sellwood, p210-11.

38. 'Report of the Naval Inspector General Regarding Irregularities Connected with the Handling of Surrendered German Submarines', US Navy Department, FF1/A17-25, 19 June 1945, available online at http://www.uboatarchive.net/U-873NIGReport.htm.

39. 'Reply from Jack H Alberti to Vice Chief of Naval Operations', 27 July 1945, available online at http://www.uboatarchive.net/U-873AlbertReply.htm.

40. 'Reply from Jack H Alberti to Vice Chief of Naval Operations', 27 July 1945.

41. Second Endorsement to Report on 'Follow Up Regarding Irregularities Connected with the Handling of Surrendered German Submarines', dated 1 September 1945, available online at http://www.uboatarchive.net/U-873FollowUp.htm.

42. James McGovern, *Crossbow and Overcast*, p104. Overcast was renamed Operation Paperclip in March 1946.

43. Sellwood, p187.

44. Wolfgang Hirschfeld, *The Secret Diary of a U-Boat*, p210.

45. Hirschfeld, p214.

46. *Surrender at Sea – Daily Updates Condensed from WHEB Radio Evening News*, Portsmouth, NH, compiled by Richard Winslow, Portsmouth-Built, Portsmouth Marine Society, 1989.

47. Extract held in U-Boot Archiv file on *U234*, taken from Robert K Wilcox, *Japan's Secret War: Japan's race against time to build its own atomic bomb*, Marlowe Publishing, 1995.

48. US National Archives NARA II, memorandum written by Jack H Alberti to Captain John L Rihaldaffer, 24 May 1945, declassified #NND903015, NARA, 12 December 1991.

49. US National Archives NARA II, document surrendered with *U234* entitled 'Verwendung ultraviolette Strahlung', FB 1598, by Hans Klumb and Bernhard Koch – N Wa 30571/44.

50. Gerhard Both, *Without Hindsight*, p259.

51. Dönitz, pp433-4.

52. H G Schütze, *Operation unter Wasser*, p232.

53. Three further divisions (in name only, barely likely to have been anywhere near divisional strength – the 3rd, 11th and 16th) were also ordered to form elements of what appears to be the 3rd, seeing some action during the final Russian drive on Berlin. However, while discussing the situation with General Generaloberst Gotthard Heinrici, charged at that time with the defence of Berlin, SS Obergruppenführer Felix Steiner, whose troops were expected to break through the Russian cordon around Berlin and lift the siege, said, 'The Navy men I can forget about, I bet they're great on ships, but they've never been trained for this kind of fighting.'

54. Interview with Ludwig Stöll.

55. Both, pp261-3.

56. Topp, pp106-7.

57. Topp, p107.

58. Both, p268.

59. Cornelius Ryan, *The Last Battle*, pp187-9. This story, and countless others, was told by Ryan, who spent months in conversations with Heinrici about the events that the German commander recalled during the Battle for Berlin.

60. Jak P Mallmann-Showell (ed), *Führer Conferences on Naval Affairs*, p 444.

61. *No Triumphant Procession*, John Russell, p111.

62. Earl of Rosse and E R Hill, *The Story of the Guards Armoured Division*.

63. Percy E Schramm, *Kriegstagebuch des OKW*, Band 8, Bernard & Graefe, 2005, p1266.

64. *History of 30AU*, p85, photographed extract from Fleming's Black List.

65. *History of 30AU*, The National Archives, Kew, ADM223/214.

66. http://www.navynews.co.uk/ww2/ve_day3.asp.

67. Joseph Goebbels, *The Goebbels Diaries 1942-1943*, ed Louis B Lochner, p52.

68. Interestingly, after Böhme surrendered in Norway, he was brought before the so-called 'Hostages Trial', a subdivision of the Nuremberg Trials, and found to be innocent of the war crimes charge associated with his time in Serbia. The Hague Convention did not actually deny the ability to execute captured partisans, and allowed the taking of civilian hostages. Furthermore, the tribunal noted that both the American and British Armies' handbooks on

land warfare allowed reprisals against civilians; the American Basic Field Manual going so far as to specify that they could be executed. Böhme was no longer alive when the verdict was delivered: on 29 May 1947 he had committed suicide by leaping from the fourth storey of the prison in which he was being held.

69. Dönitz, pp450, 456.
70. Dönitz, pp456-7.
71. 'Norway's Liberation', published as 'Norway's History', Tor Dagre, former editor of *Nytt fra Norge*, on www.norwegian-scenery.com.
72. Topp, p110.
73. Letter from Lieutenant Jack Whitton, DSC, 2 November 1986. Held at RNSM.
74. Herbert Werner, *Iron Coffins*, p307.
75. Topp, pp111-12.
76. Jak P Mallmann-Showell (ed), *Führer Conferences on Naval Affairs*, p471.
77. *Führer Conferences*, p472.
78. *Führer Conferences*, p417.
79. Admiralty translation of BdU War Diary, 1 January 1945, copy held at Royal Navy Submarine Museum.
80. When Schirlitz was taken to a prisoner-of-war camp, his French counterpart Hubert Meyer visited him in captivity. Appalled at what he saw, Meyer protested vigorously against the conditions in which the German prisoners were held. When Schirlitz asked him for news about his family, whom he believed had been killed in an air raid on Kiel, Meyer located his wife for him. Schirlitz was then falsely accused of war crimes: it was alleged that he had condoned the murder of three French prisoners-of-war by a German sergeant. Again, it was Meyer who rushed to Schirlitz's aid. Based in Lebanon at the time, he returned immediately to Bordeaux to testify before a military tribunal to the Admiral's impeccable behaviour. Schirlitz was acquitted and released.
81. Herbert Werner, *Iron Coffins*, p302.
82. Werner, pp306-7.
83. The National Archives, Kew, ref WO19/1483.
84. Interestingly, this is the same day that Britain's wartime leader Winston Churchill resigned, to be replaced by Clement Attlee.
85. Reinhard Suhren, *Teddy Suhren*, pp224-5.
86. R F Keeling, *Gruesome Harvest: The Costly Attempt to Exterminate the People of Germany*, p25. Keeling, in turn, ascribes the quotation to the London *Financial Times*, 24 May 1946, based on a report from the Swedish Minister of Foreign Trade, M Gunnar Myrdal.
87. Author interview with Georg Högel, December 2002.
88. Author interview with Jürgen Oesten, October 2005.
89. Jordan Vause, *Lone Wolf*, pp211-12.
90. *The Berlin (Potsdam) Conference, July 17–August 2, 1945; Protocol of the Proceedings, 1 August, 1945*, copy online at Yale Law School's Avalon Project (Documents in Law, History and Diplomacy), http://avalon.law.yale.edu/20th_century/decade17.asp.
91. Topp, pp116-17.
92. 'Operation Deadlight', *After The Battle* magazine, issue 36, p47.

Appendix

Appendix A

U-boats at sea when Dönitz issued the order to cease fire

Boat	Sailed	Returned	Final Destination
U190	19 February	14 May	St John's, Canada
U218	22 March	8 May	Bergen, Norway
U234	16 April	19 May	Portsmouth, USA
U244	15 March	14 May	Loch Foyle, UK
U245	9 April	9 May	Bergen, Norway
U255	8 May	19 May	Loch Alsh, UK
U278	10 April	9 May	Narvik, Norway
U287	29 April	16 May	Sunk
U293	1 April	11 May	Loch Eriboll, UK
U295	15 April	7 May	Narvik, Norway
U312	16 April	8 May	Narvik, Norway
U313	17 April	8 May	Narvik, Norway
U318	1 April	10 May	Narvik, Norway
U320	27 April	8 May	Sunk
U363	18 April	8 May	Narvik, Norway
U481	7 April	4 May	Narvik, Norway
U485	29 April	14 May	Gibraltar
U516	5 April	14 May	Loch Eriboll, UK
U530	3 March	10 July	Mara del Plata, Argentina
U532	13 January	10 May	Liverpool, UK
U534	4 May	5 May	Sunk
U541	7 April	12 May	Gibraltar
U739	1 April	13 May	Emden, Germany
U764	26 April	14 May	Loch Eriboll, UK
U776	22 March	16 May	Portland, UK
U802	28 April	11 May	Loch Eriboll, UK
U805	17 March	16 May	Boston, USA
U825	1 April	10 May	Portland, UK
U853	23 February	6 May	Sunk

U858	11 March	14 May	Cape May, New Jersey, USA
U873	30 March	17 May	Portsmouth, USA
U881	7 April	6 May	Sunk
U889	5 April	13 May	Halifax, Canada
U901	14 April	15 May	Stavanger, Norway
U907	29 April	5 May	Bergen, Norway
U956	2 April	13 May	Loch Eriboll, UK
U963	23 April	20 May	Scuttled off Portugal
U968	21 April	6 May	Harstad, Norway
U977	2 May	17 August	Mara del Plata, Argentina
U979	29 March	24 May	Scuttled off Denmark
U992	1 May	9 May	Narvik, Norway
U1005	3 May	14 May	Bergen, Norway
U1009	29 March	10 May	Loch Eriboll, UK
U1010	15 April	14 May	Loch Eriboll, UK
U1023	25 March	10 May	Weymouth, UK
U1058	28 April	10 May	Loch Eriboll, UK
U1105	12 April	10 May	Loch Eriboll, UK
U1109	17 April	12 May	Loch Eriboll, UK
U1163	15 April	9 May	Marviken, Norway
U1165	21 April	5 May	Narvik, Norway
U1228	14 April	13 May	Portsmouth, USA
U1231	27 April	14 May	Loch Foyle, UK
U1272	29 April	10 May	Bergen, Norway
U1277	21 April	3 June	Scuttled off Portugal
U1305	4 April	10 May	Loch Eriboll, UK
U2324	2 April	8 May	Stavanger, Norway
U2326	4 May	14 May	Dundee, UK
U2336	1 May	14 May	Kiel, Germany
U2511	3 May	6 May	Bergen, Norway

Appendix B

Surrender instructions transmitted to all U-boats

ANNEXURE 'A'

SURRENDER OF GERMAN U-BOAT FLEET

To all 'U' Boats at sea:

Carry out the following instructions forthwith which have been given by the Allied Representatives

Surface immediately and remain surfaced.

Report immediately in P/L your position in latitude and longitude and number of your U-boat to nearest British, US, Canadian or Soviet coast W/T station on 500 kc/s (600 metres) and to call sign GZZ 10 on one of the following high frequencies: 16845 - 12685 or 5970 kc/s.

Fly a large black or blue flag by day.

Burn navigation lights by night.

Jettison all ammunition, remove breech blocks from guns and render torpedoes safe by removing pistols.

All mines are to be rendered safe.

Make all signals in P/L [Plain Language].

Follow strictly the instructions for proceeding to Allied ports from your present area given in immediately following message.

Observe strictly the orders of Allied Representatives to refrain from scuttling or in any way damaging your U-boat.

These instructions will be repeated at two-hour intervals until further notice.

ANNEXURE 'B'

To all U-boats at sea:

Observe strictly the instructions already given to remain fully surfaced. Report your position course and speed every 8 hours. Obey any instructions that may be given to you by any Allied authority.

The following are the areas and routes for U-boats surrendering –

(1) Area 'A'

a. Bound on West by meridian 026 degs West and South by parallel 043 degs North in Barents Sea by meridian 020 degs East in Baltic Approaches by line joining the Naze and Hantsholm but excludes Irish Sea between 051 degs thirty mins and 055 degs 00 mins North and English Channel between line of Lands End Scilly Islands Ushant and line of Dover-Calais.

b. Join one of following routes at nearest point and proceed along it to Loch Eriboll (058 degs 33 minutes North 004 degs 37 mins West).

Blue route: All positions North and West unless otherwise indicated:

049 degs 00 mins 009 degs 00 mins 053 degs 00 mins
012 degs 00 mins 058 degs 00 mins 011 degs 00 mins
059 degs 00 mins 005 degs 30 mins thence to Loch Eriboll

Red route:

053 degs 45 mins North 003 degs 00 mins East
059 degs 45 mins 001 degs 00 mins 059 degs 45 mins
003 degs 00 mins thence to Loch Eriboll.

c. Arrive at Loch Eriboll between sunrise and 3 hours before sunset.

(2) Area 'B'

a. The Irish Sea between parallel of 051 degs 30 mins and 055 degs 00 mins North.

b. Proceed Beaumaris Bay (053 degs 19 mins North 003 degs 58 mins West) to arrive between sunrise and 3 hours before sunset.

(3) Area 'C'

a. The English Channel between line of Lands End - Scilly Isles - Ushant and line of Dover - Calais.

b. 'U' Boats in area 'C' are to join one of following routes at nearest point: Green route: position 'A' 049 degs 10 mins North 005 degs 40 mins West position 'B' 050 degs oo mins North 003 degs oo mins West thence escorted to Weymouth. Orange route: position 'X' 050 degs 30 mins North 000 degs 50 mins East position 'Y' 050 degs 10 mins North 001 degs 50 mins West thence escorted to Weymouth.

c. Arrive at either 'B' or 'Y' between sunrise and 3 hours before sunset.

(4) Area 'D'

a. Bound on West by lines joining The Naze and Hantsholm and on East by lines joining Lübeck and Trelleborg.

b. Proceed to Kiel.

(5) Area 'E'

a. Mediterranean Approaches bound on North by 043 degs North on South by 026 degs North and on West by 026 degs West.

b. Proceed to a rendezvous in position 'A' 036 degs oo mins North 011 degs oo mins West and await escort reporting expected time of arrival in plain language to Admiral Gibraltar on 500 kc/s.

c. Arrive in position 'A' between sunrise and noon G.M.T.

(6) Area 'F'

a. The North and South Atlantic West of 026 degs West.

b. Proceed to nearest of one of following points arriving between sunrise and 3 hours before sunset: W 043 degs 30 mins North 070 degs oo mins West approach from a point 15 miles due East X 038 degs 20 mins North 074 degs 25 mins West approach from a point 047 degs 18 mins North 051 30 mins West on a course 270 degs Z 043 31 mins North 065 degs 05 mins West approach from point 042 degs 59 mins North 054 degs 28 mins West on a course 320 degs.

Appendix C

U-boats scuttled under Operation Regenbogen

U-boat	Type	Date	Commander
U8	IIB	2 May	ObltzS Jürgen Kriegshammer
U14	IIB	2 May	Unknown
U17	IIB	5 May	Unknown
U120	IIB	2 May	ObltzS Rolf Rüdiger Bensel
U121	IIB	2 May	ObltzS Friedrich Horst
U57	IIC	3 May	ObltzS Peter Kühl
U5	IIC	3 May	ObltzS Richard Schulz
U59	IIC	3 May	LzS Herbert Walther
U60	IIC	2 May	ObltzS Herbert Giesewetter
U61	IIC	2 May	ObltzS Werner Zapf
U62	IIC	2 May	ObltzS Hans-Eckart Augustine
U137	IID	2 May	ObltzS Hans-Joachim Dierks
U139	IID	2 May	ObltzS Walter Kimmelmann
U140	IID	2 May	ObltzS Wolfgang Scherfling
U141	IID	2 May	ObltzS Heinrich-Dietrich Hoffmann
U142	IID	2 May	ObltzS Friedrich Baumgärtel

U146	IID	2 May	ObltzS Carl Schauroth
U148	IID	2 May	ObltzS Renko Tammen
U151	IID	2 May	ObltzS Graf Ferdinand von Arco
U152	IID	2 May	ObltzS Gernot Thiel
U30	VII	4 May	Unknown
U46	VIIB	4 May	Unknown
U48	VIIB	3 May	Unknown
U52	VIIB	3 May	Unknown
U71	VIIC	2 May	Unknown
U72	VIIC	2 May	Unknown
U236	VIIC	5 May	Unknown
U267	VIIC	4 May	ObltzS Bernhard Knieper
U290	VIIC	3 May	ObltzS Heinz Baum
U316	VIIC	2 May	ObltzS Gottfried König
U339	VIIC	3 May	Unknown
U349	VIIC	5 May	ObltzS Wolfgang Dähne
U351	VIIC	5 May	ObltzS Hugo Strehl
U370	VIIC	5 May	ObltzS Karl Nielsen
U382	VIIC	8 May	Unknown
U397	VIIC	5 May	Kaptlt Gerhard Groth
U428	VIIC	3 May	ObltzS Hans-Ulrich Hanitsch
U446	VIIC	3 May	Unknown
U475	VIIC	3 May	Kaptlt Otto Stoeffler
U552	VIIC	2 May	ObltzS Günther Lube
U554	VIIC	2 May	ObltzS Werner Remus
U560	VIIC	3 May	ObltzS Paul Jacobs
U612	VIIC	2 May	ObltzS Hans-Peter Dick
U704	VIIC	3 May	Unknown
U708	VIIC	3 May	ObltzS Herbert Kühn
U717	VIIC	2 May	ObltzS Siegfried Rothkirch und Panthen
U721	VIIC	4 May	ObltzS Ludwig Fabricius
U733	VIIC	5 May	ObltzS Ulrich Hammer
U746	VIIC	5 May	ObltzS Ernst Lottner
U748	VIIC	3 May	ObltzS Gottfried Dingler
U750	VIIC	5 May	ObltzS Justus Grawert
U822	VIIC	3 May	ObltzS Josef Elsinghorst
U903	VIIC	3 May	Kaptlt Otto Tinschert
U904	VIIC	4 May	ObltzS Günter Stührmann
U922	VIIC	3 May	ObltzS Erich Käselau
U924	VIIC	3 May	ObltzS Hans-Jürg Schild
U958	VIIC	3 May	ObltzS Friedrich Stege
U1056	VIIC	5 May	ObltzS Gustav Schröder
U1101	VIIC	5 May	ObltzS Rudolf Dübler
U1132	VIIC	4 May	ObltzS Walter-Bruno Koch
U1161	VIIC	4 May	Kaptlt Bruno Schwalbach
U1162	VIIC	5 May	Kaptlt Hans-Heinrich Ketels
U1192	VIIC	3 May	ObltzS Karl-Heinz Meenen
U1193	VIIC	5 May	ObltzS Joachim Guse
U1196	VIIC	3 May	ObltzS Rene Ballert
U1201	VIIC	8 May	ObltzS Reinhold Merkle

U1204	VIIC	5 May	ObltzS Erwin Jestel
U1205	VIIC	3 May	Kaptlt Hermann Zander
U1207	VIIC	5 May	ObltzS Kurt Lindemann
U323	VIIC/41	3 May	ObltzS Hans-Jürgen Dobinsky
U827	VIIC/41	5 May	Kaptlt Kurt Baberg
U828	VIIC/41	3 May	ObltzS Alfred John
U929	VIIC/41	2 May	ObltzS Werner Schulz
U999	VIIC/41	5 May	ObltzS Wolfgang Heibges
U1007	VIIC/41	2 May	Kaptlt Ernst von Witzendorff
U1008	VIIC/41	6 May	ObltzS Hans Gessner
U1016	VIIC/41	5 May	ObltzS Walther Ehrhardt
U1025	VIIC/41	5 May	ObltdR Ewald Pick
U1166	VIIC/41	3 May	Unknown. Previously decommissioned
U1168	VIIC/41	4 May	Kaptlt Hans Umlauf
U1170	VIIC/41	3 May	Kaptlt Friedrich Justi
U1275	VIIC/41	8 May	ObltzS Günther Frohberg
U1303	VIIC/41	4 May	ObltzS Helmut Herglotz
U1304	VIIC/41	4 May	ObltzS Walter Süss
U1306	VIIC/41	5 May	ObltzS Ulrich Kiessling
U1308	VIIC/41	2 May	ObltzS Heinrich Besold
U37	IX	8 May	Kaptlt Eberhard von Wenden
U38	IX	5 May	KK Georg Peters
U876	IX-D2	3 May	Kaptlt Rolf Bah
U1223	IXC/40	5 May	ObltzS Albert Kneip
U1227	IXC/40	3 May	ObltzS Friedrich Altmeier
U1234	IXC/40	5 May	ObltzS Hans-Christian Wrede
U2501	XXI	3 May	Kaptlt (Ing.) Hans Noack
U2503	XXI	4 May	Kaptlt Karl-Jürg Wächter
U2504	XXI	3 May	Oblt (Ing.) Karl-Heinz Trelle
U2505	XXI	3 May	ObltzS Joachim Düppe
U2507	XXI	5 May	Kaptlt Paul Siegmann
U2508	XXI	3 May	ObltzS Uwe Christiansen
U2510	XXI	2 May	ObltzS Werner Herrmann
U2512	XXI	3 May	Kaptlt Hubert Nordheimer
U2517	XXI	5 May	ObltzS Hermann Hansen
U2519	XXI	3 May	KK Peter-Erich Cremer
U2520	XXI	3 May	KK Rudolf Schendel
U2522	XXI	5 May	Kaptlt Horst-Thilo Queck
U2524	XXI	3 May	Kaptlt Ernst von Witzendorff
U2525	XXI	5 May	Kaptlt Paul-Friedrich Otto
U2526	XXI	2 May	ObltzS Otto Hohmann
U2527	XXI	2 May	ObltzS Hans Götze
U2528	XXI	2 May	Oblt (Ing.) Gustav Hennigs
U2531	XXI	2 May	Kaptlt Hellmut Niss
U2533	XXI	3 May	ObltzS Horst Günther
U2534	XXI	3 May	Kaptlt Ulrich Drews
U2535	XXI	3 May	Kaptlt Otto Bitter
U2536	XXI	3 May	ObltzS Ulrich Vöge
U2538	XXI	8 May	ObltzS Heinrich Klapdor
U2539	XXI	3 May	ObltzS Johann Johann

U2540	XXI	4 May	ObltzS Rudolf Schultze
U2541	XXI	5 May	Kaptlt Rolf-Birger Wahlen
U2543	XXI	3 May	ObltzS Gottfried Stolzenburg
U2544	XXI	5 May	ObltzS Rudolf Meinlschmidt
U2545	XXI	3 May	ObltzS Freiherr Hans-Bruno von Müffling
U2546	XXI	3 May	ObltzS Max Dobbert
U2548	XXI	3 May	ObltzS Karl-Erich Utischill
U2552	XXI	3 May	Kaptlt Johannes Rudolph
U3001	XXI	3 May	Kaptlt Wilhelm Peters
U3002	XXI	2 May	FK Hermann Kaiser
U3004	XXI	2 May	Kaptlt Otto Peschel
U3005	XXI	3 May	Kaptlt Johannes Hinrichs
U3010	XXI	3 May	FK Erich Topp
U3011	XXI	3 May	ObltzS Otto Fränzel
U3012	XXI	3 May	ObltzS Alfred Meier
U3013	XXI	3 May	Kaptlt Volker Simmermache
U3014	XXI	3 May	Kaptlt Karl-Heinz Marbach
U3015	XXI	5 May	Kaptlt Peter-Ottmar Grau
U3016	XXI	2 May	ObltzS Bernhard Meentzen
U3018	XXI	2 May	ObltzS Siegfried Breinlinger
U3019	XXI	2 May	ObltzS Ernst-August Racky
U3020	XXI	2 May	ObltzS Heinrich Mäueler
U3021	XXI	2 May	ObltzS Kurt van Meteren
U3022	XXI	5 May	Kaptlt Paul Weber
U3023	XXI	3 May	ObltzS Erich Harms
U3024	XXI	3 May	ObltzS Fredinand Blaich
U3025	XXI	3 May	Kaptlt Hans Vogel
U3026	XXI	3 May	ObltzS Günther Drescher
U3027	XXI	3 May	Kaptlt Karl Mehne
U3028	XXI	3 May	Kaptlt Erwin Christophersen
U3029	XXI	3 May	Kaptlt Hermann Lamby
U3030	XXI	8 May	ObltzSzS Bernhard Luttmann
U3031	XXI	3 May	ObltzSzS Heinrich Sach
U3033	XXI	4 May	ObltzSzS Peter Callsen
U3034	XXI	4 May	ObltzSzS Horst Willner
U3037	XXI	3 May	Kaptlt Gustav-Adolf Janssen
U3038	XXI	3 May	ObltzSzS Matthias Brünig
U3039	XXI	3 May	Kaptlt Günter Ruperti
U3040	XXI	3 May	ObltdR Heinz Robbert
U3044	XXI	5 May	Kaptlt Detlef von Lehsten
U3501	XXI	5 May	Kaptlt Hans-Joachim Schmidt-Weichert
U3503	XXI	8 May	ObltzS Hugo Deiring
U3504	XXI	2 May	Kaptlt Karl-Hartwig Sieboid
U3506	XXI	2 May	Kaptlt Gerhard Thäter
U3507	XXI	3 May	ObltzS Hans-Jürgen Schley
U3509	XXI	3 May	ObltzS Wilhelm Neitzsch
U3510	XXI	5 May	ObltzS Ernst-Werner Schwirley
U3511	XXI	3 May	Kaptlt Hermann Schrenk
U3513	XXI	3 May	ObltzS Richard Nachtigall
U3516	XXI	2 May	ObltzS Heinrich Grote

U3517	XXI	2 May	Kaptlt Helmut Münster
U3518	XXI	3 May	Kaptlt Herbert Brünning
U3521	XXI	2 May	ObltzS Günther Keller
U3522	XXI	2 May	ObltzS Dieter Lenzmann
U3524	XXI	5 May	KK Hans-Ludwig Witt
U3525	XXI	3 May	Kaptlt Franz Kranich
U3526	XXI	5 May	ObltzS Kurt Hilbig
U3527	XXI	5 May	Kaptlt Willy Kronenbitter
U3528	XXI	5 May	Kaptlt Heinz Zwarg
U3529	XXI	5 May	ObltzS Karl-Heinz Schmidt
U3530	XXI	3 May	ObltzS Walter-Ernst Koc
U2327	XXIII	2 May	ObltzS Hans-Walter Pahl
U2330	XXIII	3 May	ObltzS Hans Beckmann
U2333	XXIII	5 May	ObltzS Heinz Baumann
U2339	XXIII	5 May	ObltzS Germanus Woermann
U2343	XXIII	5 May	Kaptlt Hans-Ludwig Gaude
U2346	XXIII	5 May	ObltzS Hermann von der Höh
U2347	XXIII	5 May	ObltzS Willibald Ulbing
U2349	XXIII	5 May	ObltzS Hans-Georg Müller
U2352	XXIII	5 May	ObltzS Sigmund Budzyn
U2355	XXIII	3 May	ObltzS Hans-Heino Franke
U2357	XXIII	5 May	ObltzS Erwin Heinrich
U2358	XXIII	5 May	ObltzS Gerhard Breun
U2360	XXIII	5 May	ObltzS Kurt Schrobach
U2362	XXIII	5 May	ObltzS Martin Czekowski
U2364	XXIII	5 May	Kaptlt Gerhard Remus
U2365	XXIII	8 May	ObltzS Uwe Christiansen
U2365	XXIII	8 May	ObltzS Fritz-Otto Korfmann
U2366	XXIII	5 May	ObltzS Kurt Jäckel
U2368	XXIII	5 May	ObltzS Fritz Ufermann
U2369	XXIII	5 May	ObltzS Hans-Walter Pahl
U2369	XXIII	5 May	ObltzS Hermann Schulz
U2371	XXIII	3 May	ObltzS Johannes Kühne
U4701	XXIII	5 May	ObltzS Arnold Wiechmann
U4702	XXIII	5 May	ObltzS Edgar Seeliger
U4703	XXIII	5 May	ObltzS Hans-Ulrich Scholz
U4704	XXIII	5 May	ObltzS Gerhard Franceschi
U4705	XXIII	3 May	ObltzS Martin Landt-Hayen
U4707	XXIII	5 May	ObltzS Joachim Leder
U4709	XXIII	4 May	ObltzS Paul Berkemann
U4710	XXIII	5 May	ObltzS Ludwig-Ferdinand von Friedeburg
U4711	XXIII	4 May	ObltzS Siegfried Endler
U4712	XXIII	3 May	ObltzS Karl-Heinz Rohlfing
U792	XVIIA	4 May	ObltzS Hans Diederich Duis
U793	XVIIA	4 May	ObltzS Friedrich Schmidt
U794	XVIIA	5 May	ObltzS Philipp Becker
U795	XVIIA	3 May	ObltzS Horst Selle
U1405	XVIIB	5 May	ObltdR Wilhelm Rex
U1406	XVIIB	5 May	ObltzS Werner Klug
U1407	XVIIB	5 May	ObltzS Horst Heitz

Bibliography

Barnett, Correlli, *Engage the Enemy More Closely*, Hodder & Stoughton, London, 1992.

Blair, Clay, *Hitler's U-Boat War*, Cassell & Co, London, 2000.

Both, Gerhard, *Without Hindsight*, Janus Publishing, 1999.

Braeuer, Luc, *La Base Sous-Marine de Saint-Nazaire*, SPEI-Pulnoy, 2003.

Brennecke, Jochen, *Die Wende im U-Boot Krieg*, Weltbild Verlag, Augsburg, 1995.

Dönitz, Karl, *Ten Years and Twenty Days*, Weidenfeld & Nicolson, 1958.

Franks, Norman, *Search, Find and Kill*, Grub Street, London, 1995.

Goebbels, Joseph, *The Goebbels Diaries, 1942-1943*, edited by Louis B Lochner, Doubleday, New York, 1948.

Hadley, Michael L, *U-boats against Canada*, McGill-Queen's University Press, Kingston and Montreal, 1985.

Hessler, Günter, *The U-Boat War in the Atlantic*, HMSO, London, 1989.

Hirschfeld, Wolfgang, *The Secret Diary of a U-boat*, Orion Books, London, 1997.

Högel, Georg, *U-boat Emblems of World War Two*, Schiffer Military History, Atglen, PA, USA, 1999.

Keeling, R F, *Gruesome Harvest: The Costly Attempt to Exterminate the People of Germany*, Institute of American Economics, Chicago, 1947.

Kemp, Paul, *Strike from the Sea – Submarine Action*, Sutton Publishing, 1999.

Knudsen, Svein Aage, *Deutsche U-Boote vor Norwegen 1940-1945*, E S Mittler & Sohn, Hamburg, 2005.

Kramer, Reinhard and Wolfgang Müller, *Gesunken und Verschollen*, Koehlers Verlag, Herford, 1994.

Krug, Hans-Joachim, Y ichi Hirama, Berthold Sander-Nagashima, and Axel Niestlé, *Reluctant Allies*, Naval Institute Press, Annapolis, Maryland, 2001.

Leroux, Roger, *Le Morbihan en Guerre, 1939-1945*, Joseph Floch Imprimeur Editeur Mayenne, 1978.

Lohmann, W, and H H Axel Hildebrand, *Die Deutsche Kriegsmarine*, Podzun Verlag, Bad Nauheim.

Mallmann-Showell, Jak P (ed), *Führer Conferences on Naval Affairs*, Chatham Publishing, London, 2005.

McGovern, James, *Crossbow and Overcast*, W Morrow, 1964.

Neitzel, Sönke, *Die Deutschen Ubootbunker und Bunkerwerften*, Bernard & Graefe Verlag, 1991.

Niestlé, Axel, *German U-boat Losses during World War II*, US Naval Institute Press, Annapolis, 1998.

Paterson, Lawrence, *U-Boats in the Mediterranean*, Chatham Publishing, 2007.

—— *Weapons of Desperation*, Chatham Publishing, London, 2006.

Prag, Christian, *No Ordinary War: The Eventful Career of U-604*, London, 2009.

Rhode, Jens, *Die Spur des Löwen – U1202*, Self-published, Izehoe, 2000.

Rohwer, Jürgen, *Axis Submarine Successes of World War Two*, Greenhill Publishing, London, 1999.

Rosse, Earl of, and E R Hill, *The Story of the Guards Armoured Division*, Geoffrey Bles Publishing, 1956.

Rössler, Eberhard, *Die Deutschen Uboote und ihre Werften*, Bernard & Graf Verlag, Koblenz, 1990.

—— *The U-Boat*, Cassell & Co, London, 2001.

—— *U-Boottyp XXI*, Bernard & Graf Verlag, Bonn, 2001.

—— *U-Boottyp XXIII*, Bernard & Graf Verlag, Bonn, 2002.

Ruge, Friedrich, *The Soviets as Naval Opponents 1941-1945*, Naval Institute Press, Annapolis, Maryland, 1979.

Russell, John, *No Triumphant Procession*, Arms and Armour Press, 1994.

Ryan, Cornelius, *The Last Battle*, Collins, 1966.

Schäffer, Heinz, *U-Boat 977*, William Kimber and Co., London, 1952.

Schulz, Georg-Wilhelm, *Über dem Nassen Abgrund*, E S Mittler & Sohn, Hamburg, 1994.

Schütze, H G, *Operation unter Wasser*, Koehlers Verlagsgesellschaft, 1985.

Sellwood, A V, *The Warring Seas*, Universal Tandem Publishing, 1956.

Suhren, Teddy, and Fritz Brustat-Naval, *Teddy Suhren, Ace of Aces*, Chatham Publishing, 2006.

Tarrant, V E, *The Last Year of the Kriegsmarine*, Arms & Armour Press, London, 1994.

—— *The U-Boat Offensive 1914-1945*, Arms & Armour Press, London, 1989.

Terraine, John, *Business in Great Waters*, Leo Cooper Ltd, London, 1989.

Topp, Erich, *The Odyssey of a U-Boat Commander*, Praeger, Westport CT, 1992.

Vause, Jordan, *Lone Wolf*, US Naval Institute Press, Annapolis, 1991.

Werner, Herbert, *Iron Coffins*, Henry Holt and Co, New York, 1969.

West, Nigel, *MI5:British Security Service Operations 1909-1945*, Stein & Day, New York, 1982.

Wynn, Kenneth, *U-Boat Operations of the Second World War*, Chatham Publishing, London, 1998.

Index